GETTING AWAY WITH MURDER

Also by Richard D. Mahoney

Sons and Brothers: The Days of Jack and Bobby Kennedy

GETTING AWAY WITH MURDER

The Real Story behind
American Taliban John Walker Lindh
and What the U.S. Government
Had to Hide

RICHARD D. MAHONEY

Arcade Publishing • New York

FIRST EDITION

Library of Congress Cataloging-in-Publication Data

Mahoney, Richard D.
Getting away with murder : the real story behind American Taliban John Walker Lindh and what the U.S. government had to hide / by Richard Mahoney. — 1st ed.
 p. cm.
ISBN 1-55970-714-3
1. Lindh, John Walker, 1981- 2. Terrorists—United States—Biography.
3. Muslim converts from Christianity—Biography. 4. Americans—Arab countries—Biography. 5. Americans—Afghanistan—Biography. 6. United States. Central Intelligence Agency. 7. Taliban. 8. Jihad. I. Title.

HV6430.L55M34 2003
958.104'6—dc22   2003019907

Published in the United States by Arcade Publishing, Inc., New York
Distributed by Time Warner Book Group

Visit our Web site at www.arcadepub.com

10 9 8 7 6 5 4 3 2 1

EB

PRINTED IN THE UNITED STATES OF AMERICA

For Alice Doyle Mahoney with love

*He that walketh with wise men shall be wise;
but a companion of fools shall be destroyed.*

—Proverbs 13:20
1987 Winfield City High School yearbook,
dedication of Johnny Micheal Spann

*My passion holds all my wealth and all my
liabilities. . . . It is my identity. Alas, I know
of no more noble cause than to fight for that
which one has the greatest passion for. Rebellion left in the hands of good men will ultimately prevail.*

—FBI special agent John O'Neill,
letter to a friend

*The Messenger of Allah, may peace be upon
him, was asked: What deed could be an
equivalent to Jihad in the way of Allah, the
Almighty and Merciful? He answered: You
do not have the strength to do that deed.*

—Hadith, quoted by John Walker Lindh,
e-mail from Yemen, February 24, 2000

CONTENTS

ACKNOWLEDGMENTS

This book was built on the strength of friends, old and new. My friend Tim Bent had the idea of a book about the encounter between Johnny Micheal Spann and John Walker Lindh in the seconds before the bloody uprising in the prison courtyard of the Qala-e Janghi fortress. "I wonder what they said to each other?" Bent wondered over the phone one winter day in early 2003. "How they got there? How Spann really died?" I took some notes and set off on an uncharted journey.

My mother, Alice D. Mahoney, found the enterprise sufficiently interesting to read the first rough drafts and listen to my stories from the road. Three of my sisters, Sheila Patton, Noel Shambayati, and Eileen Mahoney, provided timely encouragement and valuable suggestions. My aunt Brenda Jeffers was the first to read my book proposal, and my uncle Peter Doyle was the first to see the final manuscript.

Donavon Ostrom, who has critiqued my previous histories, soldiered through this one as well. Carlotta Gall and Neil A. Lewis of the *New York Times* were kind enough to take the time to open up a couple of critical doors. Marcela Gaviria, a director and producer at Rain Media, set me up with people in Peshawar and Kabul. Anil Mehrota provided insight and material on the Pakistani connection. Toward the end of the road, I was graced to meet up by chance with an old friend, Williamette Law School professor Robin Morris Collin, who reviewed the book's final chapters. Without the resolute generosity of Johnny Spann, Mike Spann's father, this book would have lacked the true shades of its American hero. United States senator Richard C. Shelby (R-Ala.), New School president (and former U.S. senator) Bob Kerrey, and Colorado College president (and former U.S. ambassador to India) Richard F. Celeste each gave me their judgments and thereby helped shape the book's conclusions. I should also thank Army Colonel (ret.) W. Patrick Lang, the former director of human intelligence collection at the Defense Intelligence Agency, and Air Force lt. col. (ret.) Richard Francona, another lucid Arabist at DIA, for sharing their deep understanding of the application of intelligence to national security. My old classmate at the Johns Hopkins University School of Advanced International Studies, Dr. Tim Lomperis, instructed me about the extraordinary joint venture between the CIA and the Special Forces in military interventions from Vietnam to present.

Bill West, the mayor of Winfield, Alabama, and a friend of the Spann family, deserves grateful mention for guiding me through the town's unique history as well as introducing me to some of Mike Spann's former teachers. At Fort Bragg, the Green Berets I interviewed were generous in detailing their October–November 2001 operations in northeastern Afghanistan as well as describing their association with Mike Spann. "Jack," a former Green Beret who served as a military adviser to the United Front in the offensive against Al-Qaeda and the Taliban, deserves special mention for his candor and contribution. I owe a debt as well to Chris Thompson, whose scholarship on the role of the Special Forces in Afghanistan is exceptionally deep. He answered all of my many questions and opened up a few doors as well.

In the course of retracing Mike Spann's years in the United States Marine Corps, I visited Camp Lejeune where he had served in the 2nd ANGLICO. Spann's buddy, former Marine captain Michael Tapen, flew out to join me in my tour and proved indispensable in setting the scene and sharing his reminiscences. 1st Lt. Marisol Cantou was our capable guide on and off base. Two of Spann's other friends in the Corps, Lt. Col. Justin Orabona and Major Tray Ardese, also deserve grateful mention.

Without Mark Kukis's outstanding book on John Walker Lindh, "My Heart Became Attached," this book would have lacked detail and perspective regarding Lindh's strange and fateful odyssey. Four members of Lindh's defense team kindly answered questions in interview and later in e-mail. Dr. Tamara Sonn, a brilliant Islamicist who spoke at length with Lindh after his capture, was especially beneficent in her reflections.

Early on in my labors to piece together what really happened in that prison courtyard on the morning of November 25, 2001, I came to the realization that the intersection of Mike Spann and John Walker

Lindh derived from a road not taken prior to 9/11 — that of interdicting Al-Qaeda terrorists before they ever struck. One man seemed to embody not only warnings of that contingency but knowledge of Washington's corrupt inner dealings with two terrorist states thought to be American allies, Saudi Arabia and Pakistan. The story of FBI special agent John O'Neill provides a bridge for understanding what went wrong prior to 9/11 and has since. O'Neill's close friend and fellow special agent Wesley Wong was particularly frank and provident. As in my previous books in biography and foreign policy, I have adopted the practice in certain instances of maintaining confidentiality of source in this book, especially with regard to current and former special agents in the FBI, CIA officers, and key respondents in Pakistan and Afghanistan whose personal security might well be compromised if there were specific citation.

In the end, when it came time to complete the manuscript, as opposed to go back on the road again, old friends came through. Two of my former students, Brian Hirsch and Navin Gupta, pitched in, as did Teresa and Scooter Molander, Steve Brittle, Sam Vagenas, Mary Maffeo, Gene and Janey Fisher, and Mary Mahoney. Lisa Von Bargen, who signed on as my research assistant in May 2003, proved to be a great deal more than that in the last push toward the finish line. Without the steady support of my wife, Karen Longo, who cast a discerning eye on the results of my efforts throughout, I would not have completed the job.

Richard Seaver, president of Arcade, brought his superb judgment to the strategy of the book and then a sharpened pen to the protoplasmic result. He was amiable at the right times and demanding when it mattered. He remains an enduring tower on the American publishing landscape.

GETTING AWAY WITH MURDER

INTRODUCTION

At the periphery now of popular memory is the story of a gruesome prison uprising during the American invasion of Afghanistan in November 2001, a battle in which we discovered that an American was fighting for the Taliban and that another, a CIA paramilitary, was murdered by the Al-Qaeda–trained prisoners.

In the hail of coverage about the American Taliban who was captured, John Walker Lindh, and the all-American hero who died, Johnny Micheal Spann, the media presented a classic story of bravery and treason. The truth, in fact, is disturbingly different from that, and involves a tangle of deceit and misdirection that has yet to be revealed. The central questions of this book are twofold: first, did Lindh conspire to murder Spann, and if so, why did he get away with it? Even more important: why did the Bush administration, having vowed to make an example of Lindh, suddenly stop the trial hours before it was scheduled to begin? The answer is explosive.

What seems undeniable about the story is the exceptional spirit of Mike Spann, the CIA paracommando. Mildred McGuire, Spann's Sunday school teacher in the four-stoplight town of Winfield, Alabama, where he grew up, remembered him as a child wanting to "know everything about God" so he could become a soldier for him. Mike was a Marine who became a man of disguises, a CIA clandestine officer. He could use a wide range of rifles and explosives and kill in a variety of ways. But the soldier-boy, by all accounts, remained. On the eve of shipping out to Afghanistan in early October 2001, he walked into a small law office in Old Town Manassas, Virginia, and signed his last will and testament with a smile at his wife as she held their newborn son.

If Mike Spann knew from the start where he was going and what it would take to get there, John Lindh didn't, or so we were led to believe. But what emerges, at closer consideration, is a decided counterhero, stoic in his study of the Qur'an and Arabic and stubborn in his rejection of the American material wasteland. In May 2001, when he left the madrassa (an Islamic religious school) in Bannu, Pakistan, where he was studying to fight the jihad in the Himalayas for Kashmiri freedom, he was swept into a perilous current. Lindh's calling ended ignominiously, but his journey from the postmodern haven of Marin County to the premodern city of Sanaa in Yemen, thence to the teeming chaos of western Pakistan and, thereafter, into a veritable hell on earth, is a story worthy of Voltaire's *Candide.* As he passed through this bewildering gauntlet, he became a reprimitivized man — enraged, terrified, tortured, and largely singed and drowned to death at the end. When questioned moments after his capture, however, whether what he had done was worth it, he remained stoic, though wounded, starved, and half-delirious: "Definitely," he said. For those who wonder if Al-Qaeda will strike again, Lindh's journey is instructive because it mirrors the passage of thousands of young Islamists who make sharp, and usually sudden, turns toward martyrdom.

This book examines how America itself enabled the rise of terrorism. A generation before Mike Spann frog-marched* John Lindh to a place where he could interrogate him alone in the prison yard that would soon turn into a slaughter ground, the United States had conspired to arm a violent rabble of Islamic fundamentalists in order to eviscerate the Soviet Red Army in Afghanistan. When, like Frankenstein's monster, that rabble broke out and began its violent rampage, why didn't we take action? Why did we permit two of our supposedly close allies, Pakistan and Saudi Arabia, free rein in advancing and financing Al-Qaeda? Was Washington asleep at the switch, or rather, sleeping with the devil?

Much of the answer to that question is bound up in the crusade of one FBI special agent, John O'Neill, to sound the alarm in Washington before it was too late. O'Neill's struggle to contain and defeat Al-Qaeda, a struggle that ended with his death on 9/11, revealed a terrible thing: that the U.S. government itself was corruptly compromised in

---

*A military term for marching a prisoner with physical contact or envelopment.

the effort to stop terrorism. As accidental as the Spann–Lindh encounter may seem in retrospect, it was also foreordained by cynical arrangements born of Washington's own double-dealing. Even after the events of September 2001, that structure of corruption and misdirection continued. Thus, Afghanistan was invaded, but Saudi Arabia, which provided Al-Qaeda $500 million as well as fifteen of the nineteen hijackers, got off scot-free. Iraq, with no links to Al-Qaeda, was attacked, but Pakistan, a criminal state where bin Laden roams freely, was not. Why?

Getting Away with Murder requires us to reexamine our own historical character in terms of the present danger. Are we conquerors or democrats? Can we sustain an imperium without destroying our republic? The French aristocrat Alexis de Tocqueville, who studied the American scene in the 1820s, noted a certain angry and questing passion in the American, a salvation complex drawn from insurgent Protestantism. At the end of the first American century, Frederick Jackson Turner pronounced this expansive, historical personality in terms of the "frontier thesis." But those projections of the American destiny were distinctly continental and avowedly non-imperial.

Today, in the view of the historian Robert Kaplan, the "coming anarchy" in the world requires the application of "a pagan ethos" by the United States. Kaplan believes that we must train and send "expeditionary forces with men who are chameleons, modeled after the spy, linguist and master of disguise Sir Richard Francis Burton." Neoconservative analyst Robert Kagan sees 9/11 as a sort of call to destiny, assuring us that American power will grow in "ever-expanding arcs of liberty" as our legions move out to liberate the hate-strewn world.

The ethos of war and its impact on liberty were subjects the ancient Greeks also debated in their search for a balance between capabilities and commitments abroad. They too reveled in military glory and fashioned battle strategy to counter their foes. As Athens in its golden age veered disputatiously between democracy and empire, Thucydides revisited the greatest Greek war epic, the *Iliad,* to assess the promise of war and the price of security. The *Iliad* depicted a cauldron of malignancies brought on by the Achaean attack on Troy — battle glory gone corrupt in a war too far, and vengeance that, even in victory, turned on the victors. "A nation that draws too broad a difference between its

GLOSSARY

Special Activities Division (SAD): the paramilitary wing of the CIA's Directorate of Operations. It was formerly known as the Military Support Program (MSP). In foreign operations, SAD paramilitaries often attach to Special Forces squads.

Special Operations Forces (SOF): the "Special Forces" include U.S. Army Special Forces known as Green Berets, SEALs (Sea, Air, Land), a U.S. Navy/Marine unit, U.S. Air Force Special Tactics and Combat Controllers, and U.S. Army Delta Force, a force that specializes in rescue and terrorist assault missions. The U.S. Army Special Operations Command is headquartered in Fort Bragg, North Carolina.

A–Team: twelve-man U.S. Army Special Forces teams that often include U.S. Air Force Combat Controllers and CIA paramilitaries from SAD in the invasion of Afghanistan in 2001–2002.

Close Air Support (CAS): the coordination of air strikes in concert with ground assault.

ANGLICO (Air and Naval Gunfire Liaison Company): provides Marine ground forces support fire through aerial or naval bombardment.

Special Air Service (SAS): the elite British unit comparable to U.S. Special Forces.

1

MURDER

The Uprising at Qala-e Janghi Fortress

Sunday, November 25, 2001

Qala-e Janghi fortress, near Mazar-e Sharif, Afghanistan

11:06 A.M.

In an open-air courtyard in the 120-year-old pale yellow fortress built of crude brick and ocher mud, whose name, Qala-e Janghi, means "House of War," two CIA paramilitary commandos, Mike Spann, thirty-two, muscular, wearing jeans and a black sweater, with an AK-47 slung on his back and a 9 mm stuck in his belt, and Dave Tyson, about forty-five, tall, bearded, and dressed in an Afghan *kalmar shaweez,* also with a 9 mm in his belt, are interrogating non-Afghan Taliban prisoners.* They're looking for Al-Qaeda operatives either to interrogate or possibly execute. Under a "finding" signed by President George W. Bush in the third week of September, U.S. forces are permitted to assassinate Al-Qaeda personnel. There are two "kill lists" that are being carried by a handful of CIA agents during the Afghan operation: black for high priority; gray for lower priority.[1]

About 150 prisoners are kneeling, their arms bound behind them with their turbans, while Northern Alliance guards hustle other prisoners, one by one, out of the basement of a pink building toward the south of the five-hundred-yard-long courtyard.[2] Until the arrival of the 538 surrendered Taliban fighters, the great majority trained in Al-Qaeda camps, the fortress had stabled the 200 or so purebred horses that the Northern Alliance cavalry of General Abdul Rashid Dostum has used to storm Taliban positions.[3] Above the crenellated mud rampart to the northeast of the fortress stands the towering rock and ice massif of the Hindu Kush. Despite the hazy sun, it is stinging cold in the courtyard, with mist hanging in the chestnut and plane trees.

---

*Spann is an officer in the CIA's "Special Activities Division," which is part of the Agency's Directorate of Operations (DO). Formerly known as the Military Support Program (MSP), the division and Spann's training are detailed in chapter 4. Tyson, normally stationed in Tashkent, Uzbekistan, is a veteran of the Agency's Near East Division. On the ground in Afghanistan, they are known as SPECATs.

There are about a dozen Northern Alliance guards, most with AKs hitched to their shoulders, on the periphery of the mass of kneeling captives. Spann and Tyson stand mostly in front of the prisoners. From the footage taken by Afghani intelligence, it is obvious that they are trying to ascertain just who these "foreigners" are — Al-Qaeda or foreign-volunteer Taliban?

Despite a stunning series of Northern Alliance victories in Kabul, Mazar-e Sharif, and Kandahar in the previous two weeks, the American military and intelligence forces have failed to find the one man they are looking for — Osama bin Laden. There is no operational intent to capture him. He is to be killed, the way his lieutenant, Mohammed Atef, was killed on November 14 in a Predator* attack as his convoy was heading for the Pakistani border on the road from Kandahar to Quetta.[4] "What is my program?" an American adviser to the director of the Afghan CIA was said to have rhetorically asked during this time: "I want bin Laden's head in a burlap bag on Rumsfeld's desk."[5]

Spann infiltrated into northern Afghanistan in the second week of October 2001. His first mission was to establish ground contact with Northern Alliance general Dostum and provide him with several hundred thousand dollars to gather an army and mount an attack. Spann and other CIA paracommandos then set up drops, landings, and safe houses for Green Berets, Delta Forces, and U.S. Air Force combat controllers who infiltrated days later. Spann's eight-member "set" has performed outstandingly. In a matter of weeks, Special Forces units, calling in close air support (CAS) using laser-guided missiles and bombs, have literally blown the Taliban army to pieces.[6]

Spann's second mission, according to one interview done for this history, is to find and eliminate Al-Qaeda leaders who are heading for the caves and bunkers in the Hindu Kush, if not across the border to Pakistan and then into the trackless reaches of Baluchistan and the Northwest Frontier Province. Mike Spann and his partner, Dave Tyson, are accordingly operating on the basis of hours, not days.

---

*The RQ-1A/B Predator is a pilotless drone that can fly up to 25,000 feet at 150 mph. It is equipped with video cameras (watched in real time on the ground) and night vision. The purpose is reconnaissance, target acquisition, or attack with laser-guided Hellfire missiles.

In the secret videotaping done that morning by Afghani intelligence in the Qala-e Janghi courtyard, Spann appears collected and focused. He carries a pad and a camera as well as the 9 mm and AK-47. His partner Tyson, a CIA case officer, who speaks Uzbek, Dari, Farsi, and Russian, walks about in a restless, possibly preoccupied manner.[7]

If it is, in fact, preoccupation, Tyson has good reason: the previous afternoon, while the foreign, mostly Al-Qaeda–trained prisoners were getting off a truck, one of them ran toward two Northern Alliance commanders and, pulling the pin on a concealed grenade, blew them both up as well as himself.[8] The previous night in the fortress, in retaliation for that attack, a Northern Alliance guard dropped a grenade down a shaft into the basement of the pink building toward the southern end of the courtyard. The explosion killed four prisoners and wounded a dozen more. By the morning, the prisoners are like rabid wolves. "Some feared they would be killed, but most wanted to kill, and then be killed," a Northern Alliance guard, Nassum Daoudi, later commented. These were both homicidal and suicidal men — and Spann and Tyson should have known it.

What the CIA men sense about the men kneeling in front of them is not known. Dostum's soldiers, however, are murderously afraid of the prisoners. They propose to take over the interrogation. Security chief Mashal Azam says they should get rid of the press and begin shooting the prisoners, one by one, until they ferret out the Al-Qaeda individuals. These will be then handed over to the Americans. If that doesn't work, Azam tells a German reporter, they'll do it the old way. He takes out a long, notched knife and points it in his anus. "We begin here."

It is important to point out, as *Time* reporter Alex Perry later did, that from the standpoint of the Taliban the terms of their surrender were violated.[9] Six days before, after the fall of Mazar-e Sharif on November 9, Taliban commander Mullah Feisal had arranged a surrender for his troops. The terms were a $500,000 payment to General Dostum, the Northern Alliance general backed by the CIA and U.S. Special Forces. When Dostum had told him that the Americans wanted to identify and "eliminate" the Al-Qaeda men within the foreign troop, Feisal said the deal was off. What was ultimately agreed to remains a matter of debate. Either Dostum agreed that they would all be let go, or only that the Afghan Taliban, not the foreign fighters, would be re-leased.[10] Later, he repeated publicly that release of the foreign soldiers of the Taliban under UN auspices was the only way to achieve national reconciliation.[11]

At around the time Mike Spann and Dave Tyson are sorting and evaluating the prisoners, Simon Brooks, an official with the International Red Cross, approaches Northern Alliance commander Ahmed Fawzi to ask him about the negotiated transfer and widespread reports of mass executions. Enclosed trailers filled with murdered Taliban have been found, left along roads and highways. The previous week American bombs leveled an enormous madrassa in Mazar filled with "surrendered" foreign Taliban. (Evidence pointed to violent resistance by the fighters in the madrassa.) The Red Cross pulled out 450 dead.[12]

11:09 A.M.

Northern Alliance guards are pulling out suspects one by one from the ranks of the kneeling prisoners and bringing them to Spann and Tyson, who are now standing fifty feet or so behind the group. A fierce-eyed Pakistani, with a storm of hair released by his removed turban, is brought forward.[13]

TYSON (*gesturing toward the kneeling prisoners*): They are terrorists. (The prisoner seems to agree.)

TYSON (*looking out over the kneeling group*): These men are terrorists. These men are terrorists.

TYSON (*now to the prisoner*): I think you are a terrorist. You come to Afghanistan to kill people.

The prisoner, at first, shakes his head, then turns complaisant.

PRISONER: OK. I'm with you. I'm with you. (*As he is being pulled away, he appeals to Tyson.*) Wait. Wait.

11:12 A.M.

The videotape shows a tall, slender prisoner in a black knit sweater being marched out. As he approaches the camera, it is clear from his height and facial features that he is not Arab, Pakistani, or Chechen. He is pushed down to a kneeling position. Spann approaches him. The prisoner is Abdul Hamid — John Walker Lindh.

SPANN (*to Lindh*): Hey you. Right here with your head down. Look at me. Where did you get the British military sweater?

Lindh makes no reply. Two Northern Alliance soldiers approach him. One kicks him in the stomach. They stand him up, further cinching the cloth or rope binding his arms behind him, and frog-march Lindh to a place behind the other prisoners, where he is put down, cross-legged, on a large tarp.

SPANN (*squatting down*): Where are you from? Where are you from? You believe in what you're doing here that much, you're willing to be killed here? How were you recruited to come here? Who brought you here? Hey!

Spann snaps his fingers in Lindh's face, but there is no reply. Spann then kneels on one leg and aims a digital camera at Lindh, whose head is bowed and hair is blocking his face.

SPANN: Put your head up. Don't make me have to get them to hold your head up. Push your hair back. Push your hair back so I can see your face.

An Afghani intelligence officer comes over and pulls Lindh's hair away from his face. Spann snaps a picture.

SPANN: You got to talk to me. All I want to do is talk to you and find out what your story is. I know you speak English.

Tyson walks up.

TYSON: Mike.

SPANN (*standing*): Yeah, he won't talk to me.

TYSON: OK. All right. We explained what the deal is to him.

SPANN: I was explaining to the guy that we just want to talk to him, find out what his story is.

TYSON (*to Spann*): The problem is he needs to decide if he wants to live or die — and die here. I mean he don't wanna die here, he's gonna die here cause this is where we're just gonna leave him . . . he's gonna sit in prison the rest of his fucking short life. It's his decision. We can only help those guys that want to talk to us. We can only get the Red Cross to help so many guys. (*Now dismissively.*) He had his chance.

This too elicits no response from Lindh. Spann is still kneeling in front of the prisoner, gazing at him appraisingly.

SPANN: You know, you know the people. . . . Look at me. You know the people that you're here working with are terrorists? They killed other Muslims. . . . There were several hundred Muslims killed in the bombing in New York City. Is that what the Qur'an teaches? I don't think so. Are you going to talk to us?

Lindh refuses to respond and Spann stands, signaling for the guard to move the prisoner back into the ranks of the other kneeling prisoners thirty yards away.

SPANN (*to Tyson*): Did you get a chance to look at those other passports?

TYSON: There's a couple of Saudis and I didn't see the others.

SPANN (*watching the guard pull Lindh to his feet and walk him away*): I wonder what this guy's got.

CNN freelancer Robert Pelton, who has analyzed many a dangerous scene around the world, later commented that "For Dave and Mike to be in that courtyard by themselves was a major, major breach in just common sense. . . . To have two Americans way out in the middle of five-hundred foreign prisoners — it was just unbelievable."[14] On the face of it, that would seem correct. Special Forces operate on the strictest protocol of control with regard to prisoners of war, in which the searching, separation, and isolation of the prisoners are critical. Further, the complement of Northern Alliance guards, none of whom had their AK-47s trained, was only a dozen or so — a dangerously small number given the attack the previous afternoon. Research done for this book has not revealed why Spann's Special Forces comrades, who arrived later that day, were not on site that morning. The fact that the twelve-man Green Beret TIGER 02 unit had separated itself from Spann and Tyson several days before and been replaced by another mixed Special Forces unit (code-named BOXER) may have had something to do with it.

Factored into such speculation, however, should be recognition of the fact that Spann and Tyson were in hot pursuit of Al-Qaeda leaders. They were probably in the process of getting what intelligence they could before heading off to look for Al-Qaeda convoys in the white light truck Spann had parked twenty yards from the interrogation area.

In chapter 4, the training and deployment of CIA paramilitaries like Spann and Tyson is more fully set forth. Suffice it to say that over the CIA's fifty-four-year history, there has been a guaranteed namelessness to their black missions, an anonymity of person in both execution and casualty, as well as a certain illegitimacy built into their standing within the armed forces and the intelligence community. The regular military may give medals, commendations, and burial places to their valorous dead, but the CIA will only accord to each of their own fallen an anonymous black star — seventy-eight in all — on the white marble north wall of the headquarters entrance in Langley, Virginia.[15] Spann and Tyson, in terms of their mission as well as their fate, are on their own.

11:24 A.M.

The uprising begins. There are three varying accounts of what happened in the course of about the next two to three minutes. Each

account will be tested in the final chapter of this book under the rule of
"best evidence." What follow here are summaries:

• One of the prisoners kneeling in the second row stands, having
freed his arms from their binding, at the moment when there is a
grenade explosion at the entrance to the pink house where the other
prisoners are being processed. As Spann wheels to his right, unhitch-
ing his automatic rifle, to fire on the revolting prisoners, the prisoner
in front of him darts forward and, embracing Spann with one arm,
detonates a grenade, killing them both.[16]

• Spann, with Tyson behind him, is standing in front of the kneeling
prisoners, questioning them. He asks, "Why are you here?" A prisoner replies, "To kill you," and lunges at Spann, who pulls his pistol
out and shoots him dead. Another makes a move and Tyson shoots
the prisoner with his 9 mm and grabs an AK-47 from an Alliance
guard, opening fire. "According to eyewitness accounts given to the
German [camera] team, the Taliban fighters launched themselves at
Spann, scrabbling at his flesh with their hands, kicking and beating
him. Spann killed two more with his pistol before he disappeared under the crush."[17]

• Two Taliban prisoners, emerging from the basement of the pink
house, throw two grenades at two guards, killing them. They seize
the guards' weapons, shouting, "*Allah U Akbar*" (God is great). Spann
unhitches his rifle and shoots both of them dead. As more prisoners
pour out of the entrance into the yard, some of those kneeling get to
their feet and either rush at Spann and Tyson, or try to run away. One
of those who stands to run is John Walker Lindh. But in which
direction — at the CIA officers, or away from them to escape being
shot? After running six meters, Lindh is hit by a bullet to the thigh
and falls down. Spann fires a burst at those pouring into the yard,
dropping several, but a Taliban "seated on the ground throws himself
on him [Spann] while another Taliban begins beating him." Spann
disengages sufficiently to shoot three of the assailants but is soon en-
gulfed. Spann's nearly single-handed stand permits Tyson, a Northern Alliance officer, and two doctors to escape.[18]

With his partner overwhelmed and the prisoners now shouldering captured automatic rifles, Tyson flees toward the northern end of the courtyard with an AK-47 in one hand and his 9 mm (held by the barrel) in the other. When he reaches the second floor of the tower, where a German camera crew has taken refuge, he is clearly in some degree of shock, unable to stick his pistol back into his belt.[19] When reporter Arnim Stauth finds out what happened, he offers Tyson the use of his sat phone, and the CIA officer calls the U.S. embassy in Tashkent, Uzbekistan:

TYSON: We control the north end of the fort. The south end of the fort is in their hands. There's hundreds of dead here at least and I'm not — I don't know how many Americans are dead. I think one was killed. I'm not sure. I'm not sure . . .

The Taliban foreign fighters, after killing what Northern Alliance soldiers remain in the fortress (one was found days later strangled to death), break into the armory and arm themselves with automatic rifles, rocket-propelled grenades, mortars, and light machine guns. Within a half-hour of the takeover, the Taliban fighters are directing fierce fire at the upper parapets of the fortress. Dostum's troops beat a panicked retreat, sliding down the earthen berms on the outside of the fortress walls and then running through the plowed fields north of the fortress.

About fifteen minutes after the uprising starts, the British Special Air Service detachment at the Turkish school, an empty high school a few kilometers from the fortress, gets word of the fighting and the fact that a CIA paramilitary has been either captured or killed. Three SAS soldiers make their way at top speed to Qala-e Janghi to find the Northern Alliance fleeing from the prisoner assault. One SAS scales the fortress wall to get a view of the interior courtyard below and sees the body of someone who appears to be Mike Spann lying on the ground. He fires two rounds on either side of the prostrate figure. There is no movement.

2:15 P.M.

Two white minivans carrying U.S. Special Forces (both Green Berets and Delta Force) pull up on the road outside the fortress and get out.

They are wearing wraparound Predator sunglasses and baseball caps and are carrying snub-nosed M-4 automatic rifles. A minute later, a Land Rover arrives with six more SAS, dressed in jeans, Afghan scarves, and *pakuls,* the floppy woolen hats favored by the Tajiks. The SAS have a submachine gun and automatic rifles. Finally, a platoon of the Army's 10th Mountain Division, who look like they can't be more than fifteen years of age, report in for the roadside huddle. "I want sat bombs [cruise missiles] and JDAMs [guided bombs]," Major Mark Mitchell, the ground commander, says. "Tell them there will be six or seven buildings in a line in the southwest half. If they can hit that, then that would kill a whole lot of these motherfuckers."[20]

The SAS, the Special Forces A-team, the Marine platoon, and about twenty Northern Alliance soldiers move out and position themselves at the edge of the battlement of the fortress.

The U.S. radio operator gets Tyson on the radio: "Shit . . . shit . . . shit. OK. Hold on, buddy, we're coming to get you." He signs off and says to Major Mitchell, "Mike is MIA. They've taken his gun and his ammo. We have another guy. He's holed up in the north side with no ammo." There is more discussion. Then back on the radio: "Shit, let's stop fucking around and get in there." Pointing to the sky, he adds, "Tell those guys to stop scratching their balls and fly."[21]

A Northern Alliance general, Majid Rozi, has called in coordinates for a Taliban position in the fortress. The American radio operator relays these to the fighters high above: "The coordinates are north 3639984, east 06658945, elevation 1,299 feet." He tells his counterpart, "Four minutes." A minute later: "Three." And finally: "Thirty seconds." The Marines drop behind a mud wall. The spotters go flat. The Special Forces roll down in unison, opening their mouths to protect against ruptured eardrums.

Suddenly, and very briefly, a giant silver missile can be seen streaking overhead, making the sound of a braking train. There is an enormous explosion, with a concussion that seems to shake everything, even the fortress. Shrapnel sings overhead. A large plume of smoke and dust leaps up. The Northern Alliance soldiers burst into applause. The elite-force unit calls in six more cruise missiles. At the end of each, there is the same, almost defiant, clatter of Taliban machine-gun fire within the fortress.

An SAS soldier gets Dave on the radio and advises him to make his escape with the German camera crew. The Northern Alliance soldiers produce a sort of comic-opera cover fire, some standing on each other's backs to get their rifles aimed over the fortress wall. Dave advises the Germans, "Time to go." They must make their way across an open roof that has been raked with rifle fire. A one-legged Northern Alliance soldier, caught in the north tower with Tyson and the Germans, goes first. With his crutches, he hops across the roof to safety. Tyson and the German crew then do the same. Reaching the outer wall, they then slide down the sixty feet of steep earthen berm.[22]

5:10 P.M.

The twelve-man squad of SAS, Green Berets, and D-boys (Delta Force) moves back in a hurry to where their vehicles are parked, as grenades and mortar shells, lobbed over the fortress walls by the Taliban fighters, explode near enough for danger. With Tyson out, the elite force has one man to go — Mike Spann. According to author Robin Moore, there is communication between the insurrectionists in the fortress and the American Special Forces; that "they wanted Mike back and would negotiate for his release." Moore reports that the Taliban fighters refuse.[23]

The presence of the press, especially with their video cameras, adds an odd element of theater to the battle. Northern Alliance officers strike emphatic, sometimes mock-heroic, postures as they huddle with their American and British advisers in view of the camera. The British SAS studiously avoid the press and stick tightly to themselves, but the American Special Forces, once disengaged from the battle operations, exhibit a sort of self-dramatic exuberance about the great show they're putting on. Outside the fortress, one of the D-boys stops Arnim Stauth of ARD-TV with a request: "We do a lot of cool stuff and we never get to see it. Can we get a copy of your video?" Stauth gives him his card and the American gives him some friendly advice: "Listen, whatever you do tonight, don't be inside the fortress. You can be around because you're going to see an amazing show, but don't be inside the fortress tonight."

The next day, when the elite unit is preparing to go into the courtyard amid heavy fire to get Spann dead or alive, the encouragement of one of the Special Forces types to Stauth's crew is different: "Turn the cameras off, or I'm going to fucking shoot you." The Germans stand their ground, with a British voice (probably Alex Perry's) reminding the Americans, "You're not in the United States, you know. We have just as much right to be here as you do." The press stays.*

By late Sunday evening, a freezing wind coming off the great mountain clears the aerial debris enveloping the fortress. Lindh, by this time, according to two statements made by him a few days later, is in the basement of the pink building.[24] Despite the flesh wound to his thigh, he is able to hobble around.[25]

At around 11 P.M. that night, the soldiers and Special Forces camped around the fortress can hear the low hum of a blacked-out, invisible plane, an AC-130 "Warthog." The gunship flies via an array of night-vision technology, reading the heat of humans and equipment below. Circling in low elliptical orbits, it begins pouring a golden rain of explosive fire via its auto-loading 105 mm and 40 mm cannons as well as Chain and Gatling guns on the targets below. Around midnight the Warthog hits an ammo dump and a huge bright blast erupts above the fortress. The essence of America's new theater warfare is to avoid combat engagement, except when necessary, and direct laser-guided or carpet bombing of exponential explosive power against an aerially defenseless enemy.[26] After a two-sortie, four-hour "dump" of withering fire, it is the conclusion of the Americans and their Northern Alliance confreres that the battle is over.

At around 7 A.M. Monday morning, the Special Forces, consulting with Commander Rozi, begin positioning for the mop-up assault.

---

*At General Rashid Dostum's thunderously triumphant parade through the streets on Mazar-e Sharif on November 9, who should be seen seated next to Dostum as he receives, pasha-like, the sworn allegiance of local chieftains, but one of Mike Spann's CIA buddies (who, for purposes of his clandestine station, will remain nameless). The man can be seen on CNN's videotape, hulkingly muscular, swathed somewhat absurdly in Afghan costume with his wraparound Predators on, and a blazing grin on his bearded face. Whatever modular assembly the twenty-first-century centurion may require (as Robert Kaplan rather grandiosely suggests), the violation of the old rule of spies and irregular forces is basic: you don't blow cover. When you do, people die. Spann, according to interviews done for this book, was scrupulous in maintaining cover.

BOXER (the Green Beret-led unit) and three British SAS establish a forward position in the northeast tower of Qala-e Janghi. A Soviet-era T-55 tank, belonging to Dostum, clanks through the main gate and wheels its turret at the pink house. Boom. Direct hit. Then again. Northern Alliance troops edge in behind the tank. The U.S. Air Force combat controller in charge of close air support (CAS) calls up the laser-guided JDAM (Joint Direct Attack Munition), a 2,000-pound bomb with a GPS device in its nose. He "lazes" the target with his SOFLAM (Special Operations Forces Laser Marker), a beaming device that fixes the coordinates. He repeats them to the pilot tens of thousands of feet above. The pilot responds, "Be advised. You are dangerously close. You are about a hundred yards from the target." The spotter replies that they are ready now — the target lazed — to pull back. He confirms the coordinates.

PILOT: Good. Copy.

SPOTTER: Mitch [Major Mark Mitchell] and Syverson [Captain Paul R. Syverson] are making their run now. Two minutes.

The "run" the spotter refers to is the positioning of four of the Special Forces up along an inner wall of the southern edge of the fortress. When the mega-explosion detonates, they're going into the fort to get Spann, one way or another.

SPOTTER: One minute . . . Thirty seconds.

Everyone drops down, but the pilot has made a terrible mistake. He has punched in the coordinates of the *spotter*, not the target. The stupefying explosion utterly obliterates the Special Forces-Northern Alliance position. Thirty Northern Alliance soldiers are killed, some fifty wounded. Nine of the Special Forces and SAS are seriously wounded, one of the Brits perhaps mortally.[27] The T-55's turret is blown off and spins like a top above the fray. Outside the fortress, where the Marine platoon, the cameras, and various Northern Alliance forces are gathered, there is a brief cheer followed by the realization that they have taken out their own command position. The Special Forces rescue team withdraws from its mission to find Spann.

That night the AC-130 Warthog comes back pouring more fire into the courtyard. The next morning, as the anti-Taliban coalition prepares for the assault, three more JDAMs (these accurately placed) blast sections of the fortress away and, presumably, its inhabitants. The ground assault goes forward at around 1 P.M. Tuesday afternoon. Using bazookas, grenade launchers, and AKs, Northern Alliance soldiers breach the main wall and swarm into the enormous courtyard from the north. From the eastern side, the rescue team of Deltas and Green Berets goes in again. After killing several Taliban fighters, they enter one of the labyrinthine mud passageways along the inner walls of the fortress.[28] But it is a Northern Alliance soldier who finds Spann's body, lying beneath the corpse of a foreign Taliban with a booby-trapped grenade rigged against his (Spann's) stomach. One of the American Special Forces disarms it and picks up Spann's body and moves it outside the fortress.

In the yard, there is a veritable chaos of scattered human and horse flesh and limbs, the charred remains of vehicles, including Spann's light truck, and an immense litter of spent and live ordnance amid the rubble of shattered buildings and trees. Fires are burning in several locations as the Northern Alliance soldiers begin stripping the dead. Of particular value are gold teeth, whose extraction is achieved by bashing in the mouths of the corpses. They also take cigarettes, money, and the new shoes that many of the dead foreign Taliban are wearing. Two Taliban fighters are embraced in death. Dodge Billingsley, the Combat Films producer, who is making his way through this war-made hell, spots a still-living Taliban fighter whose head is being crushed with a rock by a Northern Alliance soldier. He is revolted.

The Northern Alliance forces are now pouring gasoline from five-gallon jerry cans into the shafts on the subterranean buildings and dropping grenades to ignite the gas. A T-55 tank enters the courtyard and, crunching over the corpses, proceeds to start blasting away at places suspected of housing surviving Taliban. Suddenly, from both sides of the stables on the southern end of the courtyard, squads of Taliban emerge, spraying fire on the Northern Alliance, who panic as they take serious casualties. The Northern Alliance forces flee back up the ramps to the parapet, where they mostly dive headlong down the outside of the castle walls.[29] The ferocity and close-quarter skill of the foreign Taliban are without parallel.

The Northern Alliance brings in more reinforcements, having taken some four to five hundred casualties at this point. The BOXER team does what it does best: calls in more JDAMs. General Dostum himself repairs to Qala-e Janghi on Wednesday. Thursday morning the courtyard seems secure enough for Dostum to enter, accompanied by three black-turbaned Taliban mullahs.[30] The smell of rotting flesh is overwhelming. With the mullahs imploring the chambered Taliban to give up, three health workers feel sufficiently secure to go down the steps of the stairway leading into the basement of the pink house. One is immediately shot dead and the other two are wounded.

Having failed to kill the remaining Taliban by twenty-first-century means, the Northern Alliance tries something medieval on Friday morning. By diverting a stream, they flood the basement with water and are satisfied to hear screams of drowning men emanating from below. Overnight the temperature drops below freezing. Saturday morning toward 11 A.M., there is shouting from the subterranean area. The fighters offer to surrender. The Northern Alliance, arms-aready, expecting only a handful of these devil-men to emerge, are amazed when no fewer than eighty-six of them stagger and crawl out, hirsute, stinking, many moaning terribly from wounds and burns, all severely hypothermic.[31] Someone begins giving the survivors, who are starving after having eaten only raw horsemeat for several days, fruit — bananas, apples, and pomegranates. One of the survivors, propping himself up on a stick, takes an apple from one of the soldiers and, in whispered English, thanks him.

Saturday, December 1
Qala-e Janghi fortress

By late November, more foreign journalists have died in Afghanistan (eight) than American soldiers. Between murderous thieves and raging

Taliban in retreat, journalists have become fair game. Having begged, borrowed, and stolen his way across northern Afghanistan en route to Mazar, thirty-three-year-old *Newsweek* stringer Colin Soloway, a veteran of the "shithole patrol" in places like Bosnia, walks into Qala-e Janghi at around 3 P.M. that Saturday in search of a story. Accompanied by his interpreter, Najib, Soloway comes upon Red Cross personnel getting the Taliban survivors into the backs of flatbed trucks. Northern Alliance and Green Beret soldiers are overseeing their loading. Soloway is wearing a sage green parka and jeans and has the look and the build of a CIA type. When Najib tells him that there could be an American in the back of one of the trucks, Soloway jumps up on the bumper and surveys the devastated men. A guard points him toward one, sprawled in the truck bed, who looks very different from the rest.[32]

"Are you an American?" Soloway asks. "Yeah," answers Lindh. Thus begins the short interview that would rocket back to the U.S. with an explosive impact equal to a precision-guided missile. He tells Soloway that he'd come to Afghanistan to support the Taliban because he wanted to help create a true Islamic state. When Soloway asks him if he supported the September 11 attacks, Lindh hedges: "That requires a pretty long and complicated explanation. I haven't eaten for two or three days, and my mind is not really in shape to give you a coherent answer." Soloway then presses him and Lindh adds, "Yes, I supported it."

The extraordinary photograph taken of Lindh — with his long, wild hair, cornered-animal eyes, and soot-covered face making him look like a diabolical troll — seems to sustain the admission of treachery. That afternoon, one of Dostum's commanders comes by the general's home, where adventure journalist and CNN freelancer Robert Pelton is staying with Delta Force and Green Berets seconded to Dostum. The commander says that there is an American prisoner at the hospital at Sherberghan. Accompanied by a Green Beret medic, Pelton rushes to the hospital where Lindh is being treated.[33] With his video camera rolling, he walks into the main floor of the hospital. Some eighteen fighters, some dying, some moaning, are lying on the floor. Toward the back of the room, the head of the hospital is slapping one of the survivors in the face. "What is your name?" he asks. "What is your name?" "John" is the reply.

Pelton and the Green Beret medic go over to where Lindh, vacant-eyed and intermittently delirious, is lying on the floor. The Green Beret offers to shoot Lindh. Pelton, thinking he's kidding, suggests, "Not yet."[34] They need to do the interview. Young tells Lindh that he can get him medical treatment, referring to the medic beside him. Lindh is suffering from shrapnel wounds, the bullet wound in his thigh, and has lost a toe.

LINDH (*suspiciously*): Who are you?

PELTON: CNN.

LINDH: Look, you don't have permission to film me.

PELTON (*still filming*): OK. Well, that's not our concern right now. Our concern is, uh, your welfare.

LINDH: All right. If you're concerned about my welfare then, don't film me.

PELTON: Would you like some food, Johnny? I've brought some cookies.

LINDH: Yes, please. I haven't eaten in about more than a week. I haven't eaten or slept in a long time. I can't think very clearly right now.

Young gives him a cookie, and the American medic talks to an Afghan doctor about giving Lindh a blood transfusion. (Minutes later, he is IVed with Hespan, a blood expander.) Lindh, looking very frightened, identifies himself as "Abdul Hamid."

PELTON: Abdul. Can I ask you how you ended up here?

LINDH: It's, uh, a long story.

PELTON: I'd love to hear it.

LINDH: If you asked at a different time, I could give you a better answer.

There is a pause here. The medic steps into the view of the video camera and injects Lindh, who winces. The substance has been variously described as "toranel," "morphine," or a "sedative painkiller." [35]

PELTON: Just a little happy juice.

As the opiate takes effect, Lindh warms to the exchange, first with the Green Beret medic, then with Pelton, providing full and direct responses to the questions about how he got to Afghanistan and how he joined the al-Ansar brigade.

Six minutes into the interview, Lindh's face takes on color and his eyes seem progressively clearer. Pelton then asks him to recount what happened in the uprising.

LINDH: Well, what happened was we spent the night under the basement. Then they let us out one by one. They would search each one of us. Then they tied us up and they put us out on the lawn. So, as they were taking us one by one, someone they started fighting with — starting with the grenade. One of them grabbed the Kalashnikov from one of the army forces and so the fighting began. As soon as the gunshots started, everybody stood up and ran. I ran maybe two meters and I was shot and wounded and fell down.[36]

In the final chapter of this book, we will consider what evidence there is regarding Lindh's movement when the uprising began: did he run toward Spann and participate, either in intent or act, in the assault? Or did he run away from him in an effort to save himself? The probative quality of the charge of conspiracy to murder hangs, in part, on that instant of movement.[37]

Later in the interview, Lindh appears to regret none of his actions.

PELTON: Was it your goal to be a *shaid* (martyr)?

LINDH: It's the goal of every Muslim.

PELTON: Was it your goal, though?

LINDH: Huh?

PELTON: Was it your goal at that time?

LINDH: I tell you, to be honest, every single one of us, without any exaggeration, every single one of us was 100 percent sure that we would all be *shahid,* all be martyrs . . .

PELTON: Was this what you thought it would be? Was this the right cause?

LINDH: It's exactly what I thought it would be.

December 2001
Washington, D.C.

Every network and most of the major newsmagazines run excerpts of the interview, which touches off a national paroxysm of rage. Lindh's seeming lack of repentance only stokes the fire of public fury. To a nation, as haunted as it is enraged by the Twin Towers attack, the picture of the American Taliban supplies a missing element in the mass-media passion play: betrayal. Like Lee Harvey Oswald, the biographical description of John Walker Lindh becomes chorus-like: the restless loner, the hate-filled teenager from the broken family imbibing an alien philosophy, with Marin County replacing Dallas, Texas, as the fertile seedbed of America-haters.

The right pounces on Lindh with a snarling fervor that, in many of the commentaries, borders on the comic. Rob Long in the *National Review* concludes that "he's a child of hot tubs, massage therapy, cultural relativism, amicable divorce, racial guilt, vegan diets, Chardonnay anti-Americanism, and 'Teach Peace' bumper stickers." The left mewls a bit about Lindh's "drug-induced confession" but mostly rolls over and plays dead.[38] Senator Hillary Clinton of New York identifies Lindh as a traitor, and the Bush administration lets it be known that it is considering the full range of punitive options, including the death penalty.

The unremitting cascade of lurid images — the Trade Center towers exploding, bin Laden gloating in a home video, and the "American Taliban" captured and cowering — produces what Henri Baudrillard calls, "hyperreality," a personal and public condition in which the simulacra of reality replace reality itself. Thus CNN's blazing red-white-and-blue set announcing "America at War," or President Bush's brave pose at Ground Zero, so irradiate public sentiment as to suspend a commonsense consideration of what happened and what should be done. The Bush administration, after promising a white paper on the intelligence failure regarding 9/11, uses the Afghan invasion to stampede Congress into silence.[39] As the war winds down in December, however, the Senate Democratic leadership, with support from Republican senators like Richard Shelby and John McCain, renews its call for a congressional investigation into what went wrong on 9/11. *Newsweek* reports an incendiary exchange between Majority Leader Tom Daschle and Vice President Dick Cheney, in which the latter warns him that the administration is "too busy with the war on terrorism" to cooperate in any fashion. Get with the mission, Cheney advises Daschle.[40] And the Congress, soon to be entirely in the control of the Republicans, backs down.

In the intelligence and law-enforcement communities, there is a perfect storm of bureaucratic chaos — leaks and counter-leaks between the FBI and the CIA, withering revelations of incompetence, and a complete division of the house as to whether Al-Qaeda, to use the metaphor of the period, is NBA-level organized, or "just a bunch of guys who got lucky in a pickup basketball game." One thing seems clear: CIA director George Tenet, a Clinton appointee, will be fired.[41]

Mike Spann's bravery, however real, serves to provide Tenet enough patriotic cover to keep his job. In a break with CIA tradition, the director announces Spann's death on Wednesday, November 28, within hours of recovering the body. On a closed-circuit television broadcast to CIA employees thereafter, Tenet calls Spann "an American hero."[42] On December 3, Tenet and his wife and a host of VIPs, including Senator Shelby, are on hand at the airport to escort the flag-draped coffin containing Spann's remains. Shannon Spann, ghostly thin and haggard, holding their six-month-old baby, Jacob, says that her heart "broke when it fell to the ground two Sundays ago in a place really far from here."

Tenet calls for a full-honors burial at Arlington National Cemetery and persuades Senator Shelby and the Spann family to make a direct appeal to President Bush to permit Mike Spann to be buried there. The president signs the order with a glowing tribute of his own. On December 10, a horse-drawn caisson carrying a flag-draped casket delivers Spann's remains to Section 34 on an icy, windblown day. After the three volleys of rifle shots by the Marine honor guard, Mrs. Spann accepts the folded flag and, kneeling, places a kiss with her hand onto the coffin.

Some CIA veterans, like former counterterrorism agent Larry Johnson, find the spectacle disturbing. On the *McNeil/Lehrer NewsHour,* he says that the CIA dropped Spann in Afghanistan with little support in dangerous territory and then, when he got killed, broke his cover in order to shroud themselves in glory. "It's amateur hour," Johnson says.

In the same week in which Mike Spann is buried in Arlington, John Walker Lindh's parents make a fateful decision — to retain San Francisco trial lawyer James Brosnahan to represent their son. Brosnahan, reputed to be one of the country's best litigators, immediately gets off a letter to the secretaries of state and defense as well as the attorney general, advising them of his representation. At the elegant Morrison & Foerster law firm on 425 Market Street, Brosnahan's partner, George C. Harris, puts together a team that immediately begins digging in. Their concept is simple and bold: to put the Bush administration itself on trial for the selective prosecution of Lindh.

In the days after 9/11, there are substantiated reports that the U.S. was planning to invade Afghanistan well before that event, and that CIA assets were in Afghanistan as early as June-July 2001.[43] But why? Evidence points to the fact that, after engaging in secret negotiations with the Taliban to secure a huge natural gas concession earlier in 2001, the Bush administration opted for war when those negotiations went nowhere. Furthermore, after a damning article in the *Wall Street Journal,* the administration begins stonewalling questions about the Bush family's financial relationship with the bin Laden Group, an investor in a merchant bank called the Carlyle Group, overseen by the president's father.[44] Then there's an astounding *New York Times* article filed in the third week of September 2001 about a secret emergency airlift in the days after 9/11 of bin Laden family members out of the U.S., arranged by President Bush himself. Two of the departing family members had been under active investigation by the FBI for links to Al-Qaeda, according to the BBC.[45]

In Spann's hometown of Winfield, Alabama, a four-stoplight hamlet eighty miles northwest of Birmingham, five hundred townspeople crowd into the Church of Christ to hear about Mike's shy, earnest smile, his love of southern food, his first questions about God, his determined and ultimately successful attempt to make the high school football team, and how he and Shannon kept separate journals after he shipped out to Afghanistan. Pastor James Wyers says that their town of Winfield gave Mike the right stuff. "We believe in our town. And we believe our town is but an example of the real America that is out there." Spann's father, Johnny, reads Mike's last e-mail telling everyone to stand firm "when the bodies start coming home."[46]

In the case of Sean O'Neill, thirty-four, a Cantor Fitzgerald trader killed along with the others on September 11, there is no body that comes home. His father, James O'Neill, a twenty-five-year foreign correspondent, sits in the basement of the Church of the Resurrection in Rye, New York, greeting friends and family members. Hands trembling, blinking through his tears, he comes to the point of it all, the "why" of 9/11: "What goes around, comes around."[47]

In CIA terms, this is known as "blowback." The reasons for 9/11 as well as the fate of Mike Spann are linked to a foreign policy tragically gone wrong.

2

BLOWBACK

How America Enabled the Rise of Terrorism

November 21, 1979

Near Army House

Rawalpindi, Pakistan

The distinguished men who gathered at the invitation of the Nobel
Institute in September 1995 to reflect on why Soviet-American relations had melted down in December 1979 and touched off a ferocious
war in Afghanistan that gutted the Soviet Union may have overlooked
something in the course of their deliberations: that in the bestiary of international politics, it is not always the large animals that rule; at times
it is the rats that prevail. Absent in the reflections of those Russian and
American diplomats and generals was a sense of tragic realism — of the
dangers of power as well as its utility in the international order. Could
the Americans who gathered at that conference in Oslo have imagined
that what had happened to the British empire in Afghanistan in the
nineteenth century and the Soviet empire in the twentieth could happen to the U.S. at the beginning of the twenty-first century? Could
they have sensed that America would be savaged, as it was on September 11, 2001, by a vicious band of ratlike saboteurs, armed and financed
by two of our close allies, Pakistan and Saudi Arabia? Could they have
further guessed that this, in turn, would occasion a response by Washington so overblown and disordered in its scope as to threaten the security of the American empire and the vitality of its republic?

Only a sure command of history with a sensitivity to its tragic pos-
sibilities could have alerted American leaders to such an extraordinary
cascade of danger. But the Americans, as Alexis de Tocqueville had
noted in the 1830s, were ahistoric; they wanted to invent the future, not
learn from the past.[1] Central to the cautionary tale of "blowback" is not
just betrayal by false friends but the arrogant presumption of invincibil-
ity that goes along with it. The Greeks called the latter "hubris," and for
all of the horror of 9/11 it continues.

At the beginning of the Nobel conference in 1995, the transcripts
are starchy with congratulations about the "historic importance" of the
event and the usual honorifics are exchanged by the principals, once

enemies and now just old men.[2] What follows the mutual endorsement is an orderly enunciation of the respective foreign policies of the super-powers in 1979–80. But soon the exchanges turn blunt and accusatory about who started what and why. The Americans complain of a threatening pattern of Soviet aggression in Angola, Ethiopia, Yemen, and other countries that made the Soviet invasion of Afghanistan the blow that broke détente's back. The Russians respond with their own remembered perceptions of American covert and military moves that supposedly destabilized the world and the region.

But no one at the conference speaks of November 21, 1979, the day when Pakistani president General Zia ul-Haq went for a ride on his old British army-issued bicycle in Rawalpindi at the hour when the American embassy in Islamabad was being burned to the ground by a raging mob of the Islamic faithful. It was then perhaps that the rodent of rage-filled Islam broke out — first to attack a vestige of America, and then, thanks to the connivance of General Zia, to direct itself toward Afghanistan, where it would mortally wound the Red Army and eventually cause the collapse of the Soviet empire. In a matter of years, radical Islam would turn its dreadful attention toward the very country that had enabled it to grow, the United States. We should learn something from the experience.

In the general scheme of American foreign policy during the 1970s, Afghanistan was a strategic irrelevance — a poor, landlocked state that was firmly within the sphere of influence of the Soviet Union. From 1965 to 1979, the Soviet Union had extended some $2.8 billion in economic and military aid to secure its control. The sole conduit of influence by the U.S. was through its ally, Reza Pahlavi, the Shah of Iran, who had invested over $2 billion in Afghanistan and was using his secret police, the Savak, to guard the Afghan monarch, Prince Mohammed Daoud. At least for a period, the Soviets seemed to accept the terms of the play: that Afghan opium be transshipped through Iran while Prince Daoud bowed north toward Russia on needed occasion.

In 1977, however, Prince Daoud, with Iranian encouragement, banned the Marxist People's Democratic Party and arrested its leadership. In so doing, he touched off a revolt that, with active KGB orchestration, cast him out of office in April 1978. Shortly thereafter, he was murdered. Selig Harrison (probably the best analyst of near and south Asia in the public realm at the time) wrote that "the Shah disturbed the tenuous equilibrium that had existed between the Soviet Union and the West for nearly three decades."[3] Nur Mohammed Taraki, the leader of Khalq (the hard-line Marxist faction), declared himself president of the "Democratic Republic of Afghanistan." Joining Taraki in the new republic as his second-in-command was his sometime rival, Hafizullah Amin. Two interviews done for this book reveal that Amin was an agent of Pakistan's military intelligence arm, the Inter-Services Intelligence (ISI), and was secretly listed within the CIA as a Covert American Source (CAS).[4]

Pakistan's interest in Afghanistan was based primarily on its long-standing determination to maintain a "weak neighbor" to the west, in light of the primacy of deterring its powerful neighbor to the east, India. Related to this geopolitical insecurity was Pakistan's fear of another threat: the secessionist emergence of "Pashtunistan," an ethnic enclave that might unite Pakistani Pathans (concentrated on the Afghani border) with their brother Pashtuns in Afghanistan. The additional factor in Pakistan's interest in Afghanistan was access to the cross-border shipment of opium, cultivated in the southern and western valleys of that country. With Afghanistan under the aegis of Soviet power, Pakistan had to tread lightly in manipulating its neighbor. Only with American backing could Pakistan intervene sufficiently to keep Afghanistan weak and thereby consolidate control over the opium trade. The difficulty was that in 1978 and 1979 Pakistan's relations with the United States had turned hostile, essentially because of President Jimmy Carter's foreign policy priority of the nonproliferation of nuclear weapons. In 1978, in the face of growing evidence that Pakistan was developing a nuclear bomb, Carter suspended all economic and military aid to Islamabad. Washington was also upset by the human rights behavior of General Zia, who had overthrown democratically elected premier Zulfikar Ali Bhutto in 1978, and, after a drumhead trial in March 1979, had had Bhutto hanged in a prison courtyard in Rawalpindi. Zia, a devout Muslim, was also pushing to Islamize his country.

All of this might have amounted to no more than one more foreign policy headache were it not for an event that devastated American power in the region and downright panicked the foreign policy establishment in Washington — the overthrow of the Shah of Iran. Along with Israel, Iran under the Shah was the most vital American ally in the world outside of western Europe, providing a bulwark against Soviet expansion as well as a seemingly bottomless business in arms sales and mega-infrastructural projects for those with the right connections in Washington. "When the Shah fell," wrote Colin Powell (then a colonel in the Pentagon), "our Iran policy fell with him. All the billions we had spent there only exacerbated conditions and contributed to the rise of a fundamentalist regime implacably opposed to us to this day."[5]

Thanks to an exclusive U.S. reliance on the Shah's secret police for intelligence, the Carter administration was completely blindsided by the turn of events. How could a group of bearded, unarmed ayatollahs (CIA director Stansfield Turner had to first spell, then define, "ayatollah" for the Carter National Security Council in October 1979) overcome one of the best-armed militaries outside the First World? Journalist Stephen Kinzer believes that the smoldering memory of the CIA-arranged coup in 1953 that overthrew elected premier Mohammed Mossadegh and put the Shah in power may have ignited a long-term disaster for the U.S.:

> His dictatorship [that of Mohammed Reza Pahlavi] produced the Islamic Revolution of 1979, which brought to power a passionately anti-American theocracy that embraced terrorism as a tool of statecraft. Its radicalism inspired anti-Western fanatics in many countries, most notably Afghanistan where Al-Qaeda and other terror groups found homes and bases. . . . Governments that sponsor coups, revolutions, and armed invasions usually act with the conviction that will win, and usually do. Their victories, however, will come back to haunt them, sometimes in devastating and tragic ways.[6]

In retrospect, there was probably little the U.S. could have done to save the Shah once the popular rebellion took hold. But to some, Carter's irregular application of human rights standards to the Shah's regime occasioned the worst of both worlds: it discredited the Shah for victimizing his people without forcing him to adopt the very human rights improvements that might have saved him. Furthermore, his de-stroyer, the Ayatollah Khomeini, was rapidly transforming Iran into a state that would export violent revolution while it extirpated, root and branch, every vestige of secular society.

In Washington in the fall of 1979, according to former NSC staff member (and specialist on Iran) Gary Sick, there was the perception of a domino effect in U.S. foreign policy:

> Because of Mozambique, Ethiopia, South Yemen, and certainly the events in Iran, there was in the United States a perception that, regardless of whether there was a Soviet "grand design" or not, our strategic position was collapsing. Starting about the time of the Iranian revolution, I would say, the U.S. objective was to apply a tourniquet to stop the flow of blood . . . there was a palpable sense of panic in Washington during this period; something had to be done to stop this.[7]

The balloon of radical Islam rose quickly. Days after the Iranian Revolutionary Guards (Pasdaran) seized the American embassy in Tehran, Pakistani militants marched on the U.S. embassy in Islamabad and, with General Zia's soldiers doing nothing to stop them, burned it to the ground.

Washington, by this time, was taking new measure of the man. Zia, they noted, received visitors with a courtly spit-and-polish remi-niscent of a loyal subaltern in the British colonial army (which he had been before Partition). He spoke in phrases the Americans found oddly charming: "Jolly good armor show" in response to the demonstration of an American fighting vehicle he proposed to buy. With his gap-toothed grin, slicked-back hair, and black-ringed eyes, he may have looked like the villain in an old silent film, but this was a man of a sure and savage sangfroid.

To the west across the Hindu Kush, the Marxist leaders of Afghanistan were meanwhile launching the "Saur revolution" designed to redistribute land, unveil and educate women, and secularize and so-vietize political expression. Taraki himself was determined to break up the opium business that had long empowered the feudal Islamic leaders. These initiatives were met with widespread and often violent resistance, which led to a classic Stalinist purge — the execution of some 27,000 people in secret and the "reeducation" of tens of thousands via the old Soviet technique of the auto-confession. High on the list of targets were the mullahs, both Sunni and Shiite, as well as tribal leaders who, in addition to opposing Taraki, were large landowners. Confronted with the deteriorating situation, Taraki appealed to Moscow for a contingent of Soviet troops, but Soviet premier Alexei Kosygin thought otherwise: "The entry of our troops into Afghanistan would outrage the international community. . . . This will give them [Moscow's enemies] the excuse they need to send armed bands into the country."[8]

The U.S. meanwhile was looking for an excuse to move in. A top-secret memorandum sent by the State Department to the National Security Council concluded, "The overthrow of the DRA [Democratic Republic of Afghanistan] would show the rest of the world, particularly the Third World, that the Soviets' view of the socialist course of history as being inevitable is not accurate."[9] A few days later, President Carter signed a "finding" (a secret national security order) that established a modest covert program of medical aid and propaganda to the Afghans. In the metaphor of chess, it was the movement of a mere pawn, but it signaled the start of a new and more aggressive strategy. To the players on the ground, such as CIA agent Charles Cogan, the message was to move, if very carefully.

On the day Carter signed the order, his national security adviser, Zbigniew Brzezinski, wrote the president, or so he revealed to the *Nouvel Observateur's* Vincent Javert in December 1997.[10] "I wrote a note to the President that in my opinion this aid would result in military intervention by the Soviets." Certainly, this was what America's newfound friend, General Zia, was hoping for. While Afghani premier Taraki was in Moscow, being hailed in *Pravda* in its inimitable style as "a warrior-poet working for the broad masses," Pakistani intelligence agents were in active contact with Hafizullah Amin, Taraki's second in command in Kabul.

When Taraki returned to Kabul, he was turned out of power, a fate that was made more permanent when he was strangled by one of Amin's henchmen. In the recorded account of longtime Soviet foreign minister Andrei Gromyko, the assassination of Taraki was "a terrible blow . . . L. I. Brezhnev was especially shaken by his death."[11]

What may have shaken Brezhnev as much as anything about Taraki's death was its potential effect on the restless Soviet Muslim republics on the empire's southern border. When asked in 1988 by Soviet journalist Artyom Borovnik about the reasons for the Soviet invasion, former secretary of state Alexander Haig replied, "Between the Soviet Union and Afghanistan there is only the thin line of the [river] Amu Darya. Because of this, any successful Islamic movement at your southern borders will inevitably influence the Soviet Muslim republics. I can see Brezhnev's logic."[12]

Carter, however, reeling under the rapid disintegration of American power in the wake of the Shah's fall, was concerned enough by the coup in Kabul to demand assurances of Soviet restraint in Afghanistan. At least initially, he got them from the then Russian ambassador to the U.S., Anatoly Dobrynin. But Taraki's death (and the Russian suspicion about America's relationship with Amin) obsessed the aging, alcoholic Brezhnev. "How could the world believe what Brezhnev says, if his word does not count," Brezhnev would say again and again to his aides regarding the murder of Taraki.[13]

Within the Kremlin, however, there were deep differences about the wisdom of Soviet intervention in Afghanistan. Three of the generals on the Soviet army staff were strongly opposed to the idea, but KGB chief Yuri Andropov and Defense Minister Dmitri Ustinov, with the support of Gromyko, carried the day. The day before Christmas 1979, the invasion began. United States intelligence soon got word that scores of Soviet tanks and armored personnel carriers were crossing border entry points from Uzbekistan and Tajikistan. Two days later, after little resistance, the occupation was substantially complete. When Amin publicly criticized the Russians for invading his country, Soviet commandos stormed the presidential palace and shot him dead. His replacement, Babrak Karmal, entered the country in a Soviet armored car.[14]

In his memoirs, President Carter recounts that no event, including the Iranian revolution, so shook him as did the Soviet invasion of Afghanistan with its signature of brutality.[15] Over the next weeks, he expanded the covert program to include arming anti–Soviet Afghan rebels with automatic rifles. He canceled American participation in the Moscow Olympics and slashed grain sales to the Soviet Union. He delayed submission of the SALT II treaty to the Senate for ratification and accelerated the development of the Trident and cruise missile nuclear technology. Carter then publicly pledged that he would increase the defense budget to 5 percent of GNP until the Soviets pulled out of Afghanistan, and, in the secret confines of the National Security Council, he contemplated the use of tactical nuclear weapons to stop the Russians if they advanced toward the Indian Ocean.

President Carter, in his casus belli against the Russians, had the full reportorial and editorial backing of the country's major newspapers and stations. War not only lent sudden purpose to a frightened foreign policy elite, but made for stirring press leads with a martial certainty to them. *Newsweek* wrote that the "Soviet thrust" represented a "severe threat" to U.S. interests: "Control of Afghanistan would put the Russians within 350 miles of the Arabian Sea, the oil lifeline of the West and Japan. Soviet warplanes based in Afghanistan could cut the lifeline at will." The *Washington Post* reported that military leaders hoped the invasion would "help cure the Vietnam 'never again' hangover of the American public."[16]

Pakistan was pulled off the sanctions list and military and economic aid were immediately restored. Brzezinski flew to Cairo to persuade President Anwar Sadat to ship his stockpiles of old Soviet weapons to the anti–Soviet Afghan freedom fighters. Defense Secretary Harold Brown was dispatched to Beijing on a similar mission. The Saudi royal family was encouraged on an ultra–secret basis to build a huge defense infrastructure (much of it underground) in anticipation of a Russian move into the Persian Gulf. After Brzezinski got Sadat's go-ahead, he flew to Islamabad to meet with General Zia, who must have been licking his chops. His high-stakes game of inciting war to save Pakistan and himself had worked. His country was back under the nuclear umbrella of the Americans and would be at the Islamic forefront of holy war. Zia, adroit and cunning beyond any expectation, now called the tune. He told Brzezinski that Pakistan — and Pakistan alone — would move the arms and train and deploy the rebels. The entire enterprise would be kept as secret as possible and rely on intermediaries like China and Egypt (both countries having split with the Soviet Union in the Cold War) to move the bulk of the armament. Brzezinski agreed. The die was cast.[17]

What Jimmy Carter objected to most about the Soviet invasion of Afghanistan was that Brezhnev had "lied" to him.[18] Both as a candidate for the presidency ("I'll never lie to you," Carter promised the American people) and as officeholder, Carter observed a personally sanctified and somewhat pathological code of conduct that proved consequential in the Soviet showdown. In the realm of honorable conduct, he was the Dr. Jekyll of negotiated sincerity and strict insistence on the protection of human rights both at home and abroad. If, in his view, his truthfulness was dishonored, then he tended to turn into the Mr. Hyde of righteous fury and dark tactics. This tendency was manifest in his attitude toward the CIA. "I was deeply troubled by the lies our people had been told," he wrote, "our exclusion from the shaping of American political and military policy in Vietnam, Cambodia, Chile, and other countries; and other embarrassing activities of our government, such as the CIA's role in plotting murder. . . . I was familiar with the widely-accepted arguments that we had to choose between idealism and realism, between morality and the exertion of power, but I rejected those claims. To me, the demonstration of American idealism was a practical and realistic approach to foreign affairs, and moral principles were the best foundation for the exertion of American power and influence."[19] And so it was, until Brezhnev lied to him. Then came Mr. Hyde.

Carter's foreign policy chieftains reflected this behavioral duality.[20] Secretary of State Cyrus Vance was a courtly WASP of gentlemanly mien, who sought to restore a standard of decency subverted by his predecessor, Dr. Henry Kissinger.* Basing the game of nations *primarily* on human rights (for that's what Vance said) was a laudable ideal consonant with the American tradition of "self-determination" inaugurated

---

*When then U.S. ambassador to the United Nations Daniel Patrick Moynihan told German chancellor Helmut Schmidt that Kissinger (his boss as secretary of state) was impossible to trust, Schmidt replied, "Henry will never resort to the truth when simple lying will do."

by President Woodrow Wilson and enshrined in the UN's Declaration of Human Rights.

But a foreign policy based on human rights was often difficult to square with power realities. U.S. ambassador to the United Nations Jeane J. Kirkpatrick caught the contradiction in Carter's policy toward the Shah's Iran or Somoza's Nicaragua (where the Sandinistas were routing the anti-Communist dictator from power):

> The American effort to impose liberalization and democratization on a government confronted with violent internal opposition not only failed, but actually assisted the coming to power of new regimes in which ordinary people enjoy fewer freedoms and less personal security than under the previous autocracy — regimes, moreover, hostile to American interests and policies.[21]

At the other end of the policy and personality spectrum in the Carter administration was National Security Adviser Zbigniew Brzezinski, a native Pole and devout Catholic who detested the Soviet Union's jackbooted brutality toward minority peoples and client states within the Communist empire.[22] While the rest of the American foreign policy elite, Republican and Democrat, saw the Soviet empire as a long-term fait accompli, Brzezinski did not. He would reel off a battery of "objective facts" indicating its "sclerosis." In this, his thinking, and its policy impact, were revolutionary.[23]

When Iran and Afghanistan melted down in 1978-79, the Carter administration found itself impaled on its own human rights pike while lacking the necessary instrumentalities of power. "When retired admiral Stansfield Turner went into the CIA," Colonel Charles Beckwith, the commander of the elite assault and rescue unit called Delta Force, remembered, "a lot of old whores — guys with street sense and experience — left the Agency. They had been replaced with younger, less experienced people or, worse, not replaced at all. . . . On November 12, 1979 [when Iranian Revolutionary Guards seized the American embassy] there were no American agents on the ground. Nothing could be verified."[24]

Carter's political standing at home made matters worse. By the fall of 1979, he was a president in political trouble, much of it not his fault.

A decade of fiscal profligacy had produced what was then termed "stagflation" — flat growth combined with high rates of interest and inflation. The imperial presidencies of Kennedy, Johnson, and Nixon had greatly taxed the spirit and the pockets of Americans. International greatness was generally regarded as a false idol, particularly after the horrors of Vietnam. President Carter, and his predecessor Gerald Ford, whatever their differences of party, were consigned by history to enter an Oval Office shrunken by scandal and the savagery of war.

With the national news media, led by ABC's new show *Nightline,* ticking off the days of fifty-three hostages trapped in the American embassy in Tehran, the administration attempted a hostage rescue mission in April 1980. When two of the five helicopters malfunctioned en route to the remote Great Salt Desert in Iran (in what was to be a staging ground for the rescue) and then another broke down on arrival, Carter called off "Desert One," but not before one of the surviving helicopters collided with a C-130, causing an explosion in which eight members of the rescue team were killed. Secretary of State Vance, who had been excluded from the decision to attempt the mission, promptly resigned. Carter was politically finished, but his policy of arming the mujahideen in Afghanistan went forward.

During the first presidential term of Ronald Reagan (1981–85), there was a steady upgrading of American support for the mujahideen. The Reagan administration continued its predecessor's policy of soliciting support from key allied states to back the insurgency. CIA director William Casey promised the Saudi monarch, King Fahd, that the U.S. would match Saudi support for the mujahideen. The promise proved to be little more than that until years later, but the U.S. established common cause on a military front with the Saudi regency and later (1983), over strenuous Israeli opposition, awarded the Saudis a fleet of F-16s and AWACS aircraft.

From the CIA's standpoint, the rebels could raise the price of victory by the Red Army but were given little chance to win. During the first years of the war (1981–83), there was unparalleled slaughter of Afghan combatants and innocents alike by the Soviet forces. Soviet Mi24 Hind helicopter gunships would hover in squadrons of four or five over Afghani towns and methodically, with 1,000-round-per-minute Gatling

guns and cannons that fired up to 128 rockets and napalm canisters, annihilate anything and everything that moved. The result on the ground
was a countryside that looked like cratered gray porridge. In the wake
of their aerial attacks, Soviet Hinds also littered the landscape with millions of antipersonnel explosives. By 1983, there were three million
Afghani refugees in Pakistan and another two million in Iran.

Through battlefront footage and refugee testimony, the Americans
made a concerted effort to showcase the horrors of the Russian
scorched-earth policy. In fact, Russian battlefield tactics were similar to
the "strategic hamlet/enemy village" the U.S. had used in Vietnam.
Once designated, the objective was also met with varying forms of airborne annihilation; the difference in either war between "pacification"
and "neutralization" was not noteworthy.[25]

Among the more important developments in the war, at least from
the standpoint of the U.S., was the coverage by CBS anchor Dan
Rather. From "somewhere in the Hindu Kush," Rather beamed his dispatches back to the U.S., describing the mujahideen in glorious terms
and the Soviets as war criminals. Despite a fairly high quotient of inac-
curacies and the usual self-involved heroics (the Soviets had reportedly
put out a bounty on Rather's head), the reporting by "Gunga Dan," as
one wag at the *Washington Post* nicknamed him, quickened American
public interest in the war.[26]

What transformed the trickle of covert aid into an eventual torrent
was a hard-drinking, skirt-chasing hedonist, who doubled as a Democratic congressman from the Texas Bible Belt, Representative Charlie
Wilson. Wilson launched a one-man crusade to find and deliver a surface-
to-air missile, portable enough to be used by Afghani fighters, to take
down the Hind gunships. After two years of false starts and bureaucratic
turf battles, there was a breakthrough — a seven-foot-long, thirty-
seven-pound shoulder-fired missile, produced by General Dynamics,
called the "Stinger." By 1987, the Stinger was dropping one Soviet or
Afghan government army aircraft per day. In justifying his extraordinary
efforts to force-feed the CIA with more money for the secret war in
Afghanistan, Congressman Wilson offered a single argument in defense
of supporting the mujahideen: "They're killing Russians, and that's in

everyone's interest, ours and theirs. We had fifty-eight thousand dead in Vietnam and we owe the Russians one."[27]

The CIA may have done little on the war front in terms of gathering human intelligence, but in terms of home-front disinformation there was definite progress. By the time Milt Bearden took over the CIA operation in the covert war, the story that the Russians were using toys in the form of stuffed bears and plastic butterflies to kill innocent Afghan children had taken on a life of its own. CBS duly ran the story as fact, and, according to Bearden, it became "a favorite of both CIA director William J. Casey and President Ronald Reagan. It fit into their view of the evil empire and fell into the same category as the story of the K.G.B. plotting the assassination attempt of Pope John Paul II — too good a yarn to check or dispute. So we [the CIA] ran with it for three more years. I even had copies of the Toys R Us catalog sent anonymously to the local K.G.B chief."[28]

The American CIA case officers in Pakistan, with their combination of arrogance and innocence, were the perfect prey for the crafty Zia. Few of them spoke Urdu beyond what was sufficient to order a meal or take a taxi. To the extent they infiltrated into Afghanistan, the practice was to dress up in Aghan scarves and *kalmar shaweez* for photos on the front. Failing to mount its own independent intelligence collection, the CIA station put ISI brigadier general Mian Mohammed Afzal, the director of military operations, on the CIA payroll.[29]

Despite Congressman Wilson and a handful of pro-mujahideen activists on Capitol Hill, the Reagan administration concentrated its energy and resources on another insurgency — to train and arm the so-called Contras in order to overthrow the Cuban-advised Sandinista regime in Nicaragua. The Contras, however, evinced little interest in battle, but proved adept at cornering much of the drug market in the region and using those proceeds to buy homes in the south of Florida. When Congress balked at funding the generalization of war in Central America due to human rights atrocities such as the rape and murder of four nuns in El Salvador by American-supported government troops, the Reagan administration went covert and tried to privatize the covert war.

Like the CIA's secret war in Laos in the 1960s and 1970s, the Contra operation revealed a recurring variable in the effort to conduct counterinsurgency warfare — drug trafficking. A leading international authority on the interface between war-making and drug trafficking, Dr. Alfred McCoy of the University of Wisconsin, explains how this operated in Afghanistan in the 1980s:

> During this decade, the Afghanistan borderlands were rapidly transformed into the world's largest heroin-producing zone. Literally hundreds of heroin kitchens line the Afghani-Pakistani border, supplying 60% of the U.S. heroin demand, a mushrooming market inside Pakistan, and up to 80% of European demand. During this period, the United States Drug Enforcement Administration had a large detachment of seventeen officers in the Pakistani capital of Islamabad. They attempted no investigations, no seizures, no arrests. They stayed right out of the North West Frontier Province of Pakistan, where the heroin industry was sited, because this was the base area of the CIA's secret war in Afghanistan and those traffickers were our covert-action allies. Moreover, during the 1980s, the northwestern frontier was under the control of Pakistan's Inter-Services Intelligence (ISI) — one of the organizations that armed and supplied the Taliban for the seizure of power inside Afghanistan between 1994 and 1996 — and it became the frontline agency for the CIA in the delivery of arms and training to Afghani fighters. The heroin labs operated under the control and protection of the ISI, making them enormously powerful. When these critical areas are suddenly removed from the vice-grip of prohibition, production mushrooms astronomically.[30]

The numbers are staggering. In 1981, at the beginning of the American entry into the war in Afghanistan, the country produced 200 tons of opium, according to the United Nations. By 1990, production had gone up ten times to 2,000 tons. Now trafficking in millions of dollars of weapons and operating under the CIA and Defense Department's operational umbrella, the Pakistani-sponsored mujahideen was able to create an industry heretofore unknown in either Afghanistan or Pakistan — heroin. Although the Drug Enforcement Administration (DEA) had evidence of no fewer than forty heroin syndicates and two hundred heroin labs operating in Pakistan, despite agonized appeals in

Washington, it could do nothing. American leaders were fully informed of the situation yet remained silent and merely hoped the lie would hold. In late 1980, a high-level law enforcement official in the Carter administration's Justice Department was quoted as saying, "You have the administration tiptoeing around this like it's a land mine. The issue of opium and heroin in Afghanistan is explosive. . . . In the State of the Union speech, the president mentioned drug abuse but he was very careful to avoid mentioning Afghanistan . . . why aren't we taking a more critical look at the arms we are shipping into gangs of drug runners, who are obviously going to use them to increase the efficiency of their drug-smuggling operations."[31]

The May 1984 visit of Vice President George Bush to Islamabad was emblematic of the priorities at hand. Bush headed President Reagan's National Narcotics Border Interdiction System, which brought the CIA and Special Forces military units into the "war on drugs." The Americans now had evidence that they had unintentionally participated in the creation of the newest and largest narco-regime in the world in Pakistan. Several of Zia's generals, the CIA knew, had Swiss bank accounts, each of which contained in the hundreds of millions of dollars. Nonetheless, Bush went out of his way to congratulate General Zia for his efforts to stamp out the drug trade. Hypocrisy, a constant in human affairs, is writ larger in the exigencies of politics. Still, there was something both pathetic and pernicious about a policy and its progenitors divorced from the catastrophe they were both causing and then ignoring.

Pakistan's condition of total control over the war effort in Afghanistan also led to high levels of corruption and diversion in the huge air- and sealifts of weapons. Arms-trade specialist James Adams estimated that perhaps half of the AK-47s, mortars, and rocket-propelled grenades actually reached the mujahideen.[32] The rest were appropriated by the Pakistani military (a substantial portion of which were resold on the black market) or were distributed to tribal forces to secure the drug trade. Reporter Tim Weiner wrote:

> The CIA's pipeline leaked. It leaked badly. It spilled huge quantities of weapons all over one of the world's most anarchic areas. . . . Some of the weapons fell into the hands of criminal gangs, heroin

kingpins, and the most radical faction of the Iranian military. . . . While their troops eked out hard lives in Afghanistan's mountains and deserts, the guerrillas' political leaders maintained fine villas in Peshawar and fleets of vehicles at their command.[33]

The guerrilla leader anointed by the Pakistanis was Gulbuddin Hekmatyar, a bearded, brooding Islamic fundamentalist prone to rant and even physically attack people who questioned his wish to reshroud women, close down all non-Islamic schools, and implement *hudud* (stoning, amputation, and so on for the commission of certain crimes). Hekmatyar, moreover, was a murderer who authorized the execution of emissaries from other mujahideen armies, foreign journalists, and entire uncooperative villages.[34] Thanks to the ISI, the CIA's partner, Hekmatyar controlled six heroin kitchens along the border and in 1981 gained control of the opium-rich Helmand Valley (annual production: 260 tons of raw opium).[35] It is estimated that of the $6 billion total in cash and armaments that flowed to the mujahideen during the 1980s, Hekmatyar's movement, Hizb-i-Islami, got half, $3 billion.[36]

In his splendid book on the mujahideen, Robert Kaplan faults the American role in the war. "In the end, the mujahidin's willingness to suffer to a nearly unimaginable degree eventually overcame, and thus masked, the awful mistakes of American and Pakistani policymakers." Through the words of one of the best of the insurgent commanders, Abdul Haq, Kaplan recounts the incompetence: "Hadn't the [CIA] Station Chief in Kabul, following the Soviets' December 1979 invasion, declared that the Afghans had no chance . . . that in six months the Soviets would control the entire country. . . . And hadn't the Americans decided to throw the whole operation of the war in the laps of the ISI, with little independent intelligence of their own except for satellite photographs and a handful of diplomats restricted to Kabul city?"[37]

Lack of independently derived human intelligence, as well as total operational dependence on Pakistan's ISI, prevented the U.S. from recognizing and supporting the one true moderate patriot who commanded the most effective fighting force — Ahmed Shah Massoud. A thirty-year-old (in 1980) Tajik engineer who spoke fluent French, Massoud had earned his nickname "Lion of the Panjshir" through his brilliant hit-and-run tactics in 1981 against Soviet armored brigades supported by Hind gunships.

Another personality who escaped American attention was the young Saudi Osama bin Laden, who in late 1981 arrived in Pakistan and infiltrated across the Afghani border. Outside the realm of legend (in which bin Laden reportedly fought in close-quarter encounters against Russian units), his role in Afghanistan was essentially that of financing and organizing an infusion of money, matériel, and jihadis from Arab countries.

By 1985, bin Laden had emerged as the central commander of the pan-Arab war effort and worked on a constant basis with the head of Saudi intelligence, Prince Turki al-Faisal. Saudi financing, thanks in good part to bin Laden, reached $80 million a week in 1986. The air-lifts from throughout the Muslim world, but especially from its Arab component, were bringing in hundreds of jihadis each week. Working out of Peshawar in the homes he had purchased — Beit al-Ansar and the rest — bin Laden arranged for the housing and deployment of the holy warriors. By war's end, he was a revered figure.

By 1988, the Red Army was beginning to take serious losses in the field and even in battling the mujahideen for control of some of the country's provincial cities. The once-destructive Hinds were flying so high above the ground to elude the Stingers that the Soviet infantry referred to their pilots as "cosmonauts." The pointlessness and futility of maintaining a sanguinary stalemate corroded troop morale. Russian soldiers composed and sang sad songs to allay their fear and bitterness:

> Don't call me, Father, don't disturb me:
> Don't call me, oh, don't call my name.
> We're walking down an untrodden road.
> We're drifting in fire and blood.
> I don't know if there'll be another battle:
> All I know is that the war isn't over.
> We're just grains of sand in the universe,
> And we won't see each other again.[38]

On February 15, 1989, maintaining what little decorum was left an army that had lost over 25,000 men, Soviet general Boris Gromov, stout and pale with boyish bangs framing an intensely creased face, walked over the Friendship Bridge into Uzbekistan, the last Russian to leave Afghanistan. In Washington, Congressman Charlie Wilson broke out some champagne and stood in front of his TV, watching the strange spectacle. He saluted the retreating Russian general: "Here's to you, you motherfucker." It was the beginning of the end of the Soviet Union.

American political leaders like Congressman Wilson and President Reagan believed, probably correctly, that their support for the covert war in Afghanistan had set the stage for the collapse of the Soviet empire. But for Osama bin Laden and the Afghan Arabs, as they were known, not to mention the mujahideen themselves, their victory was nothing less than a heaven-born epiphany, the moral and political equivalent of America's unconditional victories in Europe and the Pacific in 1945. For the enraged Muslim, defeated by Israel, scorned by the Americans, and brutalized by his own government, the prospect of settling accounts with the Arab regimes sustained by the West seemed suddenly within reach.

In January 1998, a French journalist asked Zbigniew Brzezinski about the consequences of the Pakistani-American covert war against the Soviet Union — the arming and unleashing of tens of thousands of radical Islamic fighters, which became the basis for the rise of the Taliban and the heinous mission of Osama bin Laden. Brzezinski was indignant in reply. "Which is more important in world history?" he asked. "The Taliban or the fall of the Soviet empire? A few over-excited Islamists or the liberation of central Europe and the end of the Cold War?"[39]

One would think Brzezinski right. Even if we mishandled the rise of Islamic fundamentalism, kicked opium and heroin production like hot coals all over the region and into our streets, at least we took down the Soviets. But that ignores one other consequence — the development of what Zia called "the Islamic H-bomb." As the covert war grew in intensity and priority for the Americans, they looked the other way as the Pakistanis developed the bomb. There is today no place in the world where the prospect of nuclear conflict is greater than in the subcontinent; and no nuclear power, including North Korea, with so unstable and explosive a political culture as that of Pakistan.[40] Today, in the aftermath of 9/11, Osama bin Laden is hiding somewhere in the tribal reaches of Pakistan. The Pakistani military dictatorship that once gave him free passage in his savage missions is back in the good graces of the U.S. and divides its time, as before, playing the terrorists against an arrogant and historically absentminded American leadership. We should have learned.

November 28, 1984
National Press Club
Washington, D.C.

When the CIA began using the term "blowback" in the late 1950s, it was to characterize the destructive consequences of operations unintended and unforeseen at their inception. The most self-destructive of such operations occurred in Vietnam, where arrogant presumption in Washington regarding the prospects of "limited war" collided with an unforeseen fact in the field — for guerrillas to win, it was only necessary for them not to lose. Blowback in Vietnam might have served as a tragic illumination of the need for future restraint, but the evidence speaks otherwise. One young infantry officer in the war, Philip J. Caputo, saw no reason "to register an objection to the war, because the war is over. We lost it, and no amount of objecting will resurrect the men who died, without redeeming anything, on calvaries like Hamburger Hill and the Rockpile. It might prevent the next generation from being crucified in the next war. But I don't think so."[41]

Since Vietnam, "imperial overstretch," as defined by Yale historian Paul M. Kennedy in *The Rise and Fall of the Great Powers,* has repeatedly put American soldiers in the middle of insoluble blood feuds while exposing the United States to the certainty of vicious retaliation as a result.[42] For the Reagan administration, the lesson regarding the limits of military intervention came tragically. On October 23, 1983, a truck loaded with explosives blew up a building that housed a Marine peacekeeping contingent near the Beirut airport, killing a total of 241 U.S. troops, nearly all of them Marines.[43] "What I saw from my perch in the Pentagon was America sticking its hand into a thousand-year-old hornet's nest with the expectation that our mere presence might pacify the hornets," then colonel Colin Powell would later write. "There are times when American lives must be risked and lost. Foreign policy cannot be paralyzed by the prospect of casualties. But lives must not be risked until we can face a parent or a spouse or a child with a clear answer to the question of why a member of that family had to die. To provide a 'symbol' or a 'presence' is not good enough."[44] The Reagan administration abandoned Lebanon.

Powell's convictions about when to intervene and when not to were derived from combat in the war in Vietnam. "Many of my generation," he later wrote, "the career captains, majors and lieutenant colonels seasoned in that war vowed that when our turn came to call the shots, we would not quietly acquiesce in halfhearted warfare for half-baked reasons that the American people could not understand or support."[45] As military assistant to Reagan's secretary of defense, Caspar Weinberger, Powell got his chance in November 1984 to draft the preconditions for future military interventions by the United States.

The memorandum that Powell put on Secretary Weinberger's desk would later be called the Powell doctrine. Weinberger delivered it in the form of a speech to the National Press Club on November 28, 1984, and it remains the most significant articulation of strategic pragmatism in the last twenty-five years.[46]

1. The proposed intervention had to be "vital to our national interests or that of our allies" or else the U.S. would not commit its forces;

2. If the U.S. did commit troops, we would do so "with the clear intention of winning";

3. The armed forces should have "clearly defined political and military objectives";

4. The relationship between ends and means "must be continuously reassessed and adjusted, if necessary";

5. "There must be a reasonable assurance we will have the support of the American people and their elected representatives in Congress";

6. "The commitment of U.S. forces to combat should be a last resort."

In later years, another precondition was added by Powell: the necessity of an "exit strategy."[47]

The benchmark of the Powell doctrine was the American experience in Vietnam. Central to that disaster was defective calculation of Vietnam's importance to "vital national interests."[48] American leaders believed that Communism was monolithic and ceaselessly expanding, an assumption that in the light of history proved grossly exaggerated. "If we do not defeat them in Vietnam," President Lyndon Johnson stated, "we will have to fight them in San Francisco." Secretary of State Dean Rusk claimed that international Communism intended to control all of Asia, Africa, and Latin America, "thus encircling and strangling the Atlantic world."[49] Once these inflated notions took on the quality of incontestable truth, no "exit strategy" was permissible, for that would have been appeasement in the face of international evil. Today we face a similar cycle of self-reinforcing overreaction with regard to the "war on terror."

Despite all the brave rhetoric, however, the policymakers of the 1960s and 1970s did not believe that Vietnam was worth a land war with China. The million-troop level that in the view of some analysts could have won the battle on the ground only reached a little more than half that, 543,400. The use of nuclear weapons to eliminate the North Vietnamese regime was never contemplated seriously by either Johnson or his successor, Richard Nixon. Vietnam wasn't worth it. As for the normative dedication to win "the hearts and minds of the Vietnamese," a Marine captain provided a more refined equation: "When you have them by the balls, their hearts and minds will follow."

The distance between "ends and means," to borrow again from Powell's preconditions for intervention, were bridged in the Vietnam War through a structured deceit. The chief architect of the war, Secretary of Defense Robert McNamara, implemented quantitative tests to measure progress in the form of enemy "body counts" and "friendly" versus "unfriendly" hamlets. American forces in the field were required to comply with this scheme, maximizing body counts (that included civilians as well as hostiles) and counting villages on an optimal basis. As a young captain, Colin Powell found that South Vietnamese army officers were constantly inflating the numbers of dead Viet Cong and North Vietnamese. When he demanded corporal proof of one dead VC, he was given a freshly cut pair of ears. Powell then summoned the company commander and his noncommissioned officer. "The rules needed refinement," he told them. "A kill meant a whole body, not component parts."[50] As one member of the Johnson administration remembered: "Numbers! There was a number mill in every military and AID installation in Vietnam. Numbers flowed into Saigon and from there into Washington like the Mekong River during flood season. Sometimes the numbers were plucked out of the air, sometimes the numbers were not accurate."[51]

"Body count" papered over strategic realities as well as the factor of men dying for no good reason. Powell would remember helping load a soldier who had stepped on a mine. His leg was hanging by a thread and his chest had been punctured. "He was just a kid, and I can never forget the expression on his face, a mixture of astonishment, fear, curiosity, and, most of all, incomprehension. He kept trying to speak but the words would not come out. His eyes seemed to be saying, why? I did not have an answer, then or now. He died in my arms before we could reach Duc Pho." Powell's conclusion was that war "should be the politics of last resort":

> And when we go to war, we should have a purpose that our people understand and support; we should mobilize the country's resources to fulfill that mission and then go in to win. In Vietnam, we had entered into a halfhearted half-war, with much of the nation indifferent, while a small fraction carried the burden.

After stints in the Carter and Reagan administrations, Powell was appointed chairman of the Joint Chiefs of Staff by President George H. W. Bush. When Saddam Hussein invaded Kuwait in August 1990, Powell had the chance — and the responsibility — to put his doctrine to the test. What, in fact, defined a "vital national interest" that required the commitment of U.S. troops? If the objective was the use of "overwhelming force" to achieve a quick victory, how did such a presence conduce to a rapid "exit strategy"? And if these complex questions were not put in simple, compelling language, how could the administration rally the American people, their Congress, and the international community, particularly with the memory of what had happened in Vietnam?

The case for invasion was far from definitive. After taking Kuwait, Saddam had 200,000 troops and 3,000 tanks less than a mile from the Saudi border. The Saudi government was exceedingly nervous and initially noncooperative about the idea of militarily repelling the invaders. It seemed that the case for sanctions against Iraq might be an alternative to military intervention.

In his inside account of the campaign, entitled *The Commanders,* Bob Woodward describes Powell as "the reluctant warrior." Although Defense Secretary Dick Cheney and General Norman Schwarzkopf wanted to go in, Powell was holding back.

Over the course of three weeks, the Bush administration, consulting constantly with Congress and its allies and checking and rechecking its intelligence estimates of the fluid scene, reached its conclusion: Saddam's invasion of Kuwait, a sovereign country that had huge oil reserves, coupled with the fact that Saudi Arabia, the oil-producing leader, was now also in danger of being invaded, necessitated direct military intervention. Iraq's actual or potential possession of weapons of mass destruction was a crucial contributing factor to the conclusion that there was a threat to "vital national interests." Bush's consultation with Congress paid off, as did his public dedication to call up the National Guard and Reserves. After a long but cordial debate, the House approved the war resolution 250 to 183, and the Senate did as well by a narrower margin, 52 to 47.

The most extraordinary aspect of the diplomatic phase of the campaign, one that should stand as an exemplar of the power of multilateral leadership, was the démarche by the president himself, who built the coalition by phoning world leaders one by one. In the end, eighty-seven nations, including Russia and every country in the Middle East except two, endorsed the invasion. No fewer than thirty-five nations participated in providing armament, manpower, and money. In "Operation Desert Storm," 200,000 coalition troops fought alongside the 300,000 American forces in a devastatingly successful military operation.

As coalition forces drove the Iraqi army out of Kuwait and swept into Iraq, Powell's gut — and his recollection of a book he had once read by Fred Ikle — was to prepare for the exit.[52] He called the president from Kuwait City on a satellite phone. "Mr. President," he said, "let's not take any more young Iraqi lives, or any more young American lives. Let's end this thing now." Bush agreed.[53] There was little resistance from the multinational high command. The mandate of Desert Storm was to free Kuwait, not occupy Iraq. On the afternoon of February 27, 1991, after forty-two days of war, Bush announced the cessation of hostilities.

In the months and years thereafter, the Bush administration was criticized for its failure to finish Saddam off and for sitting by while the Iraqi dictator ordered the slaughter of Iraqi Shiites and Kurds whom the Americans had encouraged to revolt. In his memoirs, which he co-authored with General Brent Scowcroft, President Bush provided a wise and persuasive defense:

> Trying to eliminate Saddam, extending the ground war into an oc-cupation of Iraq, would have violated our guideline about not changing objectives in midstream, engaging in "mission creep," and would have incurred incalculable human and political costs. . . . We would have been forced to occupy Baghdad and, in effect, rule Iraq. The coalition would immediately have collapsed, the Arabs deserting it in anger and other allies pulling out as well.[54]

After the war, the mood in the United States was celebratory. The Soviet Union had ceased to exist and the American military was back on top. The president, though rhetorically incapable of stirring much fervor, presided over this historic victory with a defining modesty. "We should be humble," he said again and again. He left the victory parades to his talented high command. At the cheering, honking ticker-tape pa-rade down Broadway in New York, Powell and his wife, Alma, rode be-hind the vice president and his wife in a white 1959 Buick convertible. The security detail wanted the general to wear an armored vest, but he refused. "I look chubby enough," he said. General Schwarzkopf agreed, and Cheney went along with their military judgment.[55] It was a secure and happy moment.

Within the Bush administration, however, there were stirrings of discontent that proved to be portents of future policy. Paul Wolfowitz, who was then undersecretary of defense for policy, drafted a set of internal military guidelines entitled "Defense Planning Guidance." The purpose of these is to provide military and civilian leaders with a geopolitical framework for strategic and tactical decision making. The top-secret forty-six-page draft was circulating among senior officials in the spring of 1992, when it was leaked to the *New York Times* and *Washington Post,* appearing on the front page of both papers. In the draft was a provocative term — "preemption." Wolfowitz set forth conditions in which the United States would *unilaterally* intervene with combat troops, conditions that included gaining access to oil or stopping the proliferation of weapons of mass destruction. Military intervention would be "a constant fixture" in the geopolitical landscape. Wolfowitz's draft was a de facto repeal of the Powell doctrine, and President Bush saw it as such. Through National Security Adviser Scowcroft, he ordered the document to be returned to Secretary of Defense Cheney forthwith for a redraft.[56]

William Kristol, who was then the chief assistant to Vice President Dan Quayle, later commented that the evident division in the administration was between the "realists" (Bush, Powell, and Scowcroft) and the "unilateralists" (Wolfowitz and Cheney). Perhaps it was no surprise that the "realists" were all military veterans who shared a skepticism about the promise of war, while the "unilateralists," men who had never served in the armed forces, regarded war as a strategic opportunity.

Eight years later, at the beginning of the second Bush administration, the realists reassumed control of the high ground, or so it seemed. Colin Powell was appointed secretary of state. Bush's close confidant, National Security Adviser Condoleezza Rice, made it clear as a matter of stated policy that the new administration would not be drawn into either "nation-building" or military intervention without the assurance of a decisive outcome. But the ascendancy of the realists, the record now shows, may well have been more apparent than real. Within a week of taking office, President Bush called for a "New Energy Policy" and empowered a task force to hold secret deliberations under the chairmanship of Vice President Cheney. The task force rallied to a central objective of the unilateralist cause, one that dated back to Wolfowitz's rejected draft — the cause of energy preemption. Central to the implementation of that strategy was fortifying the American corporate and military alliance with Saudi Arabia, prospecting diplomatically with the Taliban for the purpose of constructing a trans-Afghanistan gas pipeline, and the "taking down" of Saddam Hussein, the dictator of oil-rich Iraq.

What impact the cause of energy preemption may have had in terms of delaying action during the first eight months of the Bush administration against the rising challenge of Al-Qaeda will be long debated. What is certain, however, is that the Powell doctrine of international military self-restraint was conclusively eclipsed *before* 9/11. *Time* magazine entitled its cover story on September 10, 2001, "Where Have You Gone, Colin Powell?"[57] *Time's* portrait was of a great man trapped somewhere between frustration and humiliation, who maintained a soldier's dignity before the assaults on the multilateralist legacy of George H. W. Bush and his former chairman of the Joint Chiefs of Staff, General Powell. *Time* described the skein of skirmishes that had left Powell defenseless — the ripping up of arms control agreements, the ditching of the Kyoto protocol and a host of international conventions, the truculent contempt for anything associated with the UN or the European Union, and the demand for war against Iraq, Iran, and North Korea. Secretary Powell was a man who had been "blind-sided," the article said. He was a man "cut off at the knees."

What Lieutenant Philip Caputo had predicted in his brutal memoir about Vietnam, *A Rumor of War,* was right: the 58,000 men who had died in meaningless firefights in Indochina would soon be forgotten, as would the scourge of arrogant men who had sent them there. A new crop of victims would come along the way Caputo had, allergic to any sense of mortality and seduced by the old pornography put forth by another set of eager political men who were nothing more than pretenders.

Thucydides would have immediately understood the meaning of "blowback." In book 3 of *The Peloponnesian War,* Kleon, a would-be Pericles, shouts to the crowd for the mounting of an invasion to liquidate the Mytileneans. He does so, Thucydides says, with a specious intellectualism that is a mask for indulgent anger. To this Diodotos responds with a call for clemency as a practical matter; the price of slaughter and occupation is too great. According to Thucydides, Diodotos exhibits *"sôphrosunê,"* or "self-restraint."[58]

October 3, 1993
Operation Restore Hope
Mogadishu, Somalia

In October 2003, National Security Adviser Condoleezza Rice declared in a speech in New York that the historical record revealed a pattern of negligent indecision by previous administrations in forestalling the prospect of terrorist attacks against the United States. The statement came in the wake of several months of harsh international criticism about the American takeover of Iraq in addition to plummeting support at home for President Bush and his policy there. Although the national security adviser avoided any mention in her remarks about what the Bush administration itself had done or not done to take measures to prevent the September 11 attacks, her essential point was clear: "They [the terrorists] became emboldened, and the result was more terror and more victims."[59]

But *why* do terrorists become emboldened? From Vietnam to Somalia to Iraq, the record shows that U.S. force projection is the chief culprit. What Colin Powell once called "halfhearted warfare for half-baked reasons" ignites more than it quells violent grievances, and, whether it resolves or exacerbates foreign crises, the U.S. always emerges as the target. The imperial histories of Rome, Great Britain, and now the United States, demonstrate the potential fatality of such open-ended interventions, especially when military power is unchecked by civilian control and civilian leadership is enthralled with its own absolute verities.

In her remarks in New York City, Dr. Rice contradicted her own better judgment set forth in a *Foreign Affairs* article three and a half years earlier. In that article, which was widely regarded as the foreign policy blueprint of presidential candidate George W. Bush, Rice suggested that "the enemy" becomes emboldened when the U.S. ineptly intervenes.

She gave the example of Somalia in 1993, but she could have been talking about Iraq in 2003. "Using American armed forces as the world's '9/11,'" she concluded, "will degrade capabilities, bog soldiers down in peacekeeping roles, and fuel concern among other great powers. . . . This overly broad definition of America's national interest is bound to backfire."[60]

What convinced Osama bin Laden, in fact, to take his holy war to American soil was the defeat of U.S. forces in Somalia in 1993. Al-Qaeda military trainers, according to bin Laden and corroborated by two confidential interviews done for this book, were directing Somali irregulars in Mogadishu on October 3, 1993, when the Black Hawk helicopters were shot down.[61] America's withdrawal from Somalia thereafter persuaded bin Laden, and especially his second-in-command Ayman al-Zawahiri, that the superpower, if blindsided by irregular attacks on unexpected fronts, would withdraw, abandoning the "bastard regimes" Al-Qaeda itself had tried and failed to destroy. In May 1998, from a mountaintop training camp in Afghanistan, bin Laden explained this conclusion:

> After leaving Afghanistan, the Muslim fighters headed for Somalia and prepared for a long battle, thinking that the Americans were like the Russians. The youth were surprised at the low morale of the American soldiers and realized more than before that the American soldier was a paper tiger and, after a few blows, ran in defeat. And America forgot all the hoopla and media propaganda . . . about being a world leader and the leader of the New World Order, and after a few blows they forgot about this title and left, dragging behind them their corpses and their shameful defeat.[62]

The misadventure in Somalia has been depicted as a faulty military mission with confused civilian oversight. As serious an analyst as Max Boot, for example, suggests that had the U.S. left its 26,000-troop contingent in Somalia (instead of withdrawing it), this might have won the day.[63] But what about the next month or the next years?

Throughout the 1980s and 1990s, beyond the play of personality and party, there was an institutional metamorphosis taking place with far-reaching consequences: the militarization of U.S. foreign policy.

Central to the conversion of the American armed services into an imperial force was the elevation of the military commander in chief (or CINC). In addition to the five CINCs commanding regional forces throughout the world, each major U.S. military intervention also occasioned the selection of a CINC to command the operation. CINCs traveled like the president, negotiated diplomatic deals like the secretary of state, and made war with a battery of weaponry and forces unimaginable a generation before. Four-star CINCs, salaried at $135,000, lived in palatial private residences, had endless perks, with a small army of security and staff attending them. The spare quarters of a General Dwight Eisenhower or the three-man retinue of General Omar Bradley were long gone, as was the "citizens'" army that they stood for. What had replaced the likes of Eisenhower and Bradley, as *Washington Post* reporter Dana Priest described the CINCs, were "Pro Consuls of Empire."[64]

Beginning in the late 1980s, what the CINCs used most effectively in high- and low-intensity conflicts were Special Operations Forces. "Since 1987," General Carl Stiner (a retired commander of the Special Operations Forces) commented, "SOF has become the force of choice for theater CINCs and ambassadors; and SOF forces have been involved in virtually every contingency operation, as well as thousands of joint training exchanges, peacetime engagement activities, and humanitarian relief operations."[65] Their speed, skill, and flexibility of mission were critical factors in the growth of Special Forces, as were new weapons systems. As American interventions in the Balkans made clear, precision-guided munitions made strikes an instrument of policy as well as battlefield domination. By 2001, thirty-five-hundred Special Operations Forces were being deployed *per day* around the world. Imperial presidents of whichever party now had what the Constitution and the catastrophe of Vietnam had denied them: an imperial military.[66]

In the course of this praetorian advance of special forces, the CIA refined and expanded its intelligence mission, making "estimates" in terms of when to go in and how. In the course of being called on for both intelligence estimates and operational advances, the Agency overhauled and expanded its "Military Special Projects" division and renamed it the "Special Activities Division." The CIA professionalized its 150 or so "paramilitaries," whose moniker heretofore had been "door-kickers," into a force that could serve alongside Special Forces personnel. Additionally, the protocol of seconding or deputizing SEALs, Delta Forces, and Green Berets to the CIA (beyond the old practice called "sheep-dipping," in which such personnel were simply sent over to the Agency on an ad hoc basis) was broadened.[67] By the mid-1990s, the CIA's assault force was an integral, operating wing of the U.S. military's Special Operations Forces.

Authors such as Tom Clancy, Robin Moore, and Robert Kaplan have praised the virtuosity of these "twenty-first century warriors." But it was precisely the skill and speed of those forces that encouraged two presidents wary of foreign intervention (George Bush Sr. and Bill Clinton) to insert the elite units into missions without control. Neither Congress, increasingly disinterested in foreign affairs, nor the State Department, perennially incapable of fulfilling its role as primus inter pares in the foreign policy bureaucracy, could check this resort to the "quick fix" as opposed to the long-term political solution.[68] The media also contributed to the loss of critical evaluation. Instead of becoming a more considered and sophisticated forum for debate on defense and foreign policy issues, television and the print media became increasingly tame, even captive, in terms of press management by the military in successive administrations.

What happened in Somalia might be termed the "Goliath syndrome." Weak ground intelligence, faulty mission control, and the mistaken concept that leadership attacks could stabilize situations of marginal relevance to national security put American troops, led by Special Forces, in a killing zone. What is worse, we had the experience but missed the meaning of it. Condoleezza Rice would rightfully skewer the Clinton administration for "mission creep" in Somalia, and then, once in power herself, help orchestrate an even bloodier and more dangerous dead end for the U.S. in Iraq. That invasion, President Hosni Mubarak of Egypt predicted, "will produce a hundred bin Ladens."

In August 1992 the United States began airlifting tons of food to starving Somalia. Much of the food, however, was seized by gangs in the port of Mogadishu, gangs that also attacked and killed UN personnel who were managing the shipments. The press, as always, compressed the story into one between good and evil. Lost in the morality play was any reflection of the complexities and contradictions of that benighted country. The cry to "do something" became a sort of badge of moral standing for press and politicians alike. The first President Bush, by this time a lame duck with a few weeks left, approved Operation Restore Hope in late November. The plan was to land 25,400 U.S. troops in Somalia to secure the port of Mogadishu as well as the main roads into the interior of the country. National Security Adviser Brent Scowcroft was uneasy: "Sure, we can get in. But how do we get out?"[69] They were prophetic words.

Except for a phalanx of press in the middle of the night, beaming spotlights and training cameras on the incoming Special Forces, there was little complication in the landing. During the first month the operation went flawlessly. But doubters, such as Pennsylvannia congressman (and Vietnam veteran) Jack Murtha, detected a more troubling reality: that the drought, which we thought had alone caused mass starvation, was really the symptom of something else:

> The American public saw our deployment to Somalia as a straight-forward humanitarian mission to distribute food to the impoverished people seen every day on TV. The disturbing reality was that we were interjecting ourselves into a civil war among clans and subclans that were using the distribution or withholding of food as a weapon against each other.[70]

Little attention was paid to the fact that warfare against rivals, especially outsiders — from the Italians to the Ethiopians — was an enduring cultural trait of the Somalis. The American forces wryly nicknamed their excitable, jabbering natives "Skinnies," on account of their slender physiques. As so often, U.S. human intelligence (HUMINT) was itself thin and malnourished in terms of any hard calculation of reality.

What began as a humanitarian effort to secure the port and get food to the interior soon became a nation-building enterprise. Under UN Security Council Resolution 814, the multinational force was supposed to "disarm the heavily-armed gangs" and to "rebuild the Somali government, and rehabilitate the Somali economy." In early May, the UN formally took command of the overall operation and the U.S. began withdrawing its 25,400 troops. In early June, Somali irregulars from the clan of a warlord by the name of Mohammed Farah Aideed ambushed a cordon of Pakistani soldiers, killing twenty-five of them. American forces responded to this attack by sending helicopter gunships to take out a known redoubt of the Somali clan, but Aideed's forces quickly disappeared into the downtown warren of Mogadishu.

The Clinton administration then made a well-intentioned mistake, one that was later termed to have caused "mission creep" (the unintended, unplanned-for increase in a strategic mission). The U.S. ambassador to the UN, Madeleine Albright, working with the White House but not the Pentagon, persuaded the Security Council to pass a resolution directing UN forces in Somalia to arrest and prosecute those responsible for the ambush of the Pakistani UN troops.[71] Two weeks later, American helicopter gunships and AC-130s launched attacks on Aideed's villa, where he and his clan members were gathered, but failed to kill him. Somali irregulars loyal to Aideed then began ambushing U.S. forces. Both the UN and U.S. command in Mogadishu then requested U.S. Special Forces to take down Aideed and his clan leaders.

General Powell, as well as the new secretary of defense, Les Aspin, opposed the idea. "Finding Aideed in the warrens of Mogadishu was a thousand-to-one shot," Powell later wrote. "Worse, we were personalizing the conflict and getting deeper and deeper into ancient Somali rivalries."[72] Had human intelligence again been stronger, the UN mission and its American complement might have learned that Aideed's irregulars were being advised by Al-Qaeda trainers, who themselves were veterans of the mujahideen war in Afghanistan.[73] Moreover, the Clinton administration might have appreciated that, historically, leadership attacks — from Mossadegh to Lumumba to Castro to Qaddafi — have rarely worked; on the contrary, they have usually touched off vicious misadventure unforeseen at the time. Certainly the Kennedy brothers realized this when Nikita Khrushchev emplaced medium-range missiles in Cuba in October 1962 in retaliation for American attacks against Castro. President Truman and General Marshall proved wiser in this regard, electing not to bomb Emperor Hirohito's palace in 1944 for fear of reprisals against American POWs. (The emperor, as it turned out, proved to be a key broker of unconditional surrender to the Allied powers short of a full invasion of Japan.)[74] In 1993, however, the national security state was enamored of what was called "effects-based warfare" — the presumption that sophisticated weapons and shadow warriors could surgically accomplish what conventional warfare could not.

Under constant pressure to give the green light to the introduction of the Special Forces, Powell finally relented in August and dispatched the U.S. Army Rangers and the Delta Force into Somalia. The integration of these two units, in the judgment of Mark Bowden, was faulty. The Rangers were younger, generally less battle-tested, and lacked the improvisational ferocity that was (and is) the hallmark of the Delta Force.[75]

Task Force Ranger attempted no less than six sorties to take out Aideed and his commanders, without success. An emboldened Aideed then went on the radio to rally the Somali rabble. The Americans took out the radio station, but he was back on the air a few hours later via a mobile radio set. A Marine intelligence officer, John R. Murphy, captured the predicament in a single phrase: "As in so many societies, cultural differences were not taken properly into account, with disastrous results."[76]

Congressman Murtha, but few others on the Hill, made a concerted effort to get the Clinton administration to come up with a timetable for U.S. withdrawal. In a letter to the president, Murtha, then chairman of the Defense Appropriations Subcommittee, also protested the wide-ranging and insufficiently managed UN peacekeeping operations, no fewer than fourteen worldwide, in which the U.S. was both troop contributor and financier (to the tune of $1.4 billion annually). This, and other warnings, went unheeded.[77]

On a strike mission on October 3, 1993, Task Force Ranger encountered automatic rifle fire as well as rocket-propelled grenades, which downed two MH-60 Black Hawk helicopters. Efforts by the Army's 10th Mountain Division as well as the Special Forces to extricate the downed Rangers touched off a huge firefight. Eighteen American servicemen were killed and eighty-two wounded. Somali casualties ranged in the thousands. The spectacle of a naked, dead American soldier being dragged through the streets of Mogadishu stunned the

American public and brought exultation in certain parts of the Arab world. Shortly thereafter, the Clinton administration pulled the plug on the mission.

The Somali experience failed to meet the stringent preconditions to intervention set forth in the Powell doctrine. Once the operation morphed into a paramilitary (as opposed to a humanitarian) effort, the vital national-interest test in terms of American combat forces was ignored, as were "the means and the capacity to win." The exit strategy could not have been worse: defeat. Special Forces, sent in to achieve the small miracle of killing, or otherwise disestablishing, Aideed, were themselves ambushed and killed.

For all of this, the open-ended habit by the CINCs of deploying Special Forces in new operations was hard to break. Among the most popular Special Forces deployments during the 1980s and '90s were the antidrug operations in Latin America, whose consistent hallmark has been their high cost and total ineffectuality.[78] The American military was briefly held to account in 2001 when a Peruvian fighter pilot, advised by U.S. CIA surveillance, shot down a Cessna in northeastern Peru, killing Roni Bowers, the wife of a Baptist missionary, and their six-year-old daughter, Charity.

"War in a time of peace" required a disciplined and contained application of military force in situations affecting the American security interest in maintaining the balance of power. Without a strict sense of priority, military intervention was prey to disruption or defeat, as was the case in Somalia. In its first term, the Clinton administration unsuccessfully struggled to define a national security mission that could manage a wide and fluid range of security challenges. Part of the problem was the Clinton foreign policy team itself. Both Warren Christopher at State and Les Aspin at Defense — gracious and likable men though they were — had little capacity for command. Powell, who stayed on as chairman of the Joint Chiefs until July 1993, describes a meeting of the National Security Council, with the secretary of state sitting quietly to the side like a good corporate lawyer ready to respond to his client's wishes, and the brainy Aspin declaiming on matters near to and far from the subject at hand. The president, in the account of David Halberstam, was always late for these meetings for a simple reason — he could not stop talking. Junior officials, such as UN ambassador Madeleine Albright, often dominated the discussion. At one particularly sharp-edged session on Bosnia, Ambassador Albright asked Powell in frustration, "What's the point of having this superb military that you're always talking about if we can't use it?" Powell thought he would have an aneurysm: American GIs were not toy soldiers to be moved around on some sort of global game board. Two dozen times in the preceding three years, the U.S. had intervened for peacekeeping and humanitarian assistance — successfully — but always with a clear political goal matched by a military commitment to that goal. Tough political goals had to be set first.[79]

After the disaster in Somalia, the Clinton administration remained gun-shy on the subject of intervention. In Bosnia, the administration dragged its feet on authorizing NATO bombing, but then its brilliant emissary, Richard Holbrooke, was able to use a major setback for the Serbs (the Croatian seizure of Krajina), to wrest a multiethnic power-sharing arrangement for Bosnia — the so-called Dayton Accords.[80] With his extraordinary energy and creative personality, Clinton was able to achieve other successes, especially in what Joseph Nye has called "soft power." America's values, institutions, and culture — through cooperative, transparent ventures — provided a constructive current for much of the world.[81] Among other Clinton achievements were the NAFTA trade agreement and Russia's transition to the democratic, market-driven world. But in matters of war and peace, and the parameters determining intervention that lie between, the Clinton administration's struggle for a clear and compelling mission continued into his second term.[82]

The Clinton experience in the Balkans had been exhausting, erratic, but ultimately stabilizing for the region. With regard to the Pakistan-Afghanistan front, however, both the Bush and Clinton administrations failed. The question is why. We knew that Pakistan, a state with nuclear weapons, was turning into a criminal-terrorist enterprise, but U.S. intelligence habitually downgraded the danger because Pakistan was "an ally." Part of that status was undoubtedly a carryover from the Cold War, when the Muslim state served both as a counterpoise to Soviet-armed India and a catalyst of the Afghan insurgency against the Red Army.

Pakistani ambassador to the U.S. Shamshad Ahmad later blamed the U.S. for allowing the region to spin of control: "After the Soviets were forced out of Afghanistan, you [the United States] left us in the lurch with all the problems stemming from the war: an influx of refugees, the drug and gun running, a Kalashnikov culture." But such a culture, with its gun-running, drug trafficking, and the sponsoring of terrorism from the Kashmiri Harkat ul-Mujahideen to Al-Qaeda, was in fact the central business of the Pakistani government, which maintained a state of siege against India for purposes of internal order. The Indian government, through intelligence-sharing, diplomatic protests, and formal démarches in Washington and Delhi, made repeated efforts to wake up Washington, to no avail.[83]

What made the Pakistani lobby so powerful in Washington was its close association with the Saudis, who, Wahhabi or not, vindicated Voltaire's notation: "When it comes to money, every man has the same religion." The trough of Saudi money seemed inexhaustible; the military-industrial complex, as President Eisenhower had warned, proved tentacular in its greed. Former Bush secretaries of state and defense respectively, James Baker and Frank Carlucci, as well as former president Bush himself, cashed in, joining the Carlyle Group, a "merchant bank" that specialized in weapons-systems contracts, arms sales, and the takeover of defense procurement companies. One of its equity partners was the bin Laden Group. It was a sad testament to a corrupt political culture.

What brought the extreme danger of Pakistan clearly into focus was the terrorist bombing of the World Trade Center in February 1993. The explosion, which left a crater two hundred feet wide and several stories deep, was intended to topple the structure. The FBI director in New York, Robert Fox, after the capture of several of those responsible, commented that "those guys were trained by the CIA."[84] (He was immediately transferred from his position.) In the course of the investigation, it became apparent that the bomb manuals used by the terrorists were knockoffs of Agency materials and that nearly all the fanatics were trained by the Inter-Services Intelligence (ISI), the CIA's old partner in the secret war against the Red Army. Although the United States attorney's office sanitized references in the testimony of both witnesses and the accused to the Agency, the story broke several weeks later.

In September 1994, CNN correspondent Peter Arnett hosted a documentary entitled *Terror Nation? U.S. Creation?* Arnett identified the nexus between the Brooklyn-based Afghan Refuge Center and "holy war headquarters" in Peshawar, Pakistan. "It is in Peshawar that the New York terror campaign takes shape. Peshawar was the headquarters of Sheikh [Omar Abdel] Rahman's international network. Peshawar was also the headquarters of Gulbuddin Hekmatyar's party, which trained four of the key New York suspects. Hekmatyar's links to the New York suspects came as no surprise to pro-Western Afghan officials. They officially warned the U.S. government about Hekmatyar no fewer than four times. The last warning was delivered just days before the Trade Center attack."[85]

Pakistan had become what one Defense Intelligence Agency official called "our psychotic stepchild." Thanks to the latest CIA surveillance technology, Pakistan's ISI could monitor every phone call within the country and thousands outside Pakistan.[86] The military dictatorship could invade Kashmir and foment terrorist sorties into India with relative impunity because of American sponsorship. Peshawar could serve as Osama bin Laden's terrorist entrepôt until Pakistan began underwriting the financial survival of a cruel martial cult called the Taliban, which in turn would host the Saudi terrorist.

The point here is that blowback by Afghanistan's holy warriors was overwhelmingly evident *before* the 9/11 attack, as was Pakistan's double game of blackmailing the U.S. into backing its dictatorships in exchange for interdicting the token terrorist.[87] The Goliath syndrome, long on open-ended operations and extended troop presences sustained by self-serving intelligence, stimulated the very thing it was supposed to resolve — breakdowns in regional security and the rise of groups savagely disposed toward the United States. Why were 7,000 U.S. troops, for example, stationed in Saudi Arabia, the holy see of Islam? Where did force projection, as in Somalia, lead to force vulnerability, or worse?* These geopolitical questions required more than geomilitary answers. CINCs, even those as gifted and masterful as General Anthony

---

*The term "force projection" refers to the strategic capacity of the U.S. military to introduce ground, naval, and aerial forces into a given theater of operation."

Zinni, were not the ones to make those choices, but rather the president with the advice and consent of the Congress. As Benjamin Franklin said when a woman asked him at the conclusion of the Constitutional Convention, "Well, Mr. Franklin. What will it be?" Franklin's reply resounds today: "A republic — if you can keep it."

The fight to keep the republic occurred on a neglected front, and was waged by an unexpected personality. On February 7, 1995, according to Ahmed Rashid, Pakistan's most distinguished analyst of contemporary events, "nine agents of the CIA and FBI teamed up with ISI officers. Acting on a tip from a South African Muslim informer named Mustaq Parker, who won a two-million-dollar reward and a new identity in the U.S. as [further] reward, the U.S.-Pakistani team burst into a room in the Su Casa, a guesthouse in Islamabad owned by Osama bin Laden, their guns ready and drawn. Supine on the bed was the man then considered the world's most hunted terrorist, twenty-seven-year-old Ramzi Ahmed Yousef, the mastermind of the 1993 bombing of the World Trade Center."[88]

The point man in this extraordinary operation that spirited Yousef back to the U.S. was no CINC or Special Forces asset, nor was he a veteran CIA agent or State Department counterterrorism specialist, but rather an FBI special agent with about thirty-six total hours counterterrorist experience. In the coming years he would transform Washington's entire strategy on terrorism and become the most revered and detested man in the war on terror. He was the FBI's David to the Pentagon, State Department, and CIA's Goliath. His name was John Patrick O'Neill.

3

COUNTERTERRORIST
The Crusade of John O'Neill

Sunday, February 7, 1995

FBI headquarters

Washington, D.C.

B y the time he arrived in D.C. to take over the counterterrorism operation in the first week of February 1995, O'Neill's high style and hard-charging derring-do were well-known within the Bureau but hardly outside it. Within days, however, O'Neill was to achieve sudden celebrity within the highest precincts of the national security state.

After a five-scotch farewell — or so he later recounted — in Chicago, where he had served as the FBI second-in-command, O'Neill got in his car and drove all night to D.C. Arriving late Sunday morning, February 7, he went straight to FBI headquarters and found his way to the counterterrorism section. He was hanging his pictures in an empty office when he heard a phone ringing somewhere in the warren of cubicles.

The caller was Richard Clarke, head of counterterrorism at the National Security Council. When Clarke asked who was on the other end of the phone, O'Neill replied, "I'm John O'Neill. Who the hell are you?" Clarke introduced himself and told O'Neill that he had just come across some intelligence from Pakistan that Ramzi Ahmed Yousef had been spotted in Islamabad. O'Neill barely recognized the name, so Clarke filled him in. After the 1993 bombing of the World Trade Center, Yousef had moved to Manila and slipped out of sight until 1994, when Filipino police had stumbled on his trail in the course of investigating a small apartment in which there had been an accidental explosion. A laptop left behind in the apartment detailed plans to blow up eleven passenger jets and assassinate Pope John Paul II.[1]

Clarke remembered:

> He [O'Neill] had never worked on the case before, but he obviously knew the importance of it. He went into action over the course of the next two or three days; he never left the office. He worked the phones out to Pakistan. He worked the phones out to the Pentagon. He worked the phones to the State Department.[2]

O'Neill first got clearance to seize Yousef (as opposed to extradite him). He then put together a somewhat unorthodox team: a medical doctor, a fingerprint expert (to make sure it was Yousef, if they ever got him), a State Department representative, and a hostage rescue squad. The intelligence on Yousef was that he had plans to take a bus to Peshawar and then disappear into Afghanistan. The hastily assembled team flew to Islamabad and, with the cooperation of Pakistani military intelligence, was able to capture Yousef, who was flown back to the United States, where he was tried, convicted, and sentenced to 240 years in prison.[3]

It was a huge breakthrough for American intelligence and law enforcement, especially for the FBI, long regarded as the klutziest of extraterritorial agencies. In 1993 it was famous for its plodding, fruitless efforts at drug and laundered-money interdiction.

O'Neill's meeting style was soon to become the talk of clandestine Washington. After hours on the phone cajoling his counterparts at State, CIA, and Defense, he would get them into a meeting the likes of which no one could remember attending in the balkanized terrain of federal law enforcement. Radiantly dressed and beaming, O'Neill would greet them in a sort of FDR style as they entered the main conference room, with thanks, winks, and an inescapable stream of Irish blarney. He would review progress to date — then simply assign tasks and ask each participant to state timelines and execution. Bringing in two or three cell phones, he would initiate calls. Many bridled at the treatment, but Clarke remembered that O'Neill's information was so exhaustive, his preparation so meticulous, his personality so relentless, that somehow he got away with it. The word went out: "If you didn't want the job done, you didn't give it to John O'Neill. If you did want the job done, you gave it to John O'Neill, and watch out, because it was going to get done."[4]

Clarke noticed something else about O'Neill — that he was insecure. "He always needed that reassurance. At the end of meetings, he'd often ask, 'How'd I do,' or 'What did I do wrong?'"[5] Beneath the glossy, muscular aspect of the man, the relentless ebullience and the intimidating intelligence, was someone with a deep fear of failure.

Beyond his command capacity, O'Neill was also an extraordinary

forensicist, as was evident in the FBI's investigation of the TWA Flight
800 explosion and crash in July 1996 off the coast of Long Island. There
was widespread speculation at the Counterterrorism Security Group
(CSG) that multiple witness accounts of an ascending flare prior to the
explosion of the airplane indicated that a shoulder-fired missile from
shore had brought the plane down. O'Neill worked with Defense Department experts to show that the airliner was beyond the range of a
Stinger missile, at least one fired from shore. He speculated that the flare
might have been caused by the ignition of leaking fuel and persuaded
the CIA to do a video simulation of that scenario. The virtual result
paralleled eyewitness accounts. The FBI never conclusively solved the
case, but it is now accepted that mechanical failure was the cause.[6]

People around O'Neill at this time remembered him reading
everything — the transcripts, depositions, and witness reports from the
World Trade Center bombing case; CIA estimates and cables from the
field; Defense Intelligence estimates of just what degree of intelligence
cooperation we were getting from so-called friendly regimes. He expressed his view — and was advised henceforth to withhold such judgment — that the policy of the Saudi royal family was to lie to the
United States about its funding of terrorism. He wondered openly about
the CIA's incestuous relationship with the Pakistani Inter-Services Intelligence, which was advancing a fundamentalist movement called the
Taliban in Afghanistan.[7]

After the Yousef arrest and prosecution, O'Neill began speaking
directly to the press and public, saying that far beyond the blind mullah
from Brooklyn indicted in the first attack on the World Trade Center,
there was an international network of terror groups that overlapped
and, at points, interlocked. They seemed both patient and furious in
their efforts to destroy. "The intent is for a large number of casualties."[8]

It was as if O'Neill saw an immense storm on the horizon and
spoke and acted with signal urgency to avoid it. In this mission, he
spared no one above or below him. "He was smarter than everybody
else," one FBI agent observed, "and he would use that fine mind to hu-
miliate people." He rode his agents to exhaustion, demanding the same
seventy-five-hour week he maintained. Special Agent John Lipka was
one of O'Neill's horses, and recalled, "He was able to identify those

people who shared his work ethic, and then he tasked the living shit out of them, with e-mails and status briefings and phones and pagers going off all the time, to the point that I asked him, 'When do you sleep?'"[9]

On June 25, 1996, a massive bomb in a fuel truck demolished a high-rise called Khobar Towers in Dhahran, Saudi Arabia, where American servicemen were housed. Nineteen Americans died and five hundred others were injured.[10] The powerful bomb collapsed much of the building and left a huge crater at the locus of the explosion. Accompanied by FBI director Louis Freeh, O'Neill made several trips to Saudi Arabia to investigate the blast. In meetings with Saudi leaders, including some of the lesser royals, he spoke bluntly and accusingly.[11] He asked for dossier after dossier of known Saudi terrorists. He carried around photos of the mangled remains of the American soldiers to allay, as he later termed it, "the rather reverential atmosphere around the stinking place." He reminded his FBI colleagues that the last time there had been a bombing in Saudi Arabia (in 1995), the regime had beheaded the alleged perpetrators before U.S. officials could question them. The Saudis were furious and protested both in Riyadh and Washington. On the way home, O'Neill made a comment to Freeh that resonated over the years for both its offensiveness and its accuracy. "Lou," he said to Freeh sitting next to him on the government jet, in response to the director's expression of being satisfied with Saudi cooperation, "they're blowing smoke up your ass." Freeh was so galled by this remark that for the next twelve hours of the flight he refused to speak to O'Neill.[12]

ABC News producer Chris Isham, who became a close friend of O'Neill's in New York, later commented, "He felt the Saudis were definitely playing games and that the senior officials in the U.S. government, including Louis Freeh, just didn't get it." Or didn't *want* to get it. O'Neill wondered openly why more than 7,000 American officers and enlisted men were stationed on Saudi soil. The U.S., he told Clarke, had entered into a de facto military alliance with a weak, corrupt regime that bankrolled international terrorism.

The military alliance with the Saudi royal family was the direct result of the American-led multinational intervention in 1991 to expel Iraq from Kuwait and bring Saddam Hussein to heel. "Desert Storm" transformed the long-standing "oil for security" arrangement with the Saudis into a full military communion. The Clinton administration, operating with a loosely defined concept of post–Cold War U.S. national security, had allowed the relationship to grow and deepen during the balance of the 1990s.[13] There was a "stealth imperialism" afoot; without a strong definition of the national security interest from the White House, the nativists on the Hill combined with their military-industrial patrons to push defense spending to levels beyond any consonance with national defense.[14]

A year after the Khobar Towers tragedy, Secretary of Defense William S. Cohen, in a document entitled "Personal Accountability for Force Protection at Khobar Towers," would pin blame on Brigadier General Terryl Schwalier, commander of the 4404th Wing (Provisional), for dereliction of duty. There was no section of the report devoted to governmental accountability.[15]

If getting tough with the Saudis was off-limits, tracking bin Laden was not. The National Security Council tasked the CIA in 1996 to mount an operation that would measure Al-Qaeda's terrorist reach. The problem was that bin Laden, at this time, was in Sudan, running a small empire that included not only terrorist training and deployment but large-scale road and warehouse construction. He was one of the most powerful men in the country. Furthermore, the U.S. had no embassy in Khartoum or business offices to provide cover for espionage.[16] For these reasons, the CIA created a virtual station in northern Virginia, codenamed Station Alex. O'Neill asked and got the go-ahead for the FBI to joint-venture in the station.

It was a notable success in proving that bin Laden had an international network that moved money, explosives, and terrorists in no fewer than fifty-six different countries. By tracking the movements of certain individuals, Station Alex identified what NSC staffer Clarke called "a string." By tugging it, through surveillance and cross-fertilization of foreign intelligence, more and more terrorist suspects were revealed — a total of more than four hundred. Working with FBI deputy director Robert M. "Bear" Bryant, O'Neill wrote a report advocating a fundamental change in the way the FBI would fight terrorism. It called for a centralized information system and a permanent task force to predict future attacks. Agents could spend entire careers working counterterrorism cases. The recommendation, though approved, was never funded.[17]

In January 1997, O'Neill was offered the second-in-command position at the FBI's large New York office, with the special responsibility of counterterrorism and national security. He jumped at the offer and invited his longtime love interest (one of two), Valerie James, who had remained in Chicago, to join him in Manhattan.[18] Everything about the glitz, grit, and speed of New York suited O'Neill — the front table at Elaine's where he often held court until 3 A.M., the blizzard of culture on the street, on stage, and in the polished drawing rooms, the gutsy give-and-take of the place. For a devout Catholic who had grown up poor in north Jersey, mass at St. Patrick's was a quiet splendor.

On his first day in the New York office, he asked his secretary, Lorraine di Taranto, to help him schedule some "courtesy calls" to the elected and the influential, a typical practice for the FBI high command. But in O'Neill's case the list of people ran into the dozens, and he wanted to know if he could see them all within three months. And he did![19] Each week throughout his tenure in New York City, O'Neill entertained, with display and style, visiting law enforcement and intelligence officials from foreign countries. At sunset he would zoom around Manhattan in a police helicopter, followed by an intimate dinner, and then drinks at Elaine's, Bruno's, or a host of other bars and restaurants. O'Neill called it his "night job." Within a year, it is safe to say, he was the most well-known figure in the world of law enforcement, and he soon converted this into a global forensics and intelligence database that cross-fertilized investigations and terrorist profiles and tracking.[20]

Frances Townsend, Attorney General Janet Reno's deputy, described his talent:

> He had a weird combination of qualities. John was not your average agent, and that screamed itself at you when he was in a room in a meeting on a case. He was bright. He was articulate. He was very aggressive in terms of how he approached his work. He was very hard-charging, which, I think, at times, turned people off. What I think made John different was his passion for the job,

his passion for fighting for things he really believed in. . . . What made him different was his absolute single-mindedness and passion that he brought to whatever case he was working on.[21]

FBI director Freeh, to his credit, released O'Neill to take his case for national preparedness to the media. In May 1997 O'Neill announced point-blank that terrorists were organized and operating within the U.S. A month later in Chicago, before the National Strategy Forum, he described the mujahideen's defeat of the Soviets in Afghanistan as "a major watershed event," rightly predicting that they would bring their destructive skills to the West. On an A&E program in December 1997, he spoke about the primary duty of FBI agents and all law enforcement — "to protect constitutional rights, to protect civil rights," warning that in societies "with too much order, there is little liberty."[22] He and all Americans, he said, participated in "a delicate ballet that occurs every day" in the streets, cities, and courtrooms. The balance was "ordered liberty." You had to add one more wrinkle to O'Neill's complex countenance: he may have been a registered Republican with a 9 mm automatic strapped to his ankle, but he was also a social and civil liberty liberal.[23]

During that summer of 1997, there were investigative leads that revealed the dimensions of the Al-Qaeda network in New York City itself. Just before dawn on July 31, 1997, Abdel Rahman Mosabbah, a young Arab man, flagged down a police officer near the Atlantic Avenue train station in Brooklyn and told him that his roommate, Ghazi Abu Maizer, was going to suicide-bomb the station at rush hour. O'Neill was immediately alerted and the next morning the apartment was raided by an FBI SWAT team that found Maizer, a pipe bomb (assembled, fused, and ready to go), and a letter protesting U.S. support of Israel. While it wasn't clear that Maizer had been deployed by Al-Qaeda, his association with the Al-Farouq mosque seemed to indicate that. Al-Farouq had hosted the blind Egyptian cleric Sheikh Omar Abdel Rahman, who had been implicated in the 1993 attack on the World Trade Center.

In that same summer of 1997, Al-Qaeda deployed a team of "tourists" to film New York City landmarks. A twenty-nine-minute videotape was later recovered by Spanish police that shows Ghasoub al-Abrash Ghalyoun, a Syrian national, sitting next to a life-size bronze statue of a businessman in the outdoor plaza of the World Trade Center.[24] There were also long panning shots of the exterior structure of the World Trade Center towers as they rose from the ground floor. Bin Laden, though not formally educated as a structural engineer, had broad experience in using steel girders and stressed concrete in building construction.

But O'Neill and other counterterrorist agents were chipping away. When Jamal al-Fadl, one of bin Laden's closest aides from his years in Sudan, began cooperating with the U.S. government after stealing $100,000 from Al-Qaeda, O'Neill learned that the Al-Farouq mosque and the Alkifah Center in Brooklyn served as both recruiting and fundraising sites for Al-Qaeda. O'Neill spent several hours with al-Fadl, quizzing him on how bin Laden moved money, deployed key commanders, recruited suicide operatives, and concealed his own communications and movements. He began to see that beyond the hate-filled zealot, bin Laden was a sort of terrorist entrepreneur, leveraging a variety of assets and opportunities in his attack on America, and building teams that needed relatively little command-and-control once launched.[25] He was adaptive, and cunning. This was no Qaddafi.

In his exchanges with counterterrorist colleagues like Clarke, O'Neill often compared bin Laden to Hitler. He was more than an evil prophet: he combined a ratlike sense of opportunity with the pedestrian methods of a party organizer. When Hitler wrote *Mein Kampf,* O'Neill said to Clarke, "[he] was just a jerk. No one took him seriously, so no one read the book, or if they read the book, they didn't believe he would try to do what was in the book. . . . Bin Laden's just like this. . . . He's going to war with the United States."[26]

In June 1998, O'Neill learned that ABC News's John Miller had traveled to bin Laden's redoubt in Afghanistan to do an interview. He immediately called Chris Isham, an ABC producer, and demanded to see the whole interview, outtakes and all. Such a request went totally against ABC News policy, but ultimately Isham was able to persuade the network to put the whole interview online, knowing that its first viewer would be John O'Neill.[27] O'Neill watched it again and again, had the interview retranslated from Arabic to English no fewer than three times. He told his counterparts that these were not histrionic comments; they were pronouncements of policy, and they might even be something more — exhortations to action.[28]

The 2000 millennium
New York City

On May 28, 1998, at midnight, with hundreds of AK-47 rounds being fired into the air and with the smell of gasoline from rumbling generators, bin Laden's convoy of vehicles pulled up at one of his camps near Khost, Afghanistan. Out stepped the six-foot-three-inch bin Laden with his seven bodyguards. In the hail of gunfire and shouted greetings, bin Laden, accompanied by his two top aides, Mohammed Atef (later killed in a U.S. aerial bombardment in November 2001) and Ayman al-Zawahiri (the leader of Islamic Jihad, which merged with Al-Qaeda in the early 1990s), walked through the swarm of mujahideen. Despite the tumult bin Laden's eyes were "fixed and steady," in the recollection of ABC News journalist John Miller, who had traveled to Afghanistan for the interview. One of the aides waved off the gunfire the way an emcee might quell a standing ovation, but everyone kept shooting.[29]

Bin Laden walked into a long rectangular hut that had been set up for the meeting, followed by his bodyguards, aides, and the ABC crew of two. The Saudi sat down at the far end of the hut on a bench with red cushions and propped his automatic rifle against the wall. Twenty or so of the mujahideen lined the benches on either side of the room, guns on their laps or slung to the side, straining to listen to the man they referred to as "gentle Osama." Behind bin Laden was a brightly illuminated map of Africa, something that would later draw the attention of O'Neill and others.

As Miller later explained and the videotape shows, bin Laden speaks in a soft, raspy voice that sounds "like an old uncle giving good advice." He is wearing a green, roughcut military jacket and a gold shawl with a white turban on his head. He looks grave, somewhat fatigued, but coldly poised — and a good deal older than his forty-one years.

The control factor in the interview is complete. Shortly before the interview was to begin, someone in the Al-Qaeda entourage returned the camera of the ABC News photographer, Rick Bennett, that had been taken from him two days previously. Miller was advised that bin Laden would answer all the questions that the ABC reporter had submitted the day before, but that there would be no translation provided. "You can take the tape to New York and have them translate it there." Miller said that without a translation, he couldn't ask follow-up questions. "Oh, that will not be a problem," the aide said. "There will be no follow-up questions." When flies begin landing on bin Laden's face, the aides advise their leader and his armed followers as well as the Americans while they spray the hut. Moments later, in a cloud of insecticide, the interview, which is really a monologue, begins.

Arabic is among the most lyric languages in the world, with an alliterative, throaty, rolling inflection that fires the sutras of the Prophet as well as everyday speech in the street. Bin Laden's Arabic is characteristic of a Saudi aristocrat, with a strong undercurrent of religious imagery and sonorousness.[30] He speaks with a kind of lucid calm that is more reminiscent of elderly, wise mullahs than political revolutionaries. The style is discursive, not hortatory. For the most part in the ABC interview, bin Laden looks at his hands, occasionally looking up, his eyes flashing in emphasis.

When the Saudi royal family permitted the United States to use Saudi bases in the war to expel Iraq from Kuwait in 1991 (the video shown in casbahs and at Friday night prayers in thousands of mosques throughout the Middle East depicted American armored personnel carriers within sight of the holy mosque of Mecca), bin Laden believed he had the makings of Salah ad-Din's army, which had routed the Crusaders from the Holy Land in 1187. In the course of his interview with Miller, in savage, lucid language, bin Laden makes it clear his war is against the Arab regimes sustained by the United States — not the "clash of civilizations" or a Kulturkampf:

> The call to wage war against America was made because America has spearheaded the crusade against the Islamic nation, sending thousands of its troops to the land of the two holy mosques over

and above its meddling in its affairs and its support of the oppressive, corrupt, and tyrannical regime that is in control. These are the
reasons behind the singling out of America.

When asked if he supports terrorism, he responds that it is necessary for any person or nation to practice terrorism "for the purpose of
abolishing tyranny and corruption," and, eyes suddenly flashing, he
concludes:

> In today's wars, there are no morals, and it is clear that mankind has
> descended to the lowest degrees of decadence and oppression.
> They rip us of our wealth and of our resources and of our oil. Our
> religion is under attack. They kill and murder our brothers. They
> compromise our honor and our dignity, and dare we utter a single
> word of protest against injustice, we are called terrorists. This is
> compounded injustice.

Somalia was pivotally important in bin Laden's estimate of American lasting power in Islamic war zones.[31] Neither the CIA nor the Defense Intelligence Agency reported, either before or during the Somali
intervention, that experienced Al-Qaeda trainers were preparing a
shooting gallery for them to enter. It was thought that the can-do esprit
de corps of the Special Forces, with their superior firepower and ability
to maneuver, would overwhelm the Somali irregulars.[32]

What emerges from bin Laden's statements is his use of Islam as a
sort of moral armature for war against Western client regimes in Saudi
Arabia and Egypt. Thus, when asked about the Saudi regime, he says
nothing about their religious turpitude, but rather their *political* association with the infidel:

> The fate of any government which sells the interests of its own
> people and betrays the nation and commits offenses which furnish
> grounds for expulsion from Islam, is known. We expect for the
> ruler of Riyadh the same fate as the Shah of Iran. We anticipate
> this to happen to him and to the influential people who stand by
> him and who have sided with the Jews and the Christians, giving
> them free reign over the land of the two Holy Mosques. These are
> grave offenses that are grounds for expulsion from the faith. They
> shall be wiped out.

Is his fatwa directed toward the killing of all Americans, just the U.S. military, or Americans in Saudi Arabia?

> Through history, America has not been known to differentiate between the military and the civilians or between men and women, or adults and children. Those who launched atomic bombs and used weapons of mass destruction against Nagasaki and Hiroshima were the Americans. Can bombs differentiate between military and women and infants and children? America has no religion that can deter her from exterminating whole peoples. Your position against Muslims in Palestine is despicable and disgraceful. America has no shame. . . . We do not have to differentiate between military and civilian. As far as we are concerned, they are all targets.

Bin Laden's vow of violent retribution against the United States (including his pose before the brightly colored map of East Africa) was fulfilled nine weeks after the interview. On August 7, two huge bombs nearly leveled the U.S. embassies in Nairobi, Kenya, and Dar es Salaam, Tanzania, killing 224 and injuring thousands. Evidence subsequently developed in the investigation of the embassy bombings indicated that the huge explosion in Nairobi had been in the making for five years.

Within minutes of learning of the attack, O'Neill walked into the office of Lewis Schiliro, who ran the New York operation, and told him, "It's Al-Qaeda." He requested authorization to lead the FBI team of forensics experts in sourcing the explosions and building the case in East Africa. Schiliro agreed, but there was resistance in Washington. Attorney General Reno favored O'Neill, as did his powerful ally in New York, United States attorney Mary Jo White, but Thomas Pickard, who ran the Bureau's criminal division at headquarters, blocked his designation.[33] It was a slap in the face for O'Neill. "This is the World Series," Reno's assistant Fran Townsend recalled, "and he's gotten benched. That's exactly how he feels about it. He is very hurt, very upset about it and bitter."[34]

More than five hundred FBI agents traveled to Kenya and Tanzania to investigate the incident, which bore the Al-Qaeda hallmarks: precision timing (the explosions in both countries were nine minutes apart at a time of day when the vast majority of Kenyan and Tanzanian Muslims were at their mosques praying); experienced ringleaders (Mohammed Odeh; Haroun Fazil; "Abdel Rahman," the nom de guerre of Al-Qaeda's best explosives operative); and flexibly staged recruitment and deployment of the team, operated on a strict need-to-know basis. Thanks to the lucky arrests of Odeh and Mohammed al-'Owhali, the U.S. was able to source the attack within the week of its commission. O'Neill then took over the crucial preparation of evidence in the indictment and prosecution of five individuals, who were later convicted.

The investigation was a genuine success, but the Clinton administration wanted more — military action, or at least the appearance of it. After two weeks of deliberation, the National Security Council prepared a list of targets. On August 20, President Clinton broke off his vacation on Martha's Vineyard and, in a hastily assembled encounter with reporters on that island, announced that the U.S. had launched cruise missiles at bin Laden training camps in Afghanistan and Sudan. Clinton then flew back to the White House and addressed the nation. "Earlier today, the United States carried out simultaneous strikes against terrorist facilities and infrastructure in Afghanistan. . . . We have reason to believe that a gathering of key terrorist leaders was to take place there today, thus underscoring the urgency of our action."

To many, the timing of the strike, given the president's political embarrassment in the Monica Lewinsky affair (and his duplicitous testimony under oath a few days before), seemed grossly expedient. The day of the attack also happened to coincide with the release to the public of congressional evidence to impeach the president. It was later revealed that the intelligence on which the bombing of the Sudanese plant was based was inconclusive at the time and was later found to be inaccurate. The urgency for immediate retaliation was said to be based on an estimate that bin Laden was about to launch a chemical attack, but this too was later evaluated as tendentious.[35]

"Operation Infinite Reach," as it had been infelicitously named, failed to kill bin Laden, but it did manage to "wag the dog" in terms of using a military mission to drive the Lewinsky scandal off the evening news. Beyond that meretricious act, however, it also revealed fundamental flaws in a military response to mass murder. As the U.S. soon learned, bin Laden and his chief lieutenants had escaped unscathed, having cleared out of his camps with days to spare.

Peter L. Bergen argues that bin Laden was savvy enough to expect a cruise missile attack, given Clinton's established aversion to risking possible casualties in an airstrike or commando operation.[36] Perhaps the Americans hoped that, even if they didn't get bin Laden, he would be deterred from attempting some atrocity in the future — a fundamental misapprehension of the Saudi's fanatical determination.

Pakistan's Inter-Services Intelligence, as sinister and compromised as ever, supplied Washington with ground intelligence about bin Laden's movements around Khost, where four of his training camps were located. Did ISI tip Al-Qaeda off as to the timing of the attack? An hour before launch, an American general met with the ISI director-general Mahmoud Ahmad, to advise him that cruise missiles would be crossing Pakistani airspace and reassure him that they were not incoming missiles from India. (General Amad would later be linked by Indian intelligence to a payment from an ISI asset to Mohammed Atta, the ringleader in the attacks of September 11.)[37] Whether or not ISI played both sides, advance indication of an attack was there for all to see. American warships had assumed firing position off the Pakistani coast shortly after the embassy bombings. Less than a week before August 20, there was an evacuation of U.S. diplomatic personnel in Kabul and two cities in Pakistan.

The Clinton policy toward terrorism, despite admirable progress in the areas of detection and interagency coordination, was essentially one of containment. There was no real contemplation of going to the source, either in terms of a raid to eliminate Al-Qaeda's base of operation or to confront allies such as Saudi Arabia and Pakistan, which were providing critical elements of financing, as well as logistical and intelligence support.

Benjamin Barber, in his prophetic analysis of the central fault line of our age, *Jihad vs. McWorld* (1995), defines the politicized ethos of jihad: it identifies "the self by contrasting it with an alien 'other' and makes politics an exercise in exclusion and resentment."[38] When bin Laden is asked what message he would give to fellow Muslims, the reply is bitter and violent: "I have to stress the necessity of focusing on the Americans and the Jews, for they represent the spearhead with which the members of our religion have been slaughtered. Any effort directed against America and the Jews yields positive and direct results, Allah willing. It is far better for anyone to kill a single American than to squander his efforts on other activities."

What the United States had created was a context in which Al-Qaeda could thrive. As Barber argues, the dialectic preached by violent atavists like bin Laden would not be as persuasive were it not for Mc-World's dehumanized imperative of production and market "choice" that has sapped spiritual liberty, undermined democratic thought and institutions at home, and created a new form of parasitism in the developing world. American military force projection both dramatized this dependence and occasioned vulnerability to terrorist attacks on U.S. forces, as would occur in Yemen a year later.

Sometime in the middle 1990s, bin Laden made a strategic decision: to strike at the United States to shatter the pro-Western regimes in the Middle East that had repulsed and largely defeated him. He would touch off, through terror attacks, a sort of imperial cost-accounting by McWorld. Terror would bring reprisal, which would spur further recruitment of suicidal fodder. As the price of further reprisal by the West went up — with thousands of innocents dead in its wake — the U.S. would back away and its infidel clients in the Middle East would collapse and be destroyed.[39]

There was an indispensable and paradoxical aspect to his plan: namely, that as he railed against the corrupt rulers of his Saudi homeland, he would blackmail them into financing his deadly schemes beyond the kingdom. During the 1990s, Al-Qaeda would receive more than $500 million from Saudi Arabia.[40] And the reason the Saudis' superpower patron, the United States, countenanced this arrangement was simple — the Saudis, it has been well established, had greased every wheel in Washington.

Four months after the failed cruise missile attack, Station Alex, the joint CIA-FBI task force that was shadowing Al-Qaeda, proposed that a secret team of investigators, including CIA paracommandos, make a lightning strike on Al-Qaeda's base in Kandahar and arrest bin Laden.

According to Special Agent Jack Cloonan, the plan got far enough that Station Alex was dry-running landings of small aircraft in San Antonio in preparation for the sortie. Attorney General Janet Reno vetoed the plan. "They came to the decision that this plan was too dangerous," Cloonan later recounted, "that the loss of life on the ground would have been significant."[41] Just which Special Forces team (most probably Hostage Rescue Team) would spearhead the operation is not clear, but with Kandahar bristling with mujahideen in the aftermath of the failed "Operation Infinite Reach" cruise missile attacks, it had the markings of a long and risky shot.

Beyond the tactical merits of how to eliminate bin Laden, the U.S. faced a contradiction of epic proportions in the war against terrorism: two of its allies, Saudi Arabia and Pakistan, were in the top five regimes in the world that financed and facilitated international terrorism. During the Cold War, the cause of anti-Communism had suspended any consideration of this contradiction, especially in the secret effort by the three governments to arm the mujahideen in Afghanistan. But with the collapse of the Soviet Union and the rise of Al-Qaeda, the faustian bargain continued. When Pakistan began assembling a hydrogen bomb in the late 1980s, the U.S. looked the other way, abandoning a generation of bipartisan efforts to try to control the spread of nuclear weapons. When Saudi Arabia asked for high-tech air force weaponry in the form of AWACS and F-16s in 1982, they got them. In the aftermath of the Gulf War in 1991, the U.S. established military bases in Saudi Arabia and manned them with more than 7,000 servicemen.

The phenomenon driving this expansion of empire and devaluation of traditional standards of the national security interest was what President Dwight Eisenhower had warned the nation about in 1960 — "the military-industrial complex." A generation into this symbiosis, a large and voracious class of inside players and profiteers had effectively erased the difference between public and private, and between Democrat and Republican. The money trough was deep. Patriotism was profitable. Few questioned the drift, or worried about the future price.

John O'Neill did. He wasn't the only old-fashioned patriot in the endless corridors of American intelligence, defense, and law enforcement, but he was one of the most impassioned and certifiably the most blunt. His sin — and it resulted in his being passed over for three different positions and eventually shot down in an internal security investigation — was that in the chummy world of those who traffic in influence, fame, and the eventual consultancy, he was not "a team player."

His comportment in the Situation Room, though scintillating, left little room for lesser talents:

> John would enter the room and there would be a presence about him. He would go around the room like it was a ward meeting and he was an Irish politician. He'd smash everybody on the back, grin, grip, pass out cigars and, you know, the atmosphere changed. He was building a team. I [Richard A. Clarke] might have been chairing the meeting but he was building a team. And we were all on his team. He wanted to get people beyond representing their agencies and have them be friends.
>
> Then when you got around to the substance of any discussion, he always knew more about the CIA guy's brief than the CIA guy did. He knew more about the State Department guy's brief than the State Department guy. He prepared for meetings. He prepared in detail. He wanted to show everybody that his recommendation was well-founded, because he knew all the facts, he had considered all the facts. He would continue to drive, press, press, until people agreed with his recommendation.[42]

For O'Neill, Clarke, Sheehan, and the rest of the counterterrorist high command in Washington, every effort was made to step up detection based on what they knew about Al-Qaeda's long setup process. By the summer of 1999, Counterterrorism Center (CTC) and Station Alex began to pick up "chatter" (raw intercepts) that seemed to point toward some cataclysm toward the end of the year. By early December, focus shifted to the days before and after the millennium. On December 14, Ahmed Ressam, an Algerian, was intercepted at the Canadian border carrying 130 pounds of high explosive in his trunk. A search of his Montreal apartment revealed a map of California with circles around Los Angeles International and two other airports. In Ressam's pocket were several New York telephone numbers.[43]

At this point, O'Neill went, as he put it, "Cecil B. DeMille." He commandeered several hundred New York City policemen, executed some fifteen search warrants of homes and apartments in the New York area, and kept a running exchange with Interpol and law enforcement officials from several countries. He personally oversaw the stakeout of one of the names Ressam had written down on the scrap of paper found in his pocket — Abdel Ghani Meskini, an Algerian who lived in Brooklyn. When Meskini made an incriminating call overseas, O'Neill arrested him and booked him on conspiracy.

It seemed evident that Al-Qaeda was planning a multiple strike operation in several countries, including Jordan, Pakistan, Britain, and the United States. As the New Year approached, CTC got wiretap clearances orally and practically on demand from the attorney general herself. O'Neill, ever determined to put himself on the front, spent the countdown to midnight in Times Square, thought to be one of the targets.[44] In the end, incredibly enough, there were no strikes, much less organized violent incidents. The attack alert had either interrupted Al-Qaeda's chain of command or confronted its leadership with the prospect of losing team leaders deployed to unleash suicidal fodder.[45]

The millennium success never made the press, but it reflected the centrality of using targeted law enforcement techniques on an emergency basis by inspired, cross-national players to stop terrorism. It was the flip side of the cruise missile disgrace or the overwrought war of the worlds proposed by Clinton's successor, George W. Bush. The millennium interdiction demonstrated that the way to stop mass murder was through brutally difficult manhunts, not push-button missiles or military onslaughts.

O'Neill, of course, continued to be O'Neill. Shortly before the millennium, when everyone's nerves were jangling loose, someone at the FBI office in New York inadvertently buzzed a young Arab kid into the reception area. There was panic, then guns drawn. O'Neill burst through the door with his automatic in hand and confronted the young man, who was trembling terribly. He explained in halting English that his father, a busboy in a restaurant O'Neill frequented, had sent him. Could he help him find a job? O'Neill sat the boy down, called a restaurateur he knew, and got him an interview on the strength of his recommendation. He walked the young man to the door, made him stay in school, and embraced him. Everyone at the office just kind of shrugged and shook their heads. After O'Neill's death, FBI special agent Clint Guenther, who worked under him at the New York office, was asked to describe him. "John was a leprechaun," he said.[46] "He lived in his own magic world and filled it with a special kind of mischief and daring."

In the wake of the foiled or failed terrorist attacks around the millennium, Al-Qaeda regrouped to plan new operations. A secret meeting took place in Kuala Lumpur in the first week of January 2000. Thanks to a wiretap on the phone of an Al-Qaeda safe house in Yemen, the CIA had advance warning of the meeting and asked its Malaysian counterpart to surveille the participants.

Two of those attending, Khalid al-Mihdhar and Nawaf al-Hazmi, who would play key roles in the September 11 cataclysm, were permitted to slip into the United States thereafter and go forward with their plans, unhindered. And where was John O'Neill during this critical period? Fighting to save his thirty-one-year career from being sundered by a group of rivals in Washington, D.C.

October 12, 2000
Aden, Yemen

The USS *Cole* entered Aden's narrow harbor on its twenty-fifth refueling stop at around 9:30 A.M. that sultry morning. The *Cole* was a towering vessel, 505 feet long and studded with conning towers. At around 10:30 A.M., the destroyer began taking on fuel at the fuel dock. At 11:16 A.M., spotters on the bridge of the *Cole* saw an eighteen-foot fiberglass skiff called a *houri,* the typical workaday boat in the harbor, approaching at medium speed. Crew members on the bridge of the destroyer, operating in port on the second-highest level of alert in the Fifth Fleet, neither hailed nor fired warning shots at the *houri,* though the *Cole* was equipped with .25-caliber machine guns and rapid-fire cannon on deck. (Navy officials later said, incorrectly as it turned out, that the *Cole* took the *houri* for part of the mooring operation, thinking it was approaching to free the warship from the mooring tethers.)[47]

The two men standing in the skiff raised their arms up and waved at the sailors just as they entered the shadow cast on the water by the warship. Suddenly there was an enormous explosion that ripped a forty-by-sixty-foot hole in the hull of the ship. The blast killed seventeen American sailors as well as vaporizing their two assailants.

As with the embassy bombings, bin Laden had seemed to signal his intentions in advance of the attack via mass media allegory. Three weeks prior to the bombing, he and his lieutenant, Ayman al-Zawahiri, had appeared in a taped interview on the Al-Jazeera network. Al-Zawahiri had commented, "Enough of words, it is time to take action against this iniquitous and faithless force [America] which has spread its troops through Egypt, Yemen, and Saudi Arabia."[48] In the interview bin Laden is wearing traditional Hadrami robes (common in the eastern region of Yemin that was the ancestral home of the bin Laden family) with a curved Yemeni dagger on his belt.[49] Not long before the interview aired, according to *Al-Quds,* a London-based Arab-language newspaper, bin Laden had married a seventeen-year-old girl from a prominent Hadramawt family in a lavish ceremony in Kandahar, thereby cementing the familial and terrorist union.[50]

The U.S. had long known that Yemen was a terrorist haven. In December 1992, during Operation Restore Hope (to feed the starving Somalis), U.S. Air Force C-140s had landed in Aden not just to refuel but to billet U.S. soldiers. Eighty-seven U.S. soldiers were staying the night in two of Aden's best hotels when bombs set off by Yemeni veterans of the war in Afghanistan went off outside them. Although there were no casualties, it was a sign of violence to come.

Part of the Goliath syndrome involves the international parading of American instrumentalities of war — as if their simple display will conduce compliance by rogue actors. Whether in Lebanon in 1983, Somalia in 1993, or Dhahran in 1996, the history of such imperial pacification had not been reassuring. According to a National Security Council memo sent to the Pentagon in 1997 (and leaked to the *Washington Post*), the U.S. Navy had long been negligent regarding potential attacks in port. Nonetheless, in December 1998 the U.S. signed an agreement with the government of Yemen to permit the refueling of U.S. Navy warships in the port of Aden. The carrot proffered to the Yemeni government was $80 million in aid. Marine general Anthony

Zinni later said that the Navy had too many craft in the area for sea-based refueling and that Jeddah and Djibouti were riskier.[51]

When word of the bombing reached the New York office of the FBI, John O'Neill materialized in Barry Mawn's office in a matter of minutes to request — that is, demand — to lead the investigation.[52] O'Neill was practically apoplectic; he ranted and raved outside the office that they had to break through.[53] He was sure that the bombing had been done by Al-Qaeda (just about everyone in the know was as well), but he saw the investigation as having the potential to go to the source; if they probed deeply enough, they would uncover infrastructure, sources, and methods.[54] If they did that and did so quickly, the U.S. would be justified in mounting a military operation to eliminate bin Laden.[55]

Mawn tracked down FBI director Louis Freeh in New Jersey and got him to agree that O'Neill was the best guy for the job. There was little resistance to O'Neill's appointment in Washington since, according to one source, "Yemen was regarded as a vicious shithole and nobody minded seeing John sink to the bottom of it."[56] O'Neill was to find out that his own bureau was flagrantly remiss in following up on the intelligence gathered in the embassy bombings. One of the terrorists, Mohammed al-'Owhali, had confessed a year before the *Cole* was hit that Al-Qaeda's next target would be an American ship in Yemen.[57]

O'Neill was beside himself when Mawn gave him the go-ahead. He was like a kid. Thrilled. "This is it for me," he said to Fran Townsend on his way out the office door to go home to pack. "I needed this."[58] The next day, he and the first of his 150 agents, accompanied by 50 fully armed Marines, were in Aden. Over the next four days, the American investigative presence grew to 300. Although the U.S. diplomatic mission in Yemen was under explicit instructions to make the FBI investigation its highest priority, U.S. ambassador Barbara Bodine thought otherwise. O'Neill found that no arrangements had been made to house his team, so they bunked four to a room at the Goldmohur Hotel and filled the ballroom with floor mats. The hotel air-conditioning worked intermittently. Daytime temperatures hovered over 100 degrees, with 80 percent humidity. At night it was marginally cooler but just as humid.

O'Neill's next, and far more serious, problem was security. Station

Alex, thanks to intercepts picked up by the National Security Agency, telexed the possibility of an attack on the investigators.[59] A plot to bomb the hotel was reportedly in the works. Yemeni police and military could not be trusted to provide security, but Ambassador Bodine dismissed the threats as exaggerated if not fictive. She commented that the machine-gun fire the agents were hearing near the hotel could well be wedding celebrations.[60] When bomb threats continued, O'Neill decided to move most of his agents offshore, ten miles out to sea, where they billeted on the USS *Duluth*. The U.S. diplomatic mission then required that any agent, Marine, or support staff coming ashore apply first for permission.

The investigation went from bad to worse. Ambassador Bodine informed O'Neill that the Yemeni government, not the FBI, would run the investigation. When O'Neill rejected this, sources in the State Department (and possibly the FBI) started leaking comments to the *New York Times* and the *Washington Post*. The FBI investigators were said to be behaving like ignoramuses abroad. "The idea that you do whatever you like, in spite of where you are, is just silly. Not all murder cases can be solved in the space of a 50-minute show."[61] O'Neill's insistence on being present for all investigations (in part to protect against evidence produced by torture) was ridiculed in print: "Having a large Westerner standing in a room during an investigation of a Yemeni" would not happen. At this point, FBI director Freeh publicly questioned these attacks in the press and backed O'Neill and the rest of the investigative team in Yemen. Attorney General Reno reportedly spoke to the president, who sent a letter of encouragement to Yemeni president Saleh concerning cooperation in the investigation.

Ambassador Bodine, an experienced Foreign Service officer fluent in Arabic and with a distinguished career behind her, had a point, of course. The investigation risked polarizing, if not poisoning, U.S.-Yemeni relations. And how, she wondered, could a six-foot-two-inch Irish-American, going door-to-door, accomplish anything, particularly given the state of his Arabic? Lawrence Wright, in his delightful article on O'Neill in the *New Yorker,* recounts the story of O'Neill saying to a Yemeni intelligence officer, "Getting information out of you is like pulling teeth." When his comment was translated, the Yemeni's eyes widened. The translator had told him, "If you don't give me the information I want, I'm going to pull out your teeth."[62]

Even his fellow investigators thought O'Neill might be going overboard. He wanted the totality of flight and maritime manifests in order to cross-check as to who had entered Yemen during the six months previous to the bombing. (Al-Qaeda's MO was to drop in a key lieutenant to put the final touches on the operation.) Drawing on a large investigation fund, O'Neill got these from the air and sea carriers in short order. One name that came up was Mohammed Omar al-Harazi, a top Al-Qaeda lieutenant. O'Neill also asked the Yemenis to dredge the harbor. A million dollars later this too was done.

For what it was worth, the Yemenis identified the bombers themselves two weeks into the investigation and reconstructed their movements. On the morning of October 12, the two men had driven a Nissan truck down to the beach in Little Aden, towing the skiff. They were both Hadramis (whence Osama bin Laden's family hailed), one a burly man with a bushy beard, his comrade a slight man with a goatee, who rarely spoke to those who met him in the steep alleyways above Aden harbor.[63] The first man's nom de guerre was Abdullah Ahmed Khaled al-Musawah; his real name Hassan Saced Awad al-Khamri. His partner's name was never established. O'Neill immediately requested that the Yemeni relatives of al-Khamri be DNA-tested to match the DNA samples taken from the Cole.

In mid-November, the Yemenis agreed to a protocol that would govern the joint investigation. FBI special agents would attend interviews of suspects or view them through a two-way mirror. The investigation would extend to "social, political and military figures" — in short, the government. On November 30, Ambassador Bodine — of all people — and a Yemeni Interior Ministry official signed the accord.

Within days, there was a significant break in the case: six Afghan Arabs and a Yemeni were identified and arrested as participants in the bombing. These included Jamal al-Badawi, a veteran Al-Qaeda operative, who confessed that he had been dispatched from Afghanistan, and Fahd Al-Quso, a Yemeni from a prominent family whose duty it had been to videotape the bombing. There had been as many as sixty people involved in the operation, using three safe houses — one to surveille the

Cole on its previous refueling stops, one for the ringleaders, and a third to assemble and wire the explosive (some seven hundred pounds) in the hull of the *houri*.

In the course of the interrogations, the names "Khallad" and "Almihdhar" were mentioned as principals in the plot. These were two of the six men whose pictures and names the CIA had received from the Al-Qaeda meeting in Malaysia. *Had the CIA shared its information about Almihdhar with O'Neill or put his name on the terrorist watch list, he would almost certainly have been arrested on his reentry into the United States en route to the mission on September 11.*

In late November 2000, O'Neill flew back to New York. Valerie James was shocked by his haggard and exhausted appearance. He looked as if he had lost twenty pounds.[64] While he was away, Ambassador Bodine kept up the ad hominem attacks, likening O'Neill and the FBI agents in an article in Britain's Sunday *Times* to the brutish Soviets who had humiliated the Yemenis in the 1970s.[65] She was so relentless that O'Neill's old friend Fran Townsend began to have her doubts about him. She called someone stationed in Yemen and in confidence asked, "What's your take on it?" The reply was frank: "Look, I've seen John at his worst. I've seen John when he can be very difficult, and I will tell you he's doing a magnificent job. He is really bending over backwards to try and make this thing work for her [Bodine]."[66]

What galled O'Neill most was that the FBI was no longer backing him. He had been passed over for every position he wanted, passed up for the Senior Executive Service award that he deserved, given an extraordinarily challenging investigation in a hostile Arab country, and left out to twist in the wind. He felt the ceiling was being lowered on him, that he was being crushed. "He could never understand it," Chris Isham recalled. "He couldn't understand why they didn't appreciate him more. He couldn't understand why they didn't love him." What had happened to O'Neill was that in the course of his brilliant successes, he had roused a group of jealous detractors in Washington. The Yemeni investigation, with all of its headliners and bureaucratic broadsides, suddenly gave those detractors cause to subvert his career and in so doing, to cut off a trail of leads that, if followed, might have stopped 9/11.

Despite the harassment and being passed over, O'Neill soldiered on. In Quantico at the FBI training facility, Barry Mawn, the SAC who beat out O'Neill for the top job in New York, heard a knock on the door to his room one evening. He opened it up and there stood O'Neill, holding two beers. "I understand you're an Irishman and you like to drink beer," he said to Mawn. "These are for you." He handed the beers to Mawn, who laughingly invited him in. O'Neill got to the point: "Where are we at?" Mawn said he'd be happy to back O'Neill for another appointment in a city other than New York. But no, O'Neill didn't want that. He wanted to stay in New York. And he'd come by that evening to pledge his loyalty to him.

It wasn't quite in O'Neill's nature to give up, much less to assuage those who hated him. He got the U.S. Air Force to transport a dozen Yemeni law enforcement officials to New York, the same ones O'Neill had been hounding for two months. They toured the city, met the mayor, took helicopter rides, and were wined and dined to the extent that their faith permitted. When one FBI official in San'aa later asked the Yemeni commander in chief of law enforcement (the equivalent of the FBI director) about O'Neill (whom Ambassador Bodine had told everyone the Yemenis would like to gut), the man said that he respected O'Neill and wanted to continue the investigation.[67]

But a mistake O'Neill had made some months earlier in the course of attending a mandatory FBI retirement conference in July 2000 in Orlando, Florida, was coming back to haunt him. What had happened was apparently minor, but in the militarized society of the FBI, especially with J. Edgar's ilk still conniving in the building named for him, it was being worked into a major internal investigation.

The facts were these. O'Neill had gone outside the room to take a cell phone call, leaving his briefcase behind. Although he was gone for only minutes and although there were 150 agents in the room at the time, a hotel employee somehow stole the briefcase. O'Neill immediately alerted local police, who were able to arrest the thief and return the briefcase with only a pen and a lighter missing. With secret documents in the case, O'Neill felt duty-bound to report the security breach on his return to New York. A fingerprint dusting revealed that none of the documents had been touched. The Justice Department, at the urging of the FBI command, opened an investigation that went on for

months. They worked the case from every angle — personal, professional, national security. O'Neill, Fran Townsend remembered, was shaken:
"I could hear the fear in his voice. I could hear his throat tighten."
O'Neill knew the purpose of hunting parties.[68] Townsend would also remember O'Neill suffused in anger and bitterness:

> Then something extraordinary happened. He had to go to Quan-
> tico for a meeting . . . before he flew down to Norfolk — there
> was that memorial service for the victims and their families of the
> *Cole.* When he was at Quantico, the guys and gals who he was re-
> sponsible for in Yemen, his SWAT people, the special team, made
> a presentation to him. It was a picture of all the people who had
> been there at the time, gathered on the rooftop of the hotel. . . . It's
> a huge group photograph. They had it framed and had a brass
> plaque on it.

She went out to National Airport to meet with him and found him carrying the framed photograph, clutching it. He said to her, "I may never
get an award or bonus money. But this means more to me because it's
the people I served with there. If they respected me, and they thought
enough of the job I did over there to give me this, what else do I
need?"[69]

For O'Neill, Christmas 2000 was, nonetheless, tense and unpleas-
ant. He was now down to no more than six special agents in Yemen,
along with their complement of SWAT and technicians. His dedication
to make an investigative breakthrough and justify going after bin Laden
seemed like a pipe dream. He was juggling — and not especially well —
two girlfriends, each of whom he had led to believe he would spend the
rest of his life with. (The previous year Anna di Battista, whom he had
dated in D.C., had moved up to New York, thereby complicating this
undignified pas de deux.) He owed people money. For once, he was living up to his reputation as a legion drinker. The tea or grape juice he
had liked to imbibe after midnight at Elaine's was no longer that. Often
he would head to the office at 2 or 3 A.M. and work till dawn when,
hectoring and haggard, he would confront his deputies about jobs undone.
His old friend, former FBI deputy director Bear Bryant, told him to
ease up: "Relax, you're going to have a stroke." But the brilliant manic

had gone depressive. The dark combustion of poverty and namelessness that had fired the tremendous talent had waned to something of a flicker. He had become paranoid.

O'Neill was pleased that George W. Bush had won, or at least been awarded, the presidency. It meant change at the top of the FBI and the State Department. As much as he liked and respected Lou Freeh, it seemed likely that Freeh's deputy, Tom Pickard, O'Neill's bête noire, would move on in the changeover. In early January 2001, he wired down to FBI headquarters in Washington that he would be leaving for Yemen later that week. The reply devastated him: the American mission in Yemen would not permit him to reenter the country. O'Neill was persona non grata.

Almost anyone else, it would seem, would lay low for a while and try his chances with the incoming administration. But not O'Neill. When he learned that Vice President-elect Dick Cheney had convened an energy task force, he told a staffer at the National Security Council that "the Saudis — and their American partners — are going to have the run of the place." Counterterrorism would be "neutered," he predicted. He called Freeh to ask him to pull rank at the State Department so that the *Cole* investigation could continue.[70] O'Neill's call was neither taken nor returned.

There was a notion of defeat in a proud note he sent to Fran Townsend, a note in which he tried to explain his reasons for the fight: "My passion holds all my wealth and my liabilities. It is the best and the worst of me. But it is me. It is my identity. Alas, I know of no more noble cause than to fight for that which one had the greatest of passion for. Rebellion left in the hands of good men will ultimately prevail, and the costs and sufferings of the rebels will be small indeed."[71]

At the very time O'Neill's standard was falling in January 2001, there was another man on the move, a CIA "black operations" type, recently returned from Afghanistan where he had gotten close enough to Osama bin Laden to "see him shit." He was no rebel like O'Neill, but a soldier, iron-hard and poised for war. He was not from north Jersey, but north Alabama, and there being a soldier meant something, especially to him.

4

SOLDIER

The Making of Mike Spann

June 2, 1987

Winfield City High School

Winfield, Alabama

Johnny Micheal Spann's third grade teacher, Odene May, would re-member how very shy he was. But she also recalled the day he overcame that. The shoelace of one of the boys in the class broke and the child became upset and started to cry. "Mike got up from his desk went over to him and took off his own shoelace and, while the other children watched, laced in his own. He flopped around the rest of the day," Ms. May recalled, "with that quiet smile on his face."[1]

On June 2, 1987, the day he graduated from Winfield City High School, he also wore that quiet smile. Mike wasn't the valedictorian of his class and hadn't been the captain of his football team. But he had *made* the varsity football team, after giving up football after his freshman year because of his small size. He went out for football again his senior year and started at split end, finishing up All-County. "He had some talent," Coach Joe Hubbert remembered. "The rest was guts."[2] One evening Hubbert had the football team over to his house to watch *Top Gun,* the Tom Cruise movie about naval aviators. After it was over, Mike said quietly to no one in particular, "One day I'll be doing the same thing."

Hubbert learned, to his surprise, that after Mike soloed as a small-plane pilot, he buzzed the town.[3] He was a modest, somewhat mischie-vous boy who held quietly to his dreams. "An ordinary boy," his father, Johnny, described him after his death. "Mike was never the kind of per-son who wanted a lot of attention. He never did things to get attention. He just went ahead and did them."[4] Around the time Mike graduated from high school, Stu Richardson, a boyhood friend, ran into him and his cousin and classmate Lonnie Spann down at D's Pizza on Highway 78. When asked what he was up to, he said he was on his way to Auburn University. "Then I'll be a Marine and then I'll join the FBI."

When he was killed in November 2001, the press descended on the lush little railroad town that looks like a snapshot out of the 1940s, an era when the textile business produced enough local wealth for some working people to build small brick homes with white colonial trim and rolling lawns backed by enormous banks of trees. The poorer folk, whose homes tended to lie farther down in the "hollers," made do with tiny clapboard "four-roomers." When the journalists asked about Mike Spann, most people admitted that they hadn't seen him in years; that when he'd left Winfield he'd left pretty much for good. But they knew the kid, they said, and they knew him well. Town mayor Bill West, who had taught Mike history and government in the ninth grade, repeated to me what he had told the rest of the inquiring visitors: "Mike always wanted to be what he came to be. And he wanted to do right."[5] The town was the same way — and still is. Poor and proud, ready to fight for the two things that have always given it a measure of distinction — God and Country.

The first white settlers in northern Alabama were destitute Scotch-Irish, who made their way over from the Carolinas and Georgia starting in the 1750s. Some had finished their indenture, and later others had mustered out as foot soldiers in the French and Indian War. Nearly all were too poor to own slaves. As the planter society grew up in central and southern Alabama, some of the northerners became drovers and teamsters for the cotton plantations. Homesteaders scratched out a meager living in the thickly forested rolling hills of the north, the tail end of the Appalachians. "They grew corn for livestock and grew poorer for it."[6]

With the advent of the Revolutionary War, they sent their young men north to fight and then named their county Marion (formed in 1818), after the South Carolinian Francis Marion, the Swamp Fox. In 1812 the men of the north had another chance to fight, this time in the army of Andrew Jackson. As Jackson came along the "Military Road" that ran from Nashville to New Orleans, threading its way through the steep hills and roaring creeks of the western part of Marion County, they joined up. The next year (1813), the army came back, marching north along the road and celebrating its victory over the British.

Slavery divided Alabama before it divided the Union. In the north, the poor yeoman farmers resented the planters whose wealth was won from the toil of slaves. They were called "Nigger Lord Slave Owners." In 1860, of the 11,434 residents of Marion County, 856 were African-American. Ten families accounted for 40 percent of the slaveholding in the county. The rest of the white population had few or no slaves. About twenty to thirty of these African-Americans had been manumitted, freed after a period of enslavement. When Abraham Lincoln was elected president in 1860, the South, and especially the Deep South, raged for secession. But in northern Alabama, secession touched off a dispute that lingers today.

In January 1861, when the assembled delegates in Montgomery voted to secede from the Union, 39 percent of those delegates, nearly all from the north, voted against the motion.[7] In Winston County, to the east of Marion County, an Irish roustabout by the name of Bill Looney assembled between 2,500 and 3,000 drinking citizens for a meeting in his tavern. There on July 4, 1861, they moved (the precise manner of which is not recorded) to secede from Alabama because Alabama had seceded from the Union.[8]

For a period of months thereafter, Confederate and Union forces competed to conscript able-bodied males in the hill country. A Union colonel Streight, riding mostly at night in search of "Alabama Yankees," reported in his dispatch that "an old lady, Mrs. Anna Campbell, had ridden some 70 miles roundtrip and returned with 30 recruits." She had done this in thirty-six hours. In the war, 2,678 Alabama white men (almost all from the north) served in the Union army, most (2,066) in the First Alabama Cavalry. Another 1,000 to 1,200 black men from Alabama fought for the Union as well.[9]

A similar number of white men from Alabama's northern counties, according to ledgers consulted by the author, served in the Confederate army.[10] From the little town of Winfield, named after the commanding general in the Mexican-American War of 1848, Winfield Scott, the great majority of both volunteer and impressed soldiers served the South.*

The Confederates, in the analysis of James Michael Hill, were

---

*The original town name, Luxapallila, was changed to Needmore and then to Winfield. It was incorporated in 1891.

both by blood and by war style "Celtic." Hill estimates that the South was about two-thirds Celtic and that the frontier regions (from Georgia to Ohio) were entirely dominated by Irish and Scottish immigrant descendants. All were skilled with guns, either through military experience or hunting. Their temperament as soldiers was "impetuous and undisciplined," but they prized fighting, especially on the back of a horse. Robert E. Lee's Army of the Potomac, for all its splendor of maneuver, was, as the general observed, an "Armed mob . . . of undisciplined individuality." Even the "Rebel Yell," the high-pitched cry ("that terrible scream and barbarous howling," one Union soldier wrote) was a direct descendant of the Celtic war cry.[11]

Some 7,000 men — variously called "Tory hideouts," "Mossbacks," or "Bushwhackers" — went into the hills, avoiding service with either side. They are described thus:

> Blindly hating the affluent slave-holder and his "nigger" alike, they had first refused to support the cause of secession and afterwards ignored all Confederate civilian and military conscription laws. Forming themselves into bands called "The Destroying Angels," or "Prowling Brigades," they swept down out of their piney-wood strongholds to raid their more fortunate neighbors . . . they burned, murdered and raped.

The most vicious civil warfare ensued, as bad as the rampant slaughter in the Missouri Territory. The retaliation by the Confederate home guard was to set forests blazing, to attack and hang suspected collaborators, and generally to commit the same crimes as the Mossbacks themselves. By 1863 much of northern Alabama was a smoking, shrieking ruin. Nearly all women and girls had experienced rape. Thousands had been robbed and murdered in the terror.[12]

No matter how many wars later, no matter the number of men who fought and died in those subsequent conflicts, for those who sided with the Confederacy, "the war" meant only one thing — the War between the States. When Mike Spann played soldiers with friends like Dale Weeks and Randy Sanders in the thick woods behind his family's house at 701 Arrowhead Village, he always wore something gray. When he read the military accounts of the War between the States, it was always with the same fervent preference. Hadn't Lee in the final weeks, with his troops starving and low on ammunition, torn Grant's battalions to pieces at Cold Harbor? Only Sherman's scorched-earth tactics, the burning of entire towns and the killing of women and children, had ended it all. As a Marine officer, Mike Spann was known as a listener in the bull sessions on politics, sports, popular culture, and the Corps. But not about the Civil War. His convictions about the wrongs done and the good fight fought was no code for racial supremacy but rather the passed-on memories of great suffering and great courage.[13] It ran in his family's blood.

The Spann family had migrated into Marion County sometime around 1837 from North Carolina. Julius Tarpley Spann (born May 28, 1850, died October 8, 1933) was a direct forebear of Mike Spann. Some eight male Spanns served in the Confederate army. (There are complete records of four.) Most were young at incorporation, anywhere from eighteen to twenty-two, and served in the 16th Alabama Infantry. The casualties the 16th Alabama took in the later Rebel campaigns were significant, but some of the Spanns survived, one being William Benjamin Spann, who "escaped from capture" in May 1865. The 16th Alabama Infantry echoed a reprise for the dead, both during the war and after: "Brother soldiers, we have often heard these names called, and they will be precious names in the Sweet by and by."[14] Some families in northern Alabama were divided, with sons serving the North or the South; the division even extended to fathers and sons, as was the case of the famous circuit court judge Dabney Terrell, Jr., who flew the Stars and Stripes atop the Pikeville courthouse until his son was killed fighting for the Confederacy, when, heartbroken, he took it down.

The names and the stories remain, as if burned, in modern memory. Bill West, Mike Spann's history teacher and the current mayor of Winfield, is not untypical: his paternal great-grandfather, Green West, was a farrier who died at Shiloh fighting for the Union. His maternal great-grandfather, William Riley Bonds, fought as a Confederate and survived long enough to be with Lee at Appomattox Court House.

With Reconstruction came more exclusion and harsher scorn for northern Alabama. White Alabama remained overwhelmingly Democrat, but not in the north, where Republicans, whose affiliation dated

from Lincoln, stuck to their colors. The little hill towns produced a
contrary breed of politicians to match their contrary views. One such
politician was Congressman Carl Elliott, Sr., whose lonely battle to dis-
tinguish himself on the subject of racial justice graces Caroline
Kennedy's *Profiles in Courage for Our Time*.[15] Elliott, a Kennedy Democrat, mortgaged his home in Jasper and sold his car to run against the
George Wallace machine in the Democratic primary for governor in
1966. He lost and later died in total poverty, but not before putting together a compendium of historical accounts of his beloved northern
counties.[16]

With the twentieth century's world wars came opportunity, in
terms of officer commissions and enlisted service, to fight for the thing
the Alabama hill country had always held dear: national pride. War,
with its cruel and beguiling invitation to young men, was here regarded
as a blessing. Accordingly, Alabama had the highest per capita volunteer
rate in both World War I and World War II. In a sense, the soldiers and
officers from Alabama were paid back in the form of the military bases
that dot the state as well as NASA's enormous complex in Huntsville.

"We shape our buildings," Winston Churchill observed in the
House of Commons, "and then our buildings shape us."[17] If you go to
Winfield, you find two types of buildings that emerge beyond the ar-
chitectural regularity of the place — the schools and the churches. Despite a low tax base, Winfield (2003 population, 4,500) boasts first-rate
education. In a town where the per capita income is half that of some
of the well-heeled suburbs of Montgomery or Tuscaloosa, Winfield
City High School is nonetheless one of the better high schools in the
state in terms of test scores. (In a recent year, it ranked 126th out of 128
in Alabama in per-pupil funding, but fourth in test scores.) The high
school Mike attended, built in the Depression, has since been largely
torn down, replaced by a Texas-sized structure that looks more like a
community college.

The mostly Baptist churches abound, rising up steepled and imposing, often with messaged signs: "Support Our Troops!" or, "Be an
Organ Donor. Give Your Heart to Christ." The Spann family attended
the Church of Christ located near the old high school. There, Mike did
what young churchgoers do — Sunday school, youth projects, and,

above all, singing. (His father, Johnny, would recount proudly how he was able to suppress his grief at his grandfather's funeral in order to do the "lead singing" of his grandfather's favorite hymn, "Above the Bright Blue.")[18]

At Winfield High, Mike was no standout in anything — grades (mostly Bs and Cs), sports, or extracurricular activities. High school government teacher Bill West would sometimes briefly turn his class over to Mike and his cousin Lonnie for some comic relief. Mike, in his dry, offbeat way, would recount Huck Finn-style adventures that "sometimes had a moral and always brought a laugh." One such adventure was when Mike and his best friend, Randy Sanders, took their .22s down to a swampy copse of woods where they had seen some deer traversing a cleared power-line track. They took "still hunter" positions and, sure enough, spotted a tan pelt through the thick foliage. They opened fire and then ran down to view the result — "Bunk" Beasely's cow. Returning on a dead run, panic-stricken, to Mike's house, they confessed their folly. Mike's father had the boys work off the $500 it cost him for the cow in after-school projects. The idea was, if you messed up, you did right.

One story Mike did *not* tell in his government class was when he, Randy, and Dale Weeks, all about fifteen years old, went for a stroll down Cherokee Street — stark naked. When one of their teachers appeared driving down the street, Mike and Dale, who had kept their shoes on, headed for the woods. The unfortunate Randy remained behind.[19]

Later on in high school, Mike would sometimes wait until his parents went to bed to sneak out and head down the road. One night he set his alarm clock but woke up before it went off and snuck out, forgetting to turn the alarm off. When he got home, his father was waiting there in the kitchen to talk to him.

The Spanns lived comfortably, thanks to father Johnny's successful real estate and home-building business. The family home, built in 1983 at 701 Arrowhead Village, was a large two-story structure situated on a hill with a stand of woods behind it. The swimming pool went in before the house was finished, and Johnny let Mike and his friends camp out there. Johnny remembered that the boys got hold of some beer and had, by Winfield standards, a wild night that included someone getting walloped by a two-by-four in the course of a "spirited discussion." Every summer and most weekends during the school year, Mike worked in his father's home-building business, banging nails or cleaning up the job site once the house was up. During Mike's sophomore year in high school, his father formed the "Micheal Spann Construction Company."

Like his early years in Winfield, Mike's time at Auburn University was marked by good times and friendships, hard physical work, and mediocre grades. After his freshman year, he majored in criminal justice/law enforcement, with an overall GPA of 2.8. He took but one ROTC course during his four years — pistol shooting. The rest of his academic time, to quote Professor Tom Petee, "he just kind of blended in." He loved the campus, among the most beautiful in the South, with its gracious blend of nineteenth- and twentieth-century buildings (mostly brick with white trim), its sweeping colonnades and manicured lawns set off by towering magnolias and flowering pear and cherry trees. Not far from Langdon House, where Lincoln had spoken during the great debate about secession, was the Lathe, which during the war had been used to bore Confederate cannon. Here, Mike brought family and friends from out of town to pose before Auburn's most picturesque scene.

Unlike most of his fellow students, Mike never lived on campus. To save money, his father towed a trailer up from Winfield in which Mike roomed along with his friend Jason Cantrell. In his freshman year, he began dating the bubbly Barbara Burke, who along with her twin sister, Elizabeth, roommate Jason, and Jason's girlfriend, Tina, palled their way through parties, Tiger football games, and the highs and lows of the undergraduate experience. At parties, Barbara Burke remembered, Mike would "sit back and take it all in, listening sufficiently well to derive material for teasing you later." Tina remembered Mike and the gang hanging out at Touchdowns, a local pub, to drink beer and eat mozzarella sticks and hamburgers. Mike liked his hamburgers so rare that he would advise the waitress to "just hit it over the head and bring it out."[20]

At Auburn, Mike stuck close to his friends from Winfield and never joined a fraternity. His car, a used Honda Prelude, and his pad, the trailer in a working-class trailer park, summarized his lack of interest in making the scene. He did occasionally rent a plane to go flying, and began skydiving his sophomore year.[21] He liked to listen to heavy metal — Quiet Riot and Motley Crue — but every Sunday morning could be found singing at the local Church of Christ. His favorite hymn was "I'll Fly Away."

At their annual Christmas party back in Winfield, Mike and Barbara and their friends sent Mike's two sisters, Tonya and Tammy, to bed and stayed up drinking and awarding each other gag gifts. One year Mike got a bottle of Red Hots with a prescriptive label: "Take one every hour to control swearing." He liked to swear, but never in front of his parents. The trait Barbara Burke most remembered about Mike was his sense of mischief. The two remained close friends, even after Mike began dating Kathryn Ann Webb, another Winfield native. They were married his senior year. One day, Mike, not given to self-dramatic statement, took Barbara aside and said that he didn't expect to "live long enough to grow old." It was as if, in modesty, Mike had been waiting, standing on the periphery of his life for a destiny he had dreamed of as a kid. And he somehow sensed where it would lead.

Mike Spann may have been an "ordinary kid who didn't want attention," as his father described him, but there were outcroppings of ambition. After the fall semester of his sophomore year at Auburn, he went home, as always, for the Christmas holidays to Winfield. Shortly before Christmas 1989 — December 21, to be exact — he checked out a book by Andrew Tully called *CIA: The Inside Story*. Tully's book was the first exposé of its kind about America's spy agency, and stands up today in terms of its accuracy and balance. Mike must have read the book, because back at Auburn he frequently talked about it.

Among other issues, the book deals with the charge by Senator Wayne Morse (D-Ore.) that the CIA made its own policy, did whatever it wanted to, and was certainly involved in "rogue operations."[22] Tully cites a succession of "freelance" operations that so bedeviled President Kennedy that he formally reminded the State Department that it had preeminence in foreign operations and sent personal letters to all American ambassadors stating that they were in charge of all operations in the field.[23]

One such CIA covert operation Tully discusses is the overthrow of Iraq's King Faisal in 1963 by General Karim el-Kassem. In the days following the coup, the left-leaning Kassem slaughtered the king and his family. Thereafter there were disturbances that threatened Kassem's power. Radio Baghdad bristled with accusations that the CIA was organizing a counter-coup. Tully recounts the fate of one Eugene Burns of Sausalito, California, who had arrived in Iraq some days earlier, ostensibly to arrange for relief of needy children. Burns was a former newspaperman who had organized and funded an organization called American Friends of the Middle East, a CIA front organization. His truck was stopped on a Baghdad side street by a raging mob, and he was hauled out and beaten to death. The CIA disowned any association with him.

When Mike met his own fate as a CIA paramilitary in November 2001, the town rallied in every way conceivable to comfort his family and back their hero. No one asked why it had all happened, or about the terrible scene in the fortress, or why the Bush administration, after vowing treason in the case of John Walker Lindh, cut a plea bargain for the "traitor" and took a hike. You don't ask such things. You respect. You do right, the way Mike did. At the memorial service for Mike Spann on December 10, 2001, in Winfield at the Church of Christ, Pastor James Wyers spoke of their little town. Winfield, he said, stood for something *about* America that shouldn't be forgotten *by* America.[24] Toward the end of the service, Johnny, too sad to lead the singing, read from Mike's final dispatches. The communication was pure north Alabama: "stand and fight."

The following year, on November 19, 2002, the town put on a final service for Mike. The Army sent over a squadron of T-38s in "missing man formation." It seemed fitting. Mike was a soldier who lived out his town's most cherished tradition. He was also a small-plane pilot, who had once, out of mischief and possibly pride, buzzed the town.

In the summer of 2003, people passing by the Johnny Micheal Spann Park where his memorial, a block of polished black granite, stands, confessed that they didn't know much about the CIA, but they did know about that white star appearing alongside the number 79. "He got that because he fought and he died." Always that word: fight. The stone memorial sits where you might expect it to — in front of Winfield's city hall — there for all to see:

> Micheal Spann gave his life for his family, friends, and country, while defending the freedom that we all enjoy. . . . We sleep safely in our beds because brave men stand ready in the night to protect us from those who would do us harm.

Mike had given his town and his country an old thing — the debt the dead may convey to the living. The debt of honor and the obligation of memory.

March 1997
Camp Lejeune
Jacksonville, North Carolina

Mike Spann's desire to be a soldier seemed to come early. His father, Johnny, remembered walking into his bedroom and seeing the three-year-old, wearing only his father's underpants, standing in his father's combat boots with his steel helmet on his head. By age five Mike knew all the verses to the Marine hymn and would march around the backyard singing to himself. The lyrics he liked best were the last:

> In many a strife we fought for life,
> And never lost our nerve.
> If the Army and the Navy ever look on Heaven's scenes;
> They will find the streets are guarded by
> United States Marines.

By grade school, shy though he was, he would solemnly state his intention when asked what he planned to be when he grew up: "A Marine." (In high school, he added, "FBI agent.")

Three weeks after graduating from Auburn, Mike reported in at the Marines' Officer Candidate School in Quantico, Virginia. Six weeks later he started basic training to become what every Marine must — a rifleman. The competition for ranking among the other 185 officer candidates, in physical fitness, weapons training, and military tactics, was fierce. As George Will wrote, what the Marine Corps do is "make hard people in a soft age."

All the firing range practice, the stripping and cleaning of the M16A2 and other assault rifles, the classroom lecturing, was directed at preparing a Marine for the rifle squad competition. In Spann's time the competition took five days, with the competitors bivouacked in the field. On day one there was a five-hundred-question test and a weapons evaluation. On day two, the squads took off on a four-hour run, with a short break for water and rations around noon. That afternoon they began a two-day, nonstop series of patrolling, live firing, calling for fire, and offensive and defensive helicopter assaults. On the final day, the winners were announced. Mike achieved "marksman" status even though his squad finished back in the pack. Commissioned as a second lieutenant at the end of basic training, he chose artillery, even though the MOS (military occupation specialty) of traditional prestige in the Corps was infantry.

What continues to irradiate every aspect of the Marine Corps — its history, its training, and its deployment — is tenacity. "When well led, the American Marine will march down the barrel of an enemy rifle for you," Captain Paul Goodwin, a veteran of Vietnam, wrote.[25] When Captain Mike Mullins, Spann's commanding officer in Okinawa, learned of Mike's death in Afghanistan, he concluded, "Knowing Mike, it doesn't surprise me that he found his way into the middle of the fight . . . and that, when it went wrong, he stood and fought it out." That's what Marines do.

Until the Spanish-American War in 1898, the Marines, founded as a naval constabulary during the Revolutionary War, had little public standing. The legend began in World War I with the Marines' stand at Belleau Wood. The most heavily decorated American "doughboy" in that conflict was a Marine — Louis Cukela — who was best remembered for his malaproprian quote: "Next time I need some damn fool for a mission, I'll go myself."[26] The "new" Marine Corps envisioned by General John Lejeune would be an expeditionary assault force held in immediate readiness. After World War I the Marines continued to recruit, promising prospective Marines via their poster: "Be the first to fight!"

In 1992, when Mike Spann joined up, the message was basically the same. "You're America's 911 force," General Charles C. Krulak told Mike's class. The Marines were the best and the largest expeditionary assault force in the world. No matter the advancing technology of warfare, the Marines' most treasured weapon was "the eye-guided missile that comes out of the rifle barrel."[27] There was pride to be won in giving your life for your country, Krulak told them. Although Marines were only one-tenth of all U.S. armed forces in Vietnam, one in four names on that black wall is that of a United States Marine.

The messaging by the high command was relentless: "It's not the stars or bars you have, not what you wear on your sleeve and shoulder, that determines what you are," the Marines' commandant, General Carl E. Mundy, Jr., reminded them. "It's what you wear on your collar — the eagle, globe, and anchor — that puts you in the Brotherhood of Marines." Krulak, who took over from Mundy as commandant in 1995, would read a letter that his father had sent him, an encomium so familiar to the Marines of Krulak's time that many could repeat it from memory: "The American people believe that Marines are downright good for the country, that Marines are masters of unfailing alchemy which converts unoriented youths into proud, self-reliant citizens."[28]

Of the 177,000 Marines (officer and enlisted, active and reserve) serving with Spann, 30 percent of the enlisted men were black or Hispanic, with 8 percent of those, officers. The great majority of Marine officers were white, and a substantial proportion of those were southerners like Spann. The Marine Corps meritocracy proceeds from its most basic training — every Marine a rifleman — and carries over into a pride that seems to transcend the usual lines of military division, officer and enlisted, and the fault lines of race and gender. In Spann's time, women numbered about 5 percent of the enlisted and a little over 2 percent of the officers.[29] General Krulak constantly pointed out that the WMs (women Marines) had acquitted themselves in the combat zone with distinction in Desert Storm.

From the Basic Training School, Second Lieutenant Spann moved to Fort Sill, Oklahoma, for six months of artillery training. Regarding ground-fired artillery, he and other officers learned how to use the 155 mm (with a normal range of 18,000 meters or a maximum range of 30,000 meters when the projectile had a "rocket wraparound"). For Marine artillerymen, however, the critical skill in terms of the modern battlefield was "terminal fire control," using laser range finders and laser range designators to direct bombing aircraft on strikes. This would be the essence of the American war in Afghanistan in 2001.

In January 1994, Mike shipped out to Okinawa, where he was stationed for two and a half years. For the first six months, he, Ann, and two-year-old Allison shared a grim two-room apartment with a single window in downtown Naha, the capital of Okinawa, a Japanese prefecture with a population of 1.4 million. Later the Spann family moved to a high-rise overlooking Kin Bay on Marine Camp Hansen.

The Marines had some twenty training and deployment facilities scattered around the island. In terms of the overall defense of the North Pacific and force projection in conflicts such as the war in Vietnam, Okinawa was critically strategic, but the large American military presence was a source of tension and controversy for native Okinawans. In 1970, Marine captain Anthony Zinni, then recovering from wounds received in combat in Vietnam, took command of a hundred-man guard unit in Okinawa. He could hardly believe the scene. He and his men were "in hand-to-hand combat every third night" on post, sorting out race riots between Marines, as well as murders, stabbings, and robberies. "The job was hell."[30]

In September 1995, in an incident that roiled and nearly ruined U.S.-Japanese relations as well as destroyed the life of a young Okinawan and her family, two Marines and a sailor abducted and gang-raped a twelve-year-old Okinawan girl. According to the Associated Press, the court reporter "broke down upon hearing the lewd jokes made by the assailants about their bleeding, unconscious victim." Admiral Richard C. Macke, commander of all forces in the Pacific, had this to say: "I think [the rape] was absolutely stupid. For the price they paid to rent the car [to abduct the girl], they could have had a girl." (The admiral went into retirement shortly after uttering this arrogant inanity.)[31]

When U.S. authorities refused to permit the confessed rapists to be bound over to Japan's justice system, there were mass protests on the island. The Clinton administration dispatched a succession of military and civilian officials to provide diplomatic unction, with limited effect. Members of Congress warned that the U.S. might cease to underwrite Japanese defense, when in fact, according to Defense Department figures, the Japanese paid 78 percent of the total cost of keeping the 42,962 American troops on their soil.[32] Spin control decontrolled on another point. General Richard Myers made the claim that the rape was totally exceptional, that "99.99 percent" of the time U.S. troops behaved responsibly. Within weeks of the incident, however, there was another rape and two vehicular homicides in which U.S. drivers were at fault.[33]

Marine Corps commandant Charles C. "Brute" Krulak was worried enough about the situation to consider Port Darwin, Australia, as an alternative site for the Marines in the Pacific. The Marine high command ordered all officers, as a matter of urgency, to control and discipline their men. Captain Spann, who had served in a military police detail during his first weeks on the island, assured his company that he would personally court-martial them if anybody broke the law.[34] His company had no infractions.

Mike, however, took his responsibilities a step further. He started attending a Baptist church in Naha, whose faithful were entirely Okinawan, and did Bible study with teenagers after the service.[35] After he left Okinawa, he remained in touch with some of them through e-mail. Later at Camp Lejeune he served as a stand-in youth minister at the Church of Christ. Months into his clandestine training with the CIA, he was still advising young men like Aaron Catrett about how to make it in college as a Christian. "I learned that the hard way," he confessed in a two-page e-mail to Catrett.[36] Each place he went in life, Mike Spann quietly labored to make things better. In Okinawa, it wasn't all work and prayer. Captain Mike Tapen remembered going out with Mike and Ann to scuba-dive in Okinawa's rich waters.[37]

In October 1996, Spann left Okinawa for Camp Lejeune in Jacksonville, North Carolina. Begun in 1942 as a training base for Marine amphibious warfare, Camp Lejeune is a sprawling series of encampments, many reachable only by water or by exiting the base to go out to

State Route 24. Mike was assigned a little white clapboard captain's house on Seth Andrew Drive where he and Ann, with their two daughters, would live for the next two years. Lejeune had retained its World War II utilitarian character of one-story red-brick buildings with white trim set out in closely trimmed lawns, interspersed with banks of semitropical forest bristling with Carolina pines. The rutted, sandy tracks that led through the forests gave way to ponds, lagoons, and the brownish-blue bays and inlets of the Atlantic. For those 200,000 Marines who went through Lejeune in preparation for island-hopping in the South Pacific in World War II, the sweltering expanses of mud and forest in the Pacific must have looked familiar. The town itself was an inelegant gallery of small businesses along Route 24, with the usual assault of fast-food franchises. But with 75 percent of the residents retired military and Department of Defense cardholders, support and enthusiasm for the Marine base was unquestioned.

After services on Sunday, Mike sometimes went alone to the Beirut Memorial, erected in a glade near the turnoff to Camp Johnson. The monument is composed of a broken wall in which the names of the 241 dead are etched in gray granite on one end, with the notation "They Came in Peace" on the other. A bronze Marine stands on the ground in between the broken walls, holding his M-16 in readiness. Every year since the erection of the monument, there has been a candlelight ceremony at the Beirut Memorial. One survivor, Cleta Walls, whose husband, First Sergeant Tandy Walls, was among those killed, observed, "I can't get over the way the Marines and this community honor these men and never forget; every year they are here, remembering their fellow Marines."[38] It said something about the familial quality of Marines that, in addition to their great successes at Tarawa, Guadalcanal, and Hamburger Hill, they should honor a disaster as proudly as any victory.

Returning from his three-year stint in Okinawa, Captain Spann joined the 214-man Second Air Naval Gunfire Liaison Company, known by its acronym ANGLICO. Operating normally in teams of four, Spann and his fellow ANGLICO forces would ground-infiltrate, parachute, or scuba into a forward observation position to direct precise bombardment on enemy positions. In Afghanistan in October-

November 2001, the Green Beret A-team with which Mike served performed the same mission: calling in devastating, precision-guided munitions on Taliban positions.*

At Lejeune, Spann participated with Force Reconnaissance Marines in doing "water jumps." Parachuting from two thousand feet, the Marines opened their chutes at five hundred feet and, after landing into the ocean two hundred yards off Onslow Beach, released their harnesses and swam ashore.[39] Spann and others did "helicopter inserts" (as he would later do in Afghanistan in October 2001), launching off the skid at 40 feet above the ground and "fast-roping" (descending at full speed) to the ground with a hundred pounds on their backs. At noon, even in the steamy summers, he and Mike Tapen would do their daily run, averaging anywhere from eight to ten miles, at a pace of "six minutes and change."[40]

Mike's break as a Marine officer came in March 1997, when Lieutenant Colonel Mike West chose Captain Spann to be his second-in-command for a joint exercise expedition in Latin America and Africa called UNITAS. The six-month deployment began in Puerto Rico and proceeded to Venezuela, Panama, Colombia, Peru, Chile, Argentina, Brazil, South Africa, and Namibia.

As the UNITAS "XO" Mike commanded four hundred Marines and planned, participated, and, along with Lieutenant Colonel West, directed the joint operations. In Puerto Rico, along with the elite Force Reconnaissance Unit as well as jumpers from the 82nd Airborne Division from Fort Bragg, the force "attacked" Vieques Island, calling in naval gunfire (a total of 225 "puff" or marking rounds).[41] Spann, who got his jump wings in 1996 at Fort Bragg, then parachuted in with six 82nd Airborne paratroopers to establish a forward observation post. Ashore the combined forces engaged in Spann's artillery specialty, close air support — spotting targets with a laser for precision-guided bombs dropped by various aircraft. The targets were enemy tanks and surface-to-air batteries.

---

*2nd ANGLICO, with its "exportable fire control team package," served both the Royal Marines and the Third Army Infantry in the invasion of Iraq in 2003. The author was briefed by 2nd ANGLICO's commanding officer, Lieutenant Colonel John M. Owens, and his executive officer, Major Mark A. Jewell, at Camp Lejeune in July 2003.

Spann's whole training as an artillery officer paralleled the revolution in the strategy of deployment and attack by the U.S. armed forces in the '90s. The Grenada invasion in October 1983 had revealed two disastrous inefficiencies in the Marines and other assault forces — an inability to integrate attack between different forces, and an inability to accurately place bombardment. There were more "friendly fire" casualties in that operation than those by "hostile fire." A secret inquiry by the Joint Chiefs of Staff subsequent to the invasion revealed the necessity of cross-training Army, Marine, and Air Force units to integrate attack, and of developing "exportable" terminal control units that could link up with both allied and American units to direct air and artillery bombardment.[42] The concept of interchangeable "package forces" was a quiet revolution in American military strategy.[43]

As Lieutenant Colonel West remembered, he chose Mike to lead the UNITAS force for "his tremendous technical communication and coordination skills." On board the maritime pre-positioning ship, working out of the combat operations center, Spann had the duty of discussing and planning joint exercises with the host assault units in advance. In port, Spann, West, and the Latin American and African commanders would spend two days planning the joint exercise. The challenge was multiple: the national forces had a wide range of competence and training, and were often as concerned with pride of command-and-control as they were with a smooth, casualty-less exercise. The Marines themselves, sure of their own abilities, were at times disparaging of their Latin and African counterparts. The challenge for Mike and Lieutenant Colonel West was as much diplomatic and cross-cultural as it was military.

Congress's authorization of Joint Combined Exchange Training (JCET) operations in 1991 was inspired by the success of NATO war games. Prior to JCET, the U.S. military had, on occasion, exchanged officers and trained foreign armed forces, including at Fort Benning's infamous School of the Americas. But joint military exercises like UNITAS integrated up to a thousand soldiers in the war games.

Spann, always something of an insomniac, was by all accounts a worthy diplomat, pouring out letters and airlifting commendations and training medals to his Latin and African counterparts. He also earned the acclaim of his junior platoon commanders. One remembered, "He was very responsive and never let me down during our live-fire training evolutions — on time and always on the mark. Always."[44]

In May 1997, the Marine UNITAS force anchored off Cartagena, a Caribbean port in Colombia. Corporal Lance Endstrom was somewhat amazed one early morning to see Captain Spann clambering down the embedded steel ladder on the side of the ship. From the bridge Endstrom watched as Spann swam off perhaps a mile or so until he was lost, at least visually, in the swells of the open sea. About an hour later, Endstrom spotted his executive officer coming back under a steady stroke. Nearly all Marines on active duty maintain a regimen of conditioning. Mike Spann, according to his fellow captain Mike Tapen, was in another league. He was a long-distance runner and swimmer of iron-man capacity as well as both a certified pilot and diver.

Mike was a solid, though by Marine standards unheroic, drinker, a fact that probably helped him save the life of one of his junior officers in Lima. A fight started at a bar where the Marines had gathered. By the time Spann got on the scene, four Peruvians were beating and kicking one of his lieutenants. Spann flew into the middle of them and, after a succession of blows, drove them off. By this time the lieutenant, bleeding heavily, was not breathing. Spann got the man into a taxi, resuscitated him, and took him to a hospital. He saved his life. "Mike was a hero before entering the CIA," Marine captain Ross A. Parrish remembered.[45]

From many interviews done for this book, it is clear that Spann loved the overseas work, reading books and briefings on the politics, culture, and security issues in advance of the visits and seeking out military attachés and diplomatic officers while in-country. He labored on his Spanish, with limited results, but delighted in the challenges of the scene. Mike, as his commander put it, was "an adventurer at heart."

In terms of his education as a man and a Marine, Mike remained a down-the-line conservative. Shortly after he joined the Marines, the gays-in-the-military issue hit the mass media spotlight. On the day President Clinton called for a review of the status of gays in the military, Sergeant Justin Elzie (of Company B, Headquarters and Support Battalion), who was stationed at Camp Lejeune, exited the proverbial closet and professed his homosexuality on ABC News. There was an uproar throughout the military, little of it in favor of Clinton's proposed reform. General Colin Powell expressed the view of many officers, including Spann: a formalization of gay rights would give rise to an expectation of privacy in communal sleeping situations, both in the barracks and in the field. The effect would be dysfunctional to military relations and operations. Beyond bigotry against gays — who had served both faithfully and courageously in the U.S. military for two hundred years — this was a legitimate concern. Ultimately, to Clinton's and Powell's credit, what emerged from all the Sturm und Drang was an inelegant but pragmatic compromise termed "don't ask, don't tell."[46]

The other story that blew during the 1990s was the Marine practice of "blood-winging." In one of the videotapes that made its way to CNN, a helmeted Marine is seen banging the golden jump-wings pin, helmet first, into the bare chest of a grimacing, then bleeding, parachute graduate. Colonel David Hackworth, among others, sprang to the defense of the eleven accused Marines in the initial incident, pointing out that they were not "stockbrokers, but special men," who were being trained to jump, usually at night, behind enemy lines, to kill or be killed.[47] Secretary of Defense William Cohen, however, whose theories about "maneuver warfare" did not include the experience of having served in the military himself, provided a more politically correct response. He said that he was "disgusted and disturbed" by the ritual and henceforth would exact "zero tolerance" for the practice.[48] General Krulak dutifully then promulgated an order that was greeted with high humor in the Corps: "Hazing rituals that are cruel, abusive, humiliating or oppressive are banned." But what about becoming a Marine? In the backwash of controversy, Spann was spared the "cruelty" after qualifying for his jump wings, but had he been so subjected, one could assume him undergoing it with a slight smile on his face.[49]

In February 1998, Lieutenant Colonel Victor Foley selected Captain Mike Spann as the executive officer of 2nd ANGLICO at Camp Lejeune. The appointment was unusual: the XO position normally went to a major, not a captain, and to an aviator, not an artilleryman. But Spann had excelled as an officer in both field and administration. His rapport with the enlisted men was nothing less than exceptional,

Gunnery Sergeant Joe Bell remembered. that Mike was tougher than everybody, mentally and physically, and stuck up for his men and his fellow officers.[50] He wrote up his old friend Mike Tapen for a commendation after the latter returned from serving in Bosnia-Herzegovina.[51] He had always been, in the word his third grade teacher had used, "dependable." But finally, after years of blending in and getting by, Mike had made it as a leader in a force he had always dreamed of joining. His appointment as the XO of 2nd ANGLICO coincided, however, with the decision of General Krulak to disband the unit, which, after a three-year hiatus, was reconstituted.

In Mike's application to the clandestine service of the CIA, he refers in some detail to a secret Marine–Special Forces mission in which he participated in October 1997. He had applied for and received a security clearance to be briefed on the mission and in early October headed for Colombia. The American military mission in Bogotá at the time was dedicated to counternarcotics, not counterinsurgency.

Counternarcotics meant interdicting drugs, but no one believed, not even the drug-war enthusiasts during their sober moments, that militarized drug interdiction had much impact other than what Marine general George Joulwan called the hose effect: squeeze the drug supply in one place and it will pop out in another. The other insuperable problem was that seemingly everybody — the bad guys (Fuerzas Armadas Revolucionarias de Colombia, or FARC), the good guys (the Colombian government), and the guys in between (the paramilitary armies) — were all involved, to one degree or the other, in the drug trade. During Spann's mission, in fact, U.S. customs officials had seized 750 kilograms of cocaine in the belly of a Colombian air force transport plane as it sat on the runway of Opa-Locka Airport in Florida.[52] Even one of the Pentagon's defense contractors was not thought to be clean.[53]

By 1999 U.S. pilot contractors were dropping seven tons of herbicide a day on the Andean-Amazon jungle regions of Columbia. To avoid ground fire, the pilots released their loads from 10,000 feet, inundating villages, waterways, and corn and yucca fields as well as drug areas. In the provinces of Caqueta and Putumayo, where much of the bombardment was taking place, infants on their mothers' backs were being blinded by the herbicide.[54]

Spann's mission was join a detachment of Green Berets in the training of Colombian paratroopers for strikes at drug labs. In the course of the training, the Colombian armed forces got what they wanted most — Black Hawk helicopters. And the Americans? The "boys and their toys" phenomenon of officer exchanges, foreign assignment, new arms sales, weapons training, and general military pomp and circumstance provided the recompense. Leading this odd mission was the former Second Marine Expeditionary Force commander at Lejeune, General Charles Wilhelm, a broad-shouldered, much-decorated, no-nonsense Marine who became the CINC of the Southern Command in 1997. Wilhelm cheerfully summarized the ridiculousness of trying to stop the tidal flow of drugs in Colombia, a physically remote, largely trackless country of forty million that had been in a state of war for thirty-eight years: "This ain't no Vietnam," Wilhelm said. "I wish it were; it would be easier."[55]

The Marines' UNITAS deployment was the U.S. military at its best — an open, cooperatively integrated training and exercise operation with cross-national exchange of friendship and fellowship. (The Marines usually engaged as well in an athletic or humanitarian exercise in the course of each national visit.) The Special Forces' drug follies in Colombia was the military at its worst — a high-cost, ineffectual gambit with a contradicted mission and no intelligible exit strategy. In addition to the sixty-one Black Hawks (and a total of $1.3 billion of aid under "Plan Colombia") provided the Colombians, the Special Forces stationed at the Larrandia base opened a Hooters bar there at taxpayer expense.

When asked in 2003 why Mike had left the Marine Corps, Major Tray Ardese replied, "Mike wanted action." He wanted, in the tradition of his family and his town, to fight for his country. The "ordinary boy" Mike's father had described had become no ordinary Marine. He had excelled technically, physically, and in terms of leadership. But for Mike, there was something missing — the test of combat. That is why he passed up the FBI and the DEA; he saw them as "bureaucratic."

As library records at the bases where he served attest, Spann read a good deal more than his fellow Marine officers, but talked only sparingly about the intake. At Camp Hansen, he read three books about the

American invasion of Iwo Jima in early 1945, when, as Admiral Chester Nimitz said, "uncommon valor was a common virtue." For thirty-six days, the Marines and Navy corpsmen had attacked, costing the Marines 26,000 casualties, including seventeen infantry battalion commanders and scores of platoon commanders. Twenty-six Marines and Navy corpsmen won Medals of Honor in that battle. Mike also read another book, one about Ernie Pyle, "World War II's most beloved typewriter soldier," who was killed at Ie Shima, a small island west of Okinawa, during the American attack on that larger island.[56] Found on Pyle's body was a draft of his final dispatch, a column he had written for the end of the war in Europe:

> But there are many of the living who have had burned into their brains forever the unnatural sight of cold dead men scattered over the hillsides and in the ditches along the high rows of hedge throughout the world.
>
> Dead men by mass production — in one country after another — month after month and year after year. Dead men in winter and dead men in summer.
>
> Dead men in such familiar promiscuity that they become monotonous.
>
> Dead men in such monstrous infinity that you come almost to hate them. These are the things that you at home need not even try to understand. To you at home they are columns of figures, or he is a near one who went away and just didn't come back. You didn't see him lying so grotesque and pasty beside the gravel road. . . .

When Mike left to go on his first secret mission in 2000 — to hunt for Osama bin Laden — his father dropped him off in the Langley parking lot at CIA at 4 A.M. As Mike was getting out, he turned to his father: "Daddy, don't ever believe I'm dead till you see my body. Okay?"[57]

April 1999
Camp Peary
Near Williamsburg, Virginia

Mike Spann's drive to serve in the black operations wing of the CIA was part pride and part escape. The pride part he set forth in his letter to the Clandestine Service Trainee Division on January 30, 1998:

> I am seeking an elite career that will challenge my abilities and allow me to continue to serve my country. I am twenty-eight years old and currently an Officer of Marines in outstanding physical and mental condition. A proven leader, I possess ample physical and moral courage that has been strengthened through a lifetime of self-discipline and hard work. I have often made difficult decisions under the most stressful circumstances. Constant evaluation has proved that I can make the right decisions by quickly analyzing a situation and gathering needed information to act. Being a hard individual with a strong will, I can meet any challenge while keeping a positive attitude and my sense of humor. I am also a skilled writer who can organize thoughts, information, and visual data into clear and coherent written communications.[58]

The factor of escape had to do with the bitter breakup of his marriage. His wife, Ann, had found someone else. It was not possible for him, he said, to go home anymore. He was on his own.

On Monday, September 21, 1998, having received a favorable reply from the Agency, Mike drove from Jacksonville to Fayetteville for an interview at the Radisson Prince Charles on 450 Hay Street in old Fayetteville. That evening there was a presentation on the Clandestine Division by two CIA officers from the Directorate of Operations. The next morning at 9 A.M. two CIA officials from DO interviewed Mike for two hours. They gave him the highest marks.

In the second week of March 1999, Mike Spann, having accepted the offer from the Special Activities Division of the CIA, began his training. In so doing he passed up offers from the Drug Enforcement Administration and the Federal Bureau of Investigation, which would have paid him around $10,000 more to start than did the paramilitary division of the CIA.[59] Spann's dedication to work covertly with the CIA was no incidental choice. He was fascinated by the foreign scene and saw a career of paper-shuffling and political maneuvering ahead for him in the Marines — and in the FBI and DEA for that matter. Beyond personal growth, Mike confided to his father that he was joining the CIA "to make the world a better place. . . . Somebody's got to do it."[60] It sounded like the phrase a young man in the late 1940s might have used in signing up with the newly formed Central Intelligence Agency, at a time when the Cold War was thought to be a moral struggle between right and wrong and before the scourge of foreign misadventure and scandal had so stained the CIA. But Mike Spann was an old-fashioned, true-blue, do-it-right type of person, entirely uninterested in rank or remuneration, much less the attention. He wanted difficult work — and he was about to get it.

It is worth asking whether Spann knew what he was getting into in joining the operational end of the CIA as a covert operative. We know he had read books such as Andrew Tully's *CIA: The Inside Story* as well as *Inside the CIA* by Ronald Kessler (a book the Agency had suggested he read in advance of his interview).[61] Mike's reading also included four other books: *Nightmover: How Aldrich Ames Sold the CIA to the KGB for $4.6 Million,* by David Wise; *The Agency: The Rise and Decline of the CIA,* by John Ranelagh; *The Very Best Men: Four Who Dared: The Early Years of the CIA,* by Evan Thomas; and *Alternative Careers in Secret Operations: Your Guide to a New Identity, Life, Career,* by Mark W. Merritt, according to the records at the Jacksonville Public Library.[62]

The portrait of the CIA counterespionage in Wise's book is frightening. A mediocre agent, Aldrich Ames, walks in the front door of the Soviet embassy in Washington and requests $50,000 in exchange for providing the names of U.S. agents to the KGB. After betraying ten U.S. agents in Russia, all of whom are killed as a result, and after having paid $480,000 in cash for a home in Virginia and spent several hundred thousand dollars on sports cars, Ames is ultimately investigated and arrested. Ranelagh's comprehensive book deals with U.S. operations from the OSS (Office of Strategic Services, the precursor to the CIA) until the middle 1980s. In judiciously measured analysis, it details some "successes" (such as the U-2 flights, the overthrow of Mossadegh in Iran and Arbenz in Guatemala, and breakthroughs in espionage penetration of the Soviets), along with a devastating catalog of blunders (the "atomic spies," the Bay of Pigs and the Castro assassination attempts, the "secret war" in Laos, the Phoenix assassination program in Vietnam, the Angolan misadventure, and the Reagan administration's sale of weapons to Iran in exchange for Contra assistance). Thomas's book focuses on four CIA spymasters and covert operators: Richard Bissell, Frank Wisner, Tracy Barnes, and Desmond Fitzgerald. Throughout the accounts, despite variations of subject and judgment, there is a definitely negative portrayal of the paramilitary unit Mike was joining. Some of the operatives were war-loving rogues like Rip Robertson or Ted Shackley, who wrought covert havoc before their professional demise. Others, like Pete Ray, an Alabama Air National Guard pilot mustered into service for the Bay of Pigs, died officially abandoned with little compensation for his survivors.[63] In a word: expendable.

Until the mid-1990s, the practice of the Directorate of Operations in terms of black operations was to contract with necessary personnel, the majority of them ex-military. In operations against Castro, the range of recruitment had run the gamut — from Mafia chieftains like Johnny Roselli to assassins such as Rolando Masferrer. (There is some evidence that Lee Harvey Oswald himself had "asset" status).[64] In Laos in the 1970s, paramilitaries ranged from ex-missionaries like William Young to ex-Marines like Tony Poe, who described his work as "just like the Mafia." In the 1980s, after Vietnam and the array of scandals, covert operations languished, as did casework in the field.[65]

As David Wise, a longtime critic of covert operations, has argued, "The Indiana Jones role for the CIA was not intended when Congress established the agency in 1947 'to correlate and evaluate intelligence.' But the law included language allowing the agency to undertake 'other functions and duties,' a loophole through which thousands of covert operations have been launched around the globe."[66] President Kennedy was the first to rein in the CIA's independence in terms of covert operations. "How could I have been so stupid?" he asked himself in the wake of the Bay of Pigs. The artifice of "plausible deniability" (i.e., that the United States could credibly deny organizing and unleashing the anti-Castro exile force), as well as the cold calculation that the exile forces and the CIA paramilitaries who were advising them were "expendable" if something went wrong, combined to produce grossly incorrect intelligence estimates as well as poor decision making by the president. After the disaster, Kennedy vowed to "split the CIA in a thousand pieces."

When Kennedy purged CIA director Allen Dulles and his deputy Richard Bissell, he imposed stringent new rules on the Agency's ability to undertake covert activities. The latter came in the form of three top-secret "National Security Action Memoranda," all issued on June 28, 1961. NSAM 55 eliminated exclusive CIA authority over planning and executing paramilitary operations. NSAM 56 asked the secretary of defense to "inventory the paramilitary assets we have in the U.S. armed forces, consider various areas of the world where the implementation of our policy may require indigenous paramilitary forces, and thus arrive at a determination of the goals we should set in this field." NSAM 57 stated that "Any large paramilitary operation wholly or partially covert which requires significant numbers of militarily trained personnel [and] amounts of military equipment" would be construed to "exceed normal CIA-controlled stocks and/or military experience of a kind or level" needed for such operations. Larger programs would become "the primary responsibility of the Department of Defense with CIA in a supporting role."[67]

The first breach in JFK's tight harness over CIA paramilitary operations was accomplished by his brother, Attorney General Bobby Kennedy. Determined to eliminate Castro, the younger Kennedy countenanced a series of assassination sorties known as "Operation Mongoose." These brought together a veritable hell's brew of malignant personalities — Cuban-exile henchmen of Florida mafioso Santos Trafficante, black ops trainers like E. Howard Hunt, and even a squadron of snipers organized by another Mafia chieftain, Johnny Roselli. Court historians like Arthur M. Schlesinger, Jr., would primly deny it, but declassified Soviet Politburo files indicate that the overriding reason why Khrushchev secretly tried to put missiles on the island of Cuba was to protect the client state from the various depredations of Operation Mongoose. After the two superpowers nearly clashed over that event, the Kennedy brothers ordered the paramilitary operations in the south of Florida to be discontinued. But now the Mafia, with the support of CIA irregulars, had a new target — Jack Kennedy himself. At the point when the decision of whether or not to approve the assassination of Castro came up, JFK's words to his special assistant, Kenny O'Donnell, were nothing short of prophetic: "If we get into that kind of business, we'll all be targets."[68]

The critical development in the rebirth of the CIA's paramilitary wing was the renaissance of the Special Forces in the 1980s. On April 13, 1987, President Reagan authorized "Special Operations Command." The independent command of the Special Forces led to independent budgeting under a separate "Program Objective Memorandum." Under the command of General Carl Stiner, the Special Operations Command was expanded to include Psychological Operations (PSYOPS) and Civil Affairs. By the 1990s the so-called optempo (operational tempo) rose accordingly. The "shadow warriors" played critical roles in Desert Shield/Desert Storm (the operations against Saddam Hussein in 1990–91), Provide Comfort (support to the Kurdish refugees), and Restore Hope (the Somali relief operation).

The CIA Directorate of Operations contributed two decisive elements to the rise of the Special Forces: operational intelligence on the ground about "good guys and bad guys," and the ability to "plausibly deny" the use of U.S. military forces. The key component in otherwise interchangeable CIA and Special Forces personnel is this: avoidance of accountability. As John Pike of GlobalSecurity had pointed out, "The CIA's capabilities and activities are intended to be unacknowledged. They are employed in countries where the fact of an American military presence would be damaging."

In the middle 1990s, faced with a range of low- and high-intensity conflicts in which the U.S. preferred not to use mainline military forces, the Agency upgraded the selection and training of its cadre of 150 paramilitary officers. Recruitment concentrated on military "high achievers" — from the Navy SEALs, the Army Green Berets and Delta Force, and the Marines' Force Reconnaissance. These were not the "door-crashers" and the "knuckle-draggers" — as they were contemptuously referred to — of yesteryear.

The marriage of the CIA paramilitary wing to the Special Forces was critical to its survival. The practice of recruiting Special Forces personnel, known as "sheep-dipping," to use them in covert operations, expanded significantly during the tenure of General William Boykin. This seconding has generally proved successful, at least in the view of most Special Forces commanders. "The CIA gets a bad rap. People tend to think that if the CIA is involved, there must be some kind of nefarious intent," commented Lieutenant Colonel Kevin M. McDonnell, commander of the U.S. Army's 1st Battalion, 3rd Special Forces Group. "They [the CIA paramilitaries] complement our mission. But the experience in our ranks complements their mission as well. They could not do what they do without us, and we could not do what we do without them."[69]

Spann looked very much like a Special Forces type. He was trained in a range of advanced weapons systems, with a core specialty of "fire control." He was also schooled in the most advanced communications equipment and had trained and "exercised" a good dozen elite foreign combat and artillery units in the use of such equipment. For a good five years he had engaged in joint training exercises in Asia, Latin America, and Africa and had first-name relationships with thirty to forty captain- and major-rank officers overseas. He had some degree of understanding of the economies, cultures, and political systems of the countries he had visited. "My foreign service and travel have given me an invaluable set of experiences that can be useful for the clandestine service," Mike had written in his cover letter to the Agency. This author was unable to get the Agency, either formally or informally, to release Spann's records, but a former director of the Military Special Projects commented about Spann's qualifications: "On paper first-rate. What comes across is a guy who is ready for either combat or command — or both. The only weakness in his record is combat experience. The Agency was also looking for combat types with fluency in foreign language, but, at least in the U.S., that's a no-go."[70]

In 1995, the CIA's top-secret Military Special Projects was redesignated the Special Activities Staff (and later Special Activities Division) when General William G. Boykin assumed command of the division, coming to the CIA from the Army's Delta Force. The Special Activities Staff, or Special Activities Division (SAD), is part of the Directorate of

Operations, which includes other subdivisions such as Counterterrorism, Counternarcotics, Counterintelligence, Covert Actions, and Special Operations, which, in the massive hierarchy of the CIA, tasks SAD.
The SAD provides a pool of air branch (mainly pilots), maritime branch
(mainly ex-SEALs), and ground branch, for which Spann was recruited
to form a Special Operations Group (SOG). These one- to twelve-man
teams are tasked with sabotage, assassination, hostage rescue, material
(such as nuclear) snatches, and bomb damage assessment. One such
SOG operation occurred during Operation Desert Shield when a lone
SAD operative repeatedly penetrated Iraqi forces in and around Kuwait
City in order to retrieve and deliver intelligence material from the be-
sieged and surrounded U.S. embassy there.[71]

JFK's once-established order to place all the CIA's covert combat
responsibilities under the aegis of the Pentagon has been conclusively
superseded. In the invasion of Afghanistan in the fall of 2001, the CIA
was in a lead role, not a supporting role under Special Operations Command. When Mike Spann and his partner Dave Tyson left that morning
for the Qala-e Janghi fortress, they were operating independently of any
Pentagon oversight. Furthermore, at the time when they began bringing the prisoners out into the courtyard for interrogation, their normal
Special Forces complement of Green Berets, known as TIGER 02, was
off fighting on another front. They were on their own.

Mike Spann's incorporation into the paramilitary wing of the CIA
coincided with what became known inside the Agency as "the Plan" —
a "comprehensive operational plan of attack against the Bin Ladin/al-
Qa'ida target inside and outside Afghanistan." "The Plan" was a comprehensive, spare-no-cost move to get bin Laden:

> The Plan included a strong and focused intelligence collection pro-
> gram to track — and then act against — Bin Ladin and his associ-
> ates in terrorist sanctuaries. It was a blend of aggressive human
> resource collection — both unilateral and with foreign partners —
> and enhanced technical collection. . . . To execute the Plan, CTC
> [Counterterrorism Center] developed a program to select and train
> the right officers and put them in the right places. . . . We have ini-
> tiated a nation-wide program to identify, vet and hire qualified per-
> sonnel for counterterrorist assignments in hostile environments.[72]

On joining the Agency in March 1999, Mike traveled to CIA headquarters in Langley, Virginia, before reporting to Camp Peary, the 10,000-acre training base built by the Navy Seabees during World War II, known as "the Farm." There, Mike began the Basic Operations Course, which trains SAD and CIA case officers in so-called tradecraft skills, including weapons training, explosives, infiltration, and exfiltration (i.e., exiting undercover) technique. It was at the Farm that Mike met Shannon J. Verleur, who was training as a CIA case officer. Like the other ex-military assault veterans, the weapons training and the physical fitness posed no problem for Spann. For Ms. Verleur, who had never been subjected to the physical and psychological stress of military conditioning and training, however, they definitely did. Johnny Spann would later report that in her travail, she found a ready supporter in "Silent Mike," whose motivations, by this time, were clearly more than professional.

Mike Spann's surviving family and friends remain tight-lipped about the disintegration of his first marriage. What is clear is that his wife, Ann, had been frustrated by his eighty-hour-a-week devotion to his job as a Marine officer and his long absences from home as a result of his foreign trips.[73] She began seeing a man (whom she later married) sometime in 1998. Mike was devastated. The situation became sufficiently unmanageable in terms of the well-being of the two children that, in the course of Mike's CIA training, his father drove to Jacksonville and took them back to Winfield to live temporarily. Mike was not one to confide much in others, much less share his anguish, but in the course of a late-night conversation he did tell one of his fellow trainees that it was no longer possible for him to go home.[74]

Bivouacked that late spring and early summer somewhere in the vast, humid, rolling hills near Williamsburg, Mike made an overture to Shannon that, at least, got her attention. Learning that she was frightened of crickets, he snuck out of camp and found a bait shop that sold crickets as fishing bait. Back in camp, he surreptitiously dumped the crickets in her tent.[75] When he later asked if she would see a movie or have dinner with him, she declined. "As graciously as I could, I said no — then immediately regretted it. 'Boy,' I thought to myself, 'I blew it, because I really like this guy.'"[76]

Shannon later explained to journalist Edward Klein that she had been through an unhappy marriage to her high school sweetheart and had not dated since their divorce. "I had an unforgiving quality toward myself," she told him.[77] Back from the training program, at a July Fourth party celebrating their successful matriculation as CIA agents, Shannon noticed that "Silent Mike" had left the party but then returned, possibly renewing his availability. Not long thereafter, they began dating. As the relationship blossomed, Shannon found that "I had the self-confidence to withstand all the intense scrutiny. I guess being validated by someone like Mike, whom I highly respected, helped me be less hard on myself." For Mike, it was much the same. For all his personal strengths, he did not care to be alone, and in Shannon he found refuge from his hurt as well as renewal as a man.

The trainees spent nine days in Elizabeth City, North Carolina, at the Harvey Point Defense Testing Activity, known in the Agency as the Point. Here there was advanced instruction in breaking into buildings undetected (surreptitious entry), stealing and photographing documents or equipment, and "snatch and grab" techniques for kidnapping or hostage rescue. Mike also attended a course at "G8," a private-sector facility formed in 1981 that trained him in the black arts — surveillance, sniping, and other antipersonnel skills. The instruction was done by former Special Forces personnel and is known to be rough and unsparing to its students. Mike also took at least half of the "Crash and Bang" course, or Countering Terrorist Tactics Course. The students entered a potentially hostile area and had to qualify in the use of the Browning 9 mm, .38 Special, and a Winchester 1200 12-gauge shotgun. In addition to the weapons training, the candidates learned tactical vehicle interception (TVI), using weapons or the vehicle itself to stop a hostile auto as well as evasive driving (to escape an attempted carjacking or assassination attempt).[78]

Beginning in February 2000 (a little less than a year after Mike Spann joined the CIA), the Agency began inserting three- to eight-man units into southern and northern Afghanistan. Characteristically, these Special Operations Groups would have one case officer from the Near East Division fluent in Dari, Pashto, or Uzbek. The mission was to establish contact and renew alliances with Northern Alliance factions as well as to reconnoiter landing zones and safe houses for Special Forces units.[79] The CIA's covert association with the likes of Rashid Dostum eased the alliance-building. The SOG "eyes-on-the-ground capability" was enhanced significantly by the Agency's counterterrorism center, which collected, compared, and digitally sifted through the mass of information about individuals and movements reported from the field on an instantaneous basis. Whatever the CIA's lapses in terms of surveilling and interdicting Al-Qaeda in the months and weeks prior to September 11, 2001 — and they would rank alongside the intelligence failure before Pearl Harbor — by 2000 the Agency's war-fighting capacity was extraordinary. But this perhaps showcased an old problem — one seen time and time again in Cuba, Iran, and Vietnam. The Agency failed in intelligence-gathering and -estimating precisely because it was dedicated to covert action.

Spann's training at the Farm was cut short by two top-secret missions aimed at Osama bin Laden. One was to engage in a joint exercise near the border of Afghanistan in the Northwest Frontier Province of Pakistan with a six-man Special Activities Division unit. The purpose was to search for and destroy bin Laden. (There were subsequent reports that the Pakistanis, through the CIA's counterpart, ISI, merely went through the motions of cooperating in the venture.)[80] The second could have been more consequential. "We got close enough to bin Laden," Mike later told his father, "to see him shit and move around."[81] The purpose, at least as an option, was the assassination of bin Laden, but for some unknown reason, the operation never pulled the trigger.

In the account of Daniel Benjamin and Steven Simon, two counterterrorism directors on the National Security Council, President Clinton was pushing hard for action against bin Laden (though the history does not allege assassination), but the CIA was temporizing. By 2000, the Predator drone was fully operational and had taken out bin Laden's "mock house" with its Hellfire missile. The Agency pulled back, first alleging the cost of the Predator program, then the danger to its agents around the world if it hit bin Laden.[82]

By December 2000, Mike's personal life was in further turmoil. Shannon was two months pregnant and Ann, who had been diagnosed with cancer, was refusing to sign the divorce decree. Mike had custody of the girls, but it was only temporary. It must have been a frightful time for all of them — and certainly Mike's parents — but Mike, as before, shouldered the burden with stubborn grace. What kept him going was his love for Shannon. "It seems I can never find the words to fully tell you how much I sincerely love you," he e-mailed her on March 26, 2001. "The simple fact is there are no words worthy enough for you. You are certainly God's gift to a hardened and broken-down heart when I needed it the most."[83]

Six weeks later, in a briefing at the Agency, Mike was informed that he would be forward-based in Afghanistan sometime in August 2001. After failing in its secret negotiations with the Taliban to secure a concession for a trans-Afghani gas pipeline, the Bush administration was planning to take America to war — not against terrorism, but for oil.

5

JIHADI
The Journey of John Walker Lindh

November 1997

Mill Valley Islamic Center

Mill Valley, California

When John Walker Lindh was twelve years old, he was taken out of school for two years, remaining at home for his studies. One afternoon his mother, Marilyn, who was in charge of his home schooling, took him to see the Spike Lee movie *Malcolm X*. It moved the child deeply.[1] Eight years later, in an Al-Qaeda training camp, he would tell his comrades about the importance of Malcolm X as a great Muslim figure. He was a man who had suffered, who had lost his father, served time in prison, converted to Islam to commit vengeance against white America, only to find in the end — not long before he was killed — that human reconciliation was the deepest essence of both Islam and America.[2]

Marilyn Walker later said that her son was particularly moved by the scene in which Malcolm X arrives in Mecca to make his hajj. There he found people of all colors, from all countries, swept up in a great, mingling euphoria of faith. But for Lindh, Malcolm X was more than a martyr. He was and would remain a father figure.

John Walker Lindh's own father, Frank, named him after another totemic figure, John Lennon. Frank Lindh, who at the time of his son's birth was working his way through law school, remembered driving home to their dilapidated rental home in Takoma Park, Maryland, at 1 A.M. in February 1981, listening to a rousing rendition of "When Johnny Comes Marching Home Again." The next morning, he recalled, he awoke "with the thrill of John's birth still upon me. It seems strange, at first, to refer to these little creatures by the names we give them, but in time, they do come to be their names." John's earliest memory, as he told his father while he was in jail in Alexandria awaiting trial in 2002, was singing himself to sleep.[3]

What we know about the Lindh family's time in Maryland belongs in the almanac of American middle-class life — Frank making brownies that he liked to deliver (sometimes dressed up) door-to-door to neighbors, Marilyn working off and on as a nurse or retail clerk for extra money, John and his older brother Connell fighting over toys, the family making an event out of Kentucky Derby Day and attending St. Bernadette's Catholic Church together on Sundays. Nothing seemed to portend any of the difficulties to come.

John was a quiet, bookish child who began taking flute lessons at an early age. He was sufficiently precocious in grade school to be enrolled in a program for highly gifted students. He did well, but often missed school because of his asthma and allergies. Frank finished law school in 1987 and worked for two years at the Federal Energy Regulatory Commission before going into private practice.[4] When he got the chance to relocate to the firm's branch in San Francisco in May 1991, he jumped at it. The Lindhs were moving up in the world — to California, the Golden State.

As a badge of their ascending station in life, Frank and Marilyn bought a home in Marin County, which the New Yorker had once termed "the Tuscany of America." With its wooded slopes, fog-swept bluffs, and breathtaking scenes of the distant bay, Marin seems to have the best of all worlds — one of the highest per capita incomes in the country, small, chic towns with Spanish colonial touches strung like elegant bits of a necklace across Marin's broad expanses, seaside wildernesses such as Point Reyes, where the English privateer Sir Francis Drake had once landed, and, of course, commuting distance to America's most elegant city, San Francisco.

Beyond its unusual beauty, the other notable element about Marin is its political and social liberalism. Leading its well-heeled, socially conscious communities are old-time residents and onetime hippies who have made it in the material kingdom. Unlike the relentless ostentation of Beverly Hills or Grosse Pointe, the opulence of Marin is quiet and human-scale, with a pleasant touch of contrariness.[5] In one local paper in Marin, notices of divorce are run alongside marriage announcements and obituaries. Antiwar sentiments abound, with bumper stickers such as "War = Terror" and "Peace is Patriotic" affixed to lampposts, car bumpers, and even a coffee canister at the Marin Coffee Roasters café. Everyone, it seems, is willing to venture an opinion. When this author stopped to ask for directions to the Mill Valley Islamic Center, the slender, bearded man on the street corner immediately warmed to the occasion. "I just went there myself out of solidarity," he said. After giving a detailed rendition of how to get to Shell Road, where the center is located, he paused, pumpernickel half-loaf in hand. "You know what Jefferson wrote, don't you?" he asked. "Divided we stand." With a laugh and a wave, he headed down the street.[6]

The Lindhs purchased a trilevel home on tranquil, leafy Laurel Avenue, a few blocks from the quaint downtown of the small community of San Anselmo. The house is perched on a heavily wooded slope, with touches of flowers on every side. The downtown breathes a placid, self-satisfied authenticity, with an array of small shops, antique stores, day spas, espresso bars, locally owned and run bookstores, and an assortment of small, upscale restaurants. Along San Anselmo Avenue, there are no traditional churches to be seen, but rather a succession of nonprofit organizations. One such is Positive Living, started by a hemophiliac, Barney Pia, who contracted AIDS through a blood transfusion and used the proceeds of a financial settlement to open an elegant bric-a-brac store whose profits (all of them) support a health care agency next door called Positive Center. Among the beneficiaries of Positive Living/Positive Center is a seven-year-old boy suffering from cancer whose family has run out of insurance coverage. Farther down San Anselmo Avenue is Cedarchest, a nonprofit that fosters economic self-sufficiency for the developmentally disabled through weaving, animal husbandry, and professional gardening. Where the main street bends, there is a tiny building housing an equally tiny store called Paper Ships, Books & Crystals. The owner, Elaine Scheeter, remembers John Walker Lindh the teenager. "He actually looked very lonely," she said.

Joan Didion, one of America's premier essayists, published a book in 1968 that portrayed her native state of California as somehow "atomized," as she put it; with the center having fallen out, there was a human vortex of lost people swirling around in a search for fabricated meaning. The book took its title from W. B. Yeats's dark and portentous poem "Slouching towards Bethlehem." At some point between 1945 and 1967, Didion wrote:

> We had somehow neglected to tell these children the rules of the game we happened to be playing. . . . These were children who

grew up cut loose from the web of cousins and great-aunts and family doctors and lifelong neighbors who had traditionally suggested and enforced the society's rules.

These lost children, Didion thought, would become more contrarian than rebellious, more disruptive than aggressive.[7]

So it seemed with John Walker Lindh, lonely and centrifugally moving. John adjusted poorly, if at all, to his new life in Marin. He transferred from one school to the next — three in two years. He was frequently ill and always friendless. In 1993 his parents decided to keep him at home, where Marilyn would school him. The child rarely went out of the house except with his mother. On one sortie, as noted, they went to see the film *Malcolm X*.

Even with the fullest information, it is difficult to pinpoint marital complications, but Frank and Marilyn became distant and disengaged from each other. She turned to Buddhism for solace and direction. Frank, in the view of one close friend, began coming to terms with being gay.[8] Perhaps in reaction to what was happening around him, John, now twelve, took his mother's name and began navigating Internet chat rooms morning and night. He wrote brash and insulting communications under a variety of pseudonyms. Sometimes he was "Dr. J," sometimes "John Doe" or "Hine E. Craque," and at others "Brother Mujahid." His alter agos were usually African-American rapsters who wanted to get messages to "white folk."

For many young people — and some older ones as well — the Internet has become an adolescent sandbox of indulgent mischief and Walter Mitty–like poses. That John was experimenting in this realm should not be regarded as anything very unusual. Still, the characters he adopted were not remotely related to him either temperamentally or socially. As "Hip-Hop's Christ," he posted a rap sequence:

> I'm much more than merely a master,
> In fact I'm faster than the last flood disaster.

When he was fourteen, he began visiting raunchy hip-hop websites under the sobriquet "doodoo." In one e-mail, he ripped a hip-hop critic as a "worthless dickrider." In another, posing as a black man, he observed, "Our blackness should not make white people hate us. It is THEIR racism that causes the hate."[9] Then there were overtones of homophobia. In one communication, John attacked Disneyland, asking, "Isn't that the theme park that sponsored 'gay day' earlier this year?"[10] In another, he referred to J. Edgar Hoover as a "gay fascist." *Time* magazine mentions that he became fascinated with conspiracies — the CIA, UFOs, the Illuminati, and so forth.[11] His Internet alter egos show a distinctly edgy and hypercritical quality, not like the taciturn freshman at Redwood High. Responding to someone's assertion that the rapper Nas was "God," Walker asked, "If this is so, then why does he smoke blunts, drink Moet, fornicate and make dukey music? That's a rather pathetic 'god,' if you ask me."[12]

Around the time he started high school, he began visiting Islamic websites. In one e-mail he asked a group called Five Percent Islam, which promised members the achievement of bliss, "I have never seen happiness myself. Perhaps you can enlighten me . . . where I can go and sneak a peek at it." He transferred from Redwood High to Tamiscal High, an accredited "independent study" public high school in which students study art, creative writing, environmental sciences, and leadership, in addition to their state requirements.

Part of John's new independence was to embrace the trappings of Islam. Taking on the name "Suleyman al-Faris," he donned a long white Islamic kaftan with a white skullcap. For Islamic instruction he went first to the Redwood Mosque in nearby Fairfax, but found it too westernized and too much directed toward Iranian Shiites, an antipathy that he would carry with him in his journey toward jihad. He then visited the Mill Valley Islamic Center, a simple structure in a modest residential neighborhood in Mill Valley whose faithful were largely from South Asia. Here he met a director at the center, Ebrahim Nana, a man of wise and engaging gentility. Nana found Lindh different from most Americans. "Most people come here with questions. They're curious. But he came and said right away that he had done his independent study and was ready to accept Islam right then and there. That really struck me as unusual." There was something else they found unusual — John Walker had shown up without anyone having referred him. Alone. But soon the young man was there every Friday for prayers, then most afternoons, and then overnight on the weekends. He became friends with Ebrahim's son, Abdullah, and they would sit for hours stretched out on overstuffed couches in the small, cramped resting room at the mosque and talk. John was "shy but dedicated," Abdullah remembered.

Years later, after John was arrested for treason as the "American Taliban," several columnists ventured that his parents, distracted and self-involved, had failed to discipline him and had even deserted him in his time of need. Interviews done for this book do not support this theory. The postmodern disease of anxiety and meaninglessness may have swept over him, as Joan Didion had surmised three decades earlier. But Frank and Marilyn counseled and supported their son and seemed anxious to understand just what he was becoming. Frank, who joked with him about his garb and refused to call him anything but John, said, "he found this other spiritual path, and I have always supported that." The important thing for Frank Lindh was that his son's passion was serious and that he didn't lose his sense of humor. The rest he would have to figure out on his own.

In November 1997, with the two required witnesses, John Walker made his *shahada* and became a Muslim. He repeated what all Muslims repeat in their testimony accents of faith: "*la iláha illa lláh muhammadan rasúlu lláh*" — "There is no God but God, and Muhammad is the messenger of God."

As with Malcolm X and the tens of millions of non-Arab converts before him, Suleyman al-Faris was mesmerized by the sonorous, vowel-driven, hypnotic beauty of the Qur'an. Asked in 2003 about what sutra might have been Suleyman's preference, there was laughing and admission of uncertainty at the Mill Valley mosque. Then a short, bearded man who had opened up the mosque after hours for the author picked up a pamphlet in which was written the 93rd sutra. It is called "The Morning Hours":

> What is after will be better
> Than what came before
> To you the lord will be giving
> You will be content
> Did he not find you orphaned
> And give you shelter

Find you lost
And guide you
Find you in hunger
And provide for you
As for the orphan — do not oppress him
And one who asks — do not turn him away
And the grace of your lord proclaim[13]

During this same period, Suleyman read *The Autobiography of Malcolm X*, which had inspired the movie. In the book, Malcolm X wrote of his hajj in 1964, which Spike Lee later used to set the scene of a multi-racial communion in Mecca. For all of the hateful tragedy that is part of modern Islam, for all the hell John Walker would contribute to and experience, this vision would remain:

Never have I witnessed such sincere hospitality and the over-whelming spirit of true brotherhood as is practiced by people of all colors and races here in their Ancient Holy Land, the home of Abraham, Muhammad, and all the other prophets. For the past week, I have been utterly speechless and spellbound by the graciousness I see displayed around me by people *of all colors* [italics in original].

I have been blessed to visit the Holy City of Mecca. I have made my 7 circuits around the Ka'ba, drank water at the well of Zem Zem. I ran 7 times back and forth between the hills of Mount Al-Safa and Mount Al-Marwah. There were tens of thousands of pilgrims from all over the world. They were all colors from blue-eyed blondes to black-skinned Africans. But we were all participating in the same ritual, displaying a spirit of unity and brotherhood that my experience in America had led me to believe never could exist between the white and the non-white.[14]

Suleyman asked his parents in the spring of 1998 if he could study Islam and Arabic in Yemen. His mother was worried about reports of kidnappings in the country, but, probing more deeply, she learned that hundreds of Western students traveled each year to the small country at the bottom of the Arabian peninsula to study. Arrangements, both to study and to reside, were made at the Yemen Language Center, one of the best of its kind in the country. Suleyman took a high school diploma equivalency exam and passed it, not bothering to pick up his degree before departing.

Like Malcolm, he would go away to discover himself. And he would suffer. "He was in desperate need of having Allah in his heart," an elder at the Islamic Center in San Francisco remembered. "God said, 'You come to me walking. I come to you running.'" But Suleyman al-Faris, out of a lonely and rootless desperation, was not walking, as Allah would have it. He was running.

May 15, 2000
Madrassa al-Arabia
Hassanni Kalan Surani, near Bannu, Pakistan

As the prosecution and the defense prepared for trial in the first months of 2002, the journey of John Walker Lindh became central to his guilt or innocence. His movements were thought to reflect his possible intent — deadly or benign? — as well as his association with Islamic violence — deliberate or incidental? Did his movements from Yemen to Pakistan and Afghanistan reveal a growing determination to become a jihadi, to conduct war against America? Or were they merely the wanderings of a restless religious tourist who eventually blundered into a lion's den? Was his rendezvous with destiny in Qala-e Janghi the consequence of would-be terrorism, or merely a factor of being in the wrong place at the wrong time? The U.S. government sent a team of FBI agents to trace Lindh's steps, and the defense dispatched two of the best private investigators in San Francisco, David Fecheimer and Barry Simon, both with experience in the Middle East and the subcontinent.[15]

Walker made two trips to Yemen — the first in 1998, the second in 2000. On his initial visit he landed in Sanaa, the capital of Yemen, in June 1998 and enrolled as planned at the Yemen Language Center, a decorously appointed and well-run program of study, according to its former students. First impressions of the eighteen-year-old Californian (and second ones as well) were not complimentary. "First of all," Robertson Gaffney, a fellow student, remembered, "he looked like a total goof." John's South Asian Muslim get-up, which he insisted on wearing everywhere, looked weird even to the Yemenis. Then there was his Arabic-affected accent, complete with broken English.[16] If that were not enough, his fellow students had to contend with his Islamic name, which some wag at the YLC changed to "Yusuf Islam," the name of '70s pop singer and Muslim convert Cat Stevens.

Within days of starting his language studies, Suleyman began complaining to the director of the language institute, Sabri Saleem, about the fact that there were women in his class. "This is a language institute, not an Islamic madrassa," Saleem explained. The other students at the YLC liked going out at night — and this Suleyman did not like either. He posted a note on the door of fellow foreign students who lived across from his room: "Dear Inhabitants of This Room, Please abstain from getting naked in front of the window. Our neighbors from the apartment building across the street have complained to Sabri, who has ignored them. However, this is not a matter to be taken lightly. Some of our neighbors have threatened to shoot Sabri and/or the inhabitants of this room and the room next door. Please pass this message on to the inhabitants of room #2, and thank you for your decency."[17]

Not long after his arrival, Suleyman exchanged several hundred dollars for Yemeni rials. On his way back from the money market, he came upon a group of beggars and decided to do his Islamic duty and provide alms for the poor. "When you give money," one of his fellow students, Steven Hyland, recalled, "you give them about ten rials. He starts passing out two-hundred-rial notes, which is way, way, way too much." Lindh was suddenly mobbed. A woman at the school had to come out and break up the melee. "John is in the middle of this whirlwind of people. He's much taller than the average Yemeni, with a fistful of cash just raised in the air with his left hand and with his right hand just duking the Yemenis away."[18]

Suleyman came off, in short, as a boor on a bizarre cultural binge. "This is an individual," Hyland later said, "whose idealism led to ideology and he lost all ability for pragmatic thought." That much seemed true. But the problem was not just false idealism, but complete immaturity. Within weeks of beginning the six-month course, Suleyman dropped out of school, as he had done so many times before. Occasionally thereafter, students at the YLC would see him downtown or in the old city walking along in his loose-limbed way. He may have been adrift, both personally and culturally, but he was also exploring and studying with his usual single-minded intensity, heading in a direction that would prove fateful.

If ever one could find a place — parched, tribalistic, and almost jauntily violent — so radically different from the lush, sea-girt, and self-indulgent money culture of Marin County, it would have to be Yemen. The country is at once beautiful and strange, a cauldron of ancient and modern emotions stoked by Islamic and tribal differences, but quieted for the most part by something called qat (see below). Aside from tiny enclaves of McWorld in Sanaa and the old port of Aden, the country seems alive with its ancient self: the five-hundred-year-old eight-story skyscrapers of mud that look like decomposing chocolate cakes, where amber-eyed people live with their livestock; the dark, twisting passage-ways of the 1,500-year-old market Souqal-Milh, where bare-chested smithies pound out knives and even guns from blazing forges; the mud minarets around the great mosque Al-Jami' al-Kabir, where the Prophet himself is said to have worshipped.

What Suleyman found in his wanderings was not just a holy seat of Islam but a citadel of ancient civilization. The kingdom of Saba, the ancient centerpiece of modern Yemen, along with Athens, Mesopotamia, and Egypt, had been one of the great civilizations of antiquity, selling its revered resins — frankincense and myrrh — to the Egyptians, Greeks, and Romans, while maintaining its military and commercial ascendancy for fourteen centuries beginning in 1000 BC. The Sabeans were master builders, who constructed a fifty-two-foot-high dam in Ma'rib in the eighth century BC to irrigate an immense valley.

In the first century AD, the Greeks and Romans discovered that they could reach India by boat by descending the Red Sea. Yemen's ports, especially Hudaidah and what later became Aden, prospered. After a period of rule by the Persians, who brought Islam to Yemen, the country became a distant appendage of the Ottoman Empire. By the seventeenth century, European colonial powers were vying for influence and its shipping lane.

Whether in ancient Yemen or modern, under the rule of foreign conquerors or indigenous clans, beginning in late morning and extending on into the afternoon, except in a few abstemious outposts in the north, everything else would stop and the chewing of qat would begin. Qat is a mild hallucinogenic stimulant that brings both warm introspection and lively bonhomie to the user and tends to smooth away earthly troubles and political differences. The guidebooks might not say so, but qat vies with Islam as the cornerstone of Yemeni culture. David Fecheimer, one of the investigators sent to retrace Lindh's footsteps in preparation for his defense at trial, estimates that one-third of Yemen's economic product can be traced to the cultivation, harvesting, marketing, and consumption of the leaf. Fecheimer found that as popular as qat is with Yemenis and foreigners alike, John Walker Lindh never imbibed, nor did he seek the social or sexual company of women in the course of those endless, dreamy afternoons.

Another of Yemen's odd features is its time-honored industry of kidnapping. Once the captive is seized (and the most sought-after specie is, of course, the money-laden foreigner), the guns would be put down and hot tea would be served. Then the haggling would start — the kidnappers in the house and the ransoming family in the street or on the phone. After exchanges concerning the immortal themes of honor and vengeance, the parties would get to the necessary business of how much. Casualty of any kind was rare, at least until 1998, when sixteen foreign tourists were seized by the Islamic Army of Aden, a radical group aligned with Al-Qaeda. British-trained security forces took the distinctly un-Yemeni action of mounting a rescue operation. In the ensuing firefight with the kidnappers, four hostages and three kidnappers were killed. This incident did not seem to faze Suleyman, who attempted to venture on at least one occasion into the fundamentalist north, well-known as a major haven of kidnapping. Before he could enter harm's way, however, he was stopped at an army checkpoint on the outskirts of Sanaa and turned back.[19]

With the exception of Afghanistan under the Taliban, there was no country in the Muslim world where Al-Qaeda flourished more freely than Yemen. Political schisms, reinforced by sectarian cleavages, made it fertile ground for the recruitment and deployment of terrorists. After the disintegration of the Ottoman Empire following World War I, the territory of Yemen was divided between North and South, with imperial Britain maintaining its crucial port of Aden. In 1962, a group of army officers seized power and founded the Yemen Arab Republic, a secularist state on the model of Egypt. In 1967, South Yemen seceded and formed a Marxist state that was underwritten by the Soviet Union until 1990, when, with the collapse of the Soviet empire, the People's Republic rejoined greater Yemen. Despite nominal consolidation of north and south, civil war ensued.

In the early 1980s, there was a new visitor to Yemen — Osama bin Laden, whose family hailed from the eastern part of Yemen, known as Hadramawt, in the desolate, rocky valley of Wadi Doan. Bin Laden's mission was to recruit young Yemenis to fight with the Afghan mujahideen in the mountains and deserts of Afghanistan against the Soviet invaders. According to U.S. intelligence, he maintained active relations with senior military commanders such as General Ali Mohsen al-Ahmar and conservative religious imams like Abdel Meguid al-Zindani.[20] In addition to sharing jihadi fervor, there was the factor of money, enormous money, that fueled the transport (three Boeing 707s a day) of youthful holy warriors to the Afghani front. With the defeat of the Red Army in 1989, bin Laden became a sacred figure in Yemen.

The mujahideen victory set the stage for the transformation of Yemen in the 1990s. Approximately 4,000 returning Yemeni veterans joined another 7,000 so-called Afghan Arabs as shock troops in President Ali Abdallah Saleh's internal war against the remaining Communists. Within three months, the holy warriors had annihilated the opposition and, for their service, were rewarded with homes, land, and employment by Saleh's regime. Outside of Afghanistan, Al-Qaeda had no stronger ally and no safer and more sympathetic habitat than Yemen. In fact, in 1997, bin Laden had even contemplated moving his entire operation there, his father's birthplace.[21]

These political shocks polarized Yemen's *umaa* (community of Muslim believers). The Shafia Sunnis, especially in the north, espoused Wahhabism, while the prevailing belief among the Zaydi Shiites was Sufism. As with many Arab countries, the warring dreams of Islam's past were prologue to its present and future.

In the mid-eighteenth century, Mohammed ibn al-Wahhab (1703–

1792) broke away from Istanbul and Ottoman rule and established a state on the Arabian peninsula based on the "pure faith." What was especially regarded as impure was any form of mysticism or non-Arabism. These included the influences of Iran — Shiia and Sufi — as well as beliefs drawn from Roman and Western influences. Wahhab took the Qur'an and employed it to cast out infidels (*kafir*) and to discipline the faithful through the *sharia* (Islamic sacred law). Especially in the north of Yemen, in the small villages and wadis that abut Saudi Arabia, the influence of Wahhab was deep and lasting. His promise was the one Suleyman al-Faris adopted — that puritanical Islam and the rule of the early caliphs (*al-salaf al-salibin*) would replace heretical tendencies, if necessary by the sword.

Elsewhere in Yemen, especially toward the central part of the country, other Sunnis and the great majority of Shiites practiced a form of Islam in which the influence of the great Sufi mystic Ahmad ibn Idris (1780–1836) was evident. Idris, a Moroccan, believed in education and spiritual self-sufficiency. He traveled to Yemen, instructing people in their own dialect and teaching the proper manner of ritual prayers (*salat*). Essential to his instruction was a devaluation of sacred Islamic law (*fiqh*) and the importance of keeping church and state separate (*tawhid*) in the development of Muslim society. The distinctive characteristics of Sufism were evident in his teaching: humanism and mysticism. It was not the mullah or imam who would transform the believer, but rather the believer himself. There was a distinctly pastoral, inclusive, and egalitarian quality to this practice of Islam, one that made Ma'rib and later Sanaa and Aden important centers of education and culture in the Arab world. Jews and Christians were treated as protected subjects (*dhimmis*), in keeping with the Prophet's instruction that they were "people of the book." Thus, during Suleyman's first visit to Yemen, a group of Israelis flew into Sanaa to visit the small Jewish community that had existed in Yemen for the better part of three centuries.[22] It is a sad, though revealing, item of Western ignorance that the humanistic liturgy and history of *most* of Islam is overlooked and the hateful creed of Wahhabism, abetted ironically enough by American sponsorship of the Saudi royal family, is emphasized instead.[23]

As the Islamist scholar Karen Armstrong has noted, the struggle between Wahhabism and Sufism in the eighteenth century had a great deal to do with the eclipse of the Islamic Ottoman Empire in the face of an expanding Christian Europe.[24] Wahhabism stood to revive the old to exclude the new. Sufism proposed to welcome the new to enrich the old. The concept of jihad (the Arabic word for "striving" that the Prophet Muhammad had defined variously as meaning either personal struggle to improve oneself, or the duty to defend the faith by force of arms) would be employed at cross-purposes: the Sufis advocating the struggle within and the Wahhabis the struggle without before the advancing West.[25]

In his journey toward surrender (*islam*) as a Muslim and especially in plural, tolerant Yemen, Suleyman could have chosen a gentler and more tolerant form of Islam than he did. His willful election of the radical, austere, and anti-Western Wahhabi form of Islam called Salafi shaped and deepened his growing hostility toward the United States. He contemptuously avoided the Shiite mosques that clustered around the old city, with their tiled Persian arcades and arches and enormous, richly colored carpets, in favor of the Ahl Kheir mosque, with its plain beige bricks, windows of paneled iron, and unadorned, whitewashed interior.[26]

Consistent with his decided preference for the autarkic Salafi sect was Suleyman's enrollment at Al-Iman University. The director of Al-Iman, Sheikh Abdel Meguid al-Zindani, was a loyalist and comrade of Osama bin Laden. Sheikh al-Zindani also headed the radical wing of the Islah party in Yemen and was known for his incendiary speeches against "Western devilry" at the conclusion of Friday prayers.[27] The university, a plain, shopworn affair on a hill at one end of the city, had some eight hundred foreign students among its six thousand enrolled students. Suleyman took religious courses and somehow got along, despite his poor Arabic. The university was a hotbed of protest and activism on the usual lightning-rod issues among young radical Arabs — the plight of Palestine, the U.S. "desecration" of Saudi Arabia, the violent repression of Islamic insurgency in Algeria, and the like.[28] In its background brief on John Walker Lindh's travels and associations, the FBI would feature his time at Al-Iman as indicative of violent tendencies, but such tendencies lay in the realm of association, not commission —

and that difference in criminal justice is crucial. In one e-mail to his mother, dated September 23, 1998, he suggests, doubtless based on faulty information fed him by his Muslim sources, that the embassy bombings "seem far more likely to have been carried out by the American government than by any Muslims," placing the bombings mistakenly in West Africa, not East Africa.[29]

Among the students and professors at Al-Iman, there were two patron saints of jihad — Osama bin Laden and Abdullah Azzam, Osama's former professor and his mentor in jihad until he was blown up by a car bomb in Peshawar in November 1989. Azzam was the instigator of the great Arab crusade to liberate Afghanistan from the Russians, and a matchless orator. No one articulated the cause of the Muslim warrior more compellingly in both Islamic jurisprudence (of which he was a doctor) and sociological analysis of current events. Bin Laden described him a man "worth a nation."[30]

Suleyman was one of millions of young Muslims to read Azzam's book *Join the Caravan,* and probably watched him on videotape, as so many others did, after Friday prayers on campus.

> I shall turn my face away from a land which has made my tongue ineffective and locked up my heart. A man's clear resolution and common sense dictate that he turn away from the sun's glare. Jihad and emigration to Jihad have a deep-rooted role which cannot be separated from the constitution of this religion. A religion which does not have Jihad cannot become established in any land, nor can it strengthen its flame. The steadfast Jihad, which is one of the innermost constituents of this religion and which has its weight in the Scales of the Lord of the Worlds, is not a contingent phenomenon peculiar to the period in which the Koran was revealed; it is in fact a necessity accompanying the caravan which this religion guides.[31]

Ultimately, Suleyman's mother, Marilyn, persuaded him to come home to California, something, he later said, he regretted.[32] As always, he ran hot and cold on even the most elementary of matters. Writing home in October 1998, he intimated that, despite his austere principles, going back wasn't such a bad idea. "Although I'm not particularly fond of the idea of returning to America, I do have a four-month vacation in about six months. This means you'll probably be seeing me again before you expected." When he tried to leave Yemen, however, he was detained on the grounds of an expired visa. Yemen Language Center director Sabri Saleem interceded to clear things up and found Suleyman utterly spent. "His face was awful. I think he was tired of Yemen, tired of everything and wanted to go home." In May 1999 he flew home to find his family falling apart.

A month after Suleyman returned to California, his father, Frank, who had previously moved out of the house while his son was away and announced that he was gay, filed for divorce. What impact this may have had on John is not known, but knowledge of it later ignited a fierce little exchange between San Francisco's two major newspapers. *San Francisco Examiner* columnist P. J. Corkery claimed that Frank Lindh had actually moved in with his male companion in 1997. "Sources close to the family say the father's turn of life from married man to modern gay man startled and flustered the then sixteen-year-old." The *Chronicle,* in turn, characterized such sentiments as taking "attacks on the family to a new and disgusting level." A leading gay columnist in New York, Michelangelo Signorile, was able to sort his way through the minefield of unresolved emotion and Kulturkampf to make a simple point. "If Lindh had left his wife for another woman and his son were traumatized, it would certainly be discussed in the media. So if Lindh did leave his wife for a man and it affected Walker, it should similarly be reported on."[33]

Back with his friends at the Mill Valley Islamic Center, Suleyman never talked about his family, only about his devotion to his younger sister, Naomi. On many weekends he simply stayed at the center. He told his old mentor at the mosque, Ebrahim Nana, that Yemen hadn't met his expectations. "They weren't as orthodox as he thought — they weren't as strict on Islam as he thought."[34] During that summer of 1999, he began traveling to San Francisco to worship in mosques that emphasized the Salafi creed. Salafis are strict and puritanical followers of al-Wahhab. Unlike the Islamic Center in Mill Valley, the Majid Darussalam mosque, located on the third floor of a building on Jones Street just up the block from Market Street, preached jihad, as did the San Francisco Islamic Center on Crescent Street in Bernal Heights.

One might surmise that the source of the call to war against the United States and the West had its origin in Muslim countries known for their anti-American fervor — Iran, Syria, Libya, or Algeria. On the contrary, the two countries that trafficked most extensively and effectively in hectoring against America were America's two most important "allies" in the Muslim world: Saudi Arabia and Pakistan.

In the case of Saudi Arabia, the paradox was simply this: as Saudi king Fahd became increasingly dependent on America's military backing, he felt obliged to satisfy the demands of the Wahhabi clerics who were critical to his fragile claim to power.

The clerics could preach revolution, but only with regard to places like the U.S., Israel, and western Europe (i.e., not in Saudi Arabia). Over time the Wahhabi creed — and its hateful messaging — moved abroad into the mosques of the religiously tolerant West. The conduit of Wahhabi propagation into these mosques were Saudi charities, the three largest of which were World Assembly of Muslim Youth (WAMY), the International Islamic Relief Organization (IIRO), and al-Haramain. In addition to building mosques, Islamic centers, and schools, these organizations published tracts and journals that targeted infidels such as the Zionists and the Shiites. WAMY, for example, distributed a book (in both Arabic and English) entitled *The Differences between the Shi'ites and the Majority of Muslim Scholars,* which claims that "the cornerstone of the Shi'ite faith, as well as its dimensions and evidence, are false and baseless." Shiism, it states, is rather the product of a Jewish conspiracy.

The United States has been, of course, constitutionally indulgent of such spoken or published idiocies, be they Muslim, Christian, or other. But in the case of the Saudis, it was not just posturing, as the FBI discovered in the bombing of the World Trade Center in 1993. The blind sheikh Abdel Rahman, who was indicted for his role in the bombing, drew on a sinister network known as the Muslim Brothers. In subsequent plots, such as those that occurred around the millennium, the investigations more often than not led to Saudi-supported mosques. At Tucson's Islamic Center, for example, Wadih el-Hage, a naturalized American citizen who had worked in Sudan as Osama bin Laden's personal secretary, recruited for Al-Qaeda. In 1991, Hani Hanjour would join the Islamic Center and enroll at the University of Arizona. Ten years later, he would be back in Arizona before being deployed to pilot one of the airliners on 9/11.

The official position of the Saudi royal family was that Osama bin Laden and Al-Qaeda were as repugnant to Saudi Arabia as they were to the United States. But this was a pose, and the American intelligence community knew it. CIA Clandestine Service officer Robert Baer concluded on the basis of hard intelligence that some six hundred Islamic extremists in Saudi Arabia and Yemen were linked with Al-Qaeda.[35] After the Khobar Towers attack, there was an understanding between bin Laden and the Saudi royals — namely that the kingdom would remain off-limits for terrorist acts if it provided financing for Al-Qaeda and sanctuary for its operatives. Most of the money funneled to Al-Qaeda moved through the charities. Dick Ganon, the State Department's director of operations for counterterrorism, stated in 1998, "We've got information about who's backing bin Laden, and in a lot of cases it goes back to the royal family." Former Israeli ambassador to the UN Dore Gold is correct — prior to 9/11, Saudi Arabia, every bit as much as Afghanistan, was an Al-Qaeda base of operations.[36] Only Washington's compromised devotion to the Saudi royal family permitted two administrations to pretend otherwise.

Central to American self-deception was the oft-repeated claim that Osama bin Laden was a man ostracized by his family. The U.S. intelligence community, however, knew better. Osama's brother-in-law Muhammad Jamal Khalifa headed a Saudi charity in the Philippines which was known as a center of Al-Qaeda support. Osama's brother Abdullah was a director for WAMY in Washington. In the early 1990s he was placed under surveillance by the FBI for presumed terrorist links. On September 13, 2001, he was spirited out of the United States in an airlift of Saudi VIPs that was authorized by the White House itself.

The Pakistanis played the same sort of double game as the Saudis, toeing Washington's line on certain international issues in exchange for access to sophisticated weapons, huge amounts of Washington-sanctioned economic and financial aid, and a permissive attitude toward their sponsorship of terrorist organizations. As far as terrorism was concerned, the two countries were close. In addition to the Saudi-Pakistani joint venture in the war against the Red Army in the 1980s and their backing of the Taliban in the mid-1990s, there was a religious alliance between Saudi Wahhabism and the Pakistani Deobandi sect. The two regimes shared an active hatred of Shia and countenanced the slaughter of Hazara Shiites in northern Afghanistan in 1998.

Among the most powerful Pakistani-based Muslim movements was the Tablighi Jamaat. In October 1999, Tablighi missionaries arrived at the Mill Valley mosque. That visit would prove to be a turning point in Suleyman's life. The seven visiting Tablighi Jamaat missionaries were on a one-year trek (*aik saal*) from mosque to mosque, reviving the faithful. One member of the group was a Pakistani businessman from Bannu, Khizar Hayat, a tall, broad-shouldered man in his early thirties with a domineering demeanor. Suleyman was so taken with Hayat that he asked for his address and telephone number at their first encounter — something Suleyman later related to his spiritual mentor in Pakistan, Mufti Mohammad Iltimas Khan. Iltimas would remember that Suleyman's relationship with Hayat was "the beginning of the dangerous journey, the first jaunt, the pleasure journey."[37]

Tablighi Jamaat was founded in India in the 1880s as an Islamist revival movement. Members are enjoined to dedicate their time to proselytize the strict observance of Sunni Islam, recruiting converts and bringing back the fallen-away. Since Islam is a religion characterized by disparate sects and practices, as well as the lack of a single ecclesiastical authority, Tablighi's multinational character (in 2000 it had more than seventy-three country chapters) has made it unique in the Muslim world.[38] The movement publishes no information, avoids interaction with the media, brings out no journals, and disseminates no propaganda. It relies solely on person-to-person mobilization and word-of-mouth communication, both of which are powerful enough to draw over a million Muslims to its annual convention in Raiwind in the Pakistani Punjab each year.

With the founding of the state of Pakistan in 1947, Tablighi Jamaat took on an increasingly political role, especially within the Pakistani military. With the advent of the mass recruitment of mujahideen from the Muslim world in the early 1980s, the movement became additionally political, serving as a recruiting apparatus, a role that continued into the 1990s with the Pakistani-supported insurgency in Kashmir, the Harkat ul-Mujahideen, the guerrilla movement John Walker Lindh would join in May 2001.[39] Tablighi's members were implicated in a plot in October 1995 to assassinate Prime Minister Benazir Bhutto and establish a theocracy in Pakistan. Tablighi's links to Al-Qaeda have been considerably looser than to Pakistani-based insurgencies. Michael J. Helmback, the deputy chief of the FBI's international counterterrorism section, has been quoted as saying that Al-Qaeda used Tablighi Jamaat for "recruiting," but the conclusion of Canadian intelligence is probably closer to the mark — namely that Al-Qaeda evaded law enforcement by seeding its operatives within Tablighi Jamaat's generally benign religious activities.[40]

According to one account, Suleyman traveled with Khizar Hayat to Nevada and possibly elsewhere as part of their circuit of religious revival.[41] Not long thereafter, Suleyman applied again for a visa to visit Yemen. Three months later, on February 1, 2000, a few days before his nineteenth birthday, he was back in Sanaa. One can interpret his return alternatively as merely a continuation of his religious studies at Al-Iman or as the initiation of his journey toward jihad.

In terms of those alternative routes, much depends on whether Suleyman traveled to the hotbed of fundamentalist action in the north of Yemen, in particular to the town of Dammaj near the city of Sa'da. Attorneys and investigators who made up his defense team insist he did not.[42] The FBI, and at least one source in Yemen, concluded that he did.[43] We know, at least, two matters for certain: first, that in his previous visit to Yemen, Suleyman *tried* to travel north, and second, that Dammaj was a recruitment and training site for jihad. In the prosecution of John Walker Lindh in 2002, the government claimed it could show that Lindh's training in Dammaj was a key step in his eventual decision to go to war against the United States.

In Dammaj was the Salifi madrassa Wad'aa, a long, whitewashed hall for prayers and lectures. Sheikh Moqbul al-Wadi'I presided over the madrassa, preaching and practicing strict *sharia,* or Islamic law based on the Qur'an. The school educated (or indoctrinated) thousands of young Muslims from many countries, including a few from Germany, France, and the United States.[44] News reports from within Yemen indicated that there was military training at the camp as well as recruitment of the young men to serve Islamic insurgencies in places like Chechnya and Afghanistan. Incidences of violence at the madrassa were frequent. A young British student whom Lindh may have encountered, Hosea Walker, age fifteen, was shot to death in July 2000 at the school. It was said to have been an accident, but the "Unofficial Communiqué" of the Yemen *Gateway* website thought otherwise.[45]

Suleyman's communications to his parents during his second visit to Yemen took on an explicitly anti-American tone. "I don't really want to see America again," he wrote his mother on February 8, 2000. When the USS *Cole* was bombed, Frank Lindh e-mailed his son, saying he felt terrible for the sailors who were killed and their families. His son replied that the attack was justified because the *Cole* was docked in an Islamic country. It was "an act of war."[46]

Within weeks of arriving in Yemen, Suleyman was back in touch with Khizar Hayat, inquiring about study in Pakistan. In October, Hayat received a call from Suleyman, saying he had booked a flight to Islamabad. Would Hayat pick him up? Hayat agreed. When Suleyman arrived in Islamabad in late October 2000, Hayat was there to meet him and they set off on the Pakistani's 150 cc Honda motorcyle first to Peshawar and then to Bannu, Hayat's hometown, in search of the right madrassa. But Suleyman passed on each school as a potential place to study the Qur'an. After several days of looking, Hayat returned to Bannu and put Suleyman up in his parents' house.

What happened thereafter is a matter of contention. Hayat confided to a *Time* reporter that he and Suleyman had a sexual relationship, a recollection he subsequently repeated. "He was liking me very much. All the time he wants to be with me. I was loving him. Because love begets love, you know." Hayat later retracted this, however, in a CNN interview, saying, "we never had any such relationship."[47]

In December 2000, after a month or so in Hayat's company, Suleyman elected to study at the nearby al-Arabia madrassa run by Mufti Iltimas Khan, who was a friend of Hayat's. Lindh's purpose at the madrassa was to memorize the Qur'an, to interiorize, in the centuries-old fashion of scholars, the music and the extraordinary vitality of the early revelations. The madrassa is located in Hassani Kalan Surani, a small village of almost biblical simplicity made up of mud houses and wandering livestock on a high, dusty plain. Iltimas, a charming, charismatic man in his early thirties, thought Suleyman handsome — "a lovely face he had, John Walker" — and greatly admired the young American's sincerity. They often talked into the night, lying on their cots in Iltimas's small office.

Suleyman remained there for six months, living a sweet and genial poverty that journalist Mark Kukis well describes:

> ... the sound of boys chanting Koran verses in the hall hummed through walls thickened with layer over layer of white paint hopelessly grimed by desert dust. Occasionally, one of the younger boys would peal into long, high wails above the others for a few verses, carrying the chorus of chants sharply into the mosque's courtyard over bricks worn smooth by the dust ground into them under worshippers' knees. When the steady chants fell off as students broke between lessons, the only sounds in the hush of the madrassa were the faucets dripping into mossy drains and the buzzing of flies, which flit off drying laundry and pillbox prayer caps hung on wall pegs. Here was the quiet place Lindh sought. To an outsider, the madrassa's dingy austerity might be off-putting. But Lindh saw everything he wanted within the tiny school's four walls: a bed, a space to pray, and a peaceful place to read.[48]

But Suleyman wanted more than the contemplative life of a Muslim scholar. He wanted to test himself the way tens of thousands of other young Muslims had been tested — through jihad. "We shall always make jihad," he wrote in his notebook at the time. In May 2001 he answered the summoning, writing his mother that he was leaving the madrassa to move "somewhere cooler for the summer" and asking his father to send him another $1,200, which he did.

On May 15, Hayat drove out to the school to pick him up. Suleyman set off on the back of the motorcycle, wearing his *kalmar shaweez* and carrying a small backpack. They headed to Peshawar. From there, Suleyman traveled to Kashmir to be trained for war.

The group Suleyman joined was called the Harkat ul-Mujahideen (HUM), which represented itself as an insurgency to free Kashmir from the control of India. The reality, as Suleyman would eventually realize, was far different. HUM was rather a force organized and trained by Pakistan's ISI and deployed in Kashmir to accomplish a range of atrocities, including the capture and execution of foreign tourists. In October 1997, the State Department formally declared HUM to be a terrorist organization. Under 18 U.S.C. sects. 2339B and 2, any individual under the jurisdiction of the United States who did "knowingly provide and attempt to provide material support and resources" to the group committed an imprisonable felony.[49] Of course, the U.S. government itself, in the interests of "good relations" with the government of Pakistan, refused to link economic or military aid to shutting down HUM.[50] This would take place only after 9/11.

Did Suleyman's twenty-four or so days training at a camp outside a town called Mansehra constitute the commission of such a felony? There is no doubt he trained there with several weapons and prepared for clandestine deployment in Kashmir. But two things stood in his favor: HUM commanders had passed him over for more advanced training (thinking him unprepared), and after his three weeks at the camp he asked to leave.[51] Suleyman would later tell Dr. Tamara Sonn, an Islamic expert retained by the Lindh defense attorneys, that shortly before telling camp leaders he wanted out, he had spied a map in the Pakistani military camp across the road. It showed Kashmir annexed to Pakistan. This was not the cause for which he cared to fight. In early June he left Mansehra and made his way to Peshawar, carrying a letter of introduction from HUM to the Taliban. From Peshawar, he moved by both truck and foot through the Khyber Pass into Afghanistan.

When Suleyman arrived in Kabul, a shattered city teeming with homeless people, he went to two gutted palaces known as Dar ul-Anan, where the Taliban had its recruitment offices.[52] He asked for permission to go directly to the front to fight the Northern Alliance, but Taliban authorities thought he needed more training. Because he could speak no Dari or Pashto but could communicate in Arabic, they sent him to the Arab section of a foreign brigade called al-Ansar (the Helpers).

In support of its ten criminal counts against John Walker Lindh, the affidavit prepared by the U.S. government and released in February 2002 alleged that he stated he knew at the time that "Bin Laden and Al-Qaeda were against America and the government of Saudi Arabia."[53] Whether this was true or not was undermined by the FBI's misrepresentation that "al-Ansar" was the same as the elite terrorist strike force known as "Al-Qaeda." They were, in fact, different, as the U.S. government was forced to concede before Lindh's trial the following year. Suleyman's key points of contact with Al-Qaeda were rather at the Kandahar guesthouse built by Al-Qaeda where he stayed and the al-Farooq camp where he later trained.

By the time David Fecheimer and his partner Barry Simon reached al-Farooq the following year, in their quest to reconstruct Lindh's movements and associations, they found it reduced to rubble by American bombing. Over the ruined camp was an acronym painted in huge letters on a cliff by the American invading force in November–December 2001 — "USMC." At al-Farooq, the al-Ansar recruits were put through a rigorous course of weapons training, physical conditioning, and lectures in the evening. On three occasions, as honored guest and lecturer, Osama bin Laden visited the al-Farooq camp. On his third visit he conversed with Suleyman. Just what was said between the two would be as laden with symbolic as well as potentially criminal consequences as were John Walker Lindh's brief minutes in the fortress courtyard with Mike Spann.

At the end of Suleyman's training, there was another momentous encounter. Abu Mohammed al-Misri, an Al-Qaeda lieutenant who worked at the camp as a trainer, approached Suleyman for a one-to-one conversation. They went into a room together, al-Misri taking a seat alongside Suleyman. "Would he do a martyrdom mission against the United States or Israel?" al-Misri asked. Suleyman said no. He wanted to fight for the Taliban.[54] Several days later, Suleyman got his wish. He was flown to Kunduz and made his way to the northern front outside the abandoned town of Chichkeh near the Tajik border. He took his position in a shallow foxhole and got ready for an attack. It was September 6 or 7, 2001. A few days later, someone brought news from a radio. There had been an attack on America.

6

PREEMPTION
2000–2001

September 11, 2001

South Tower, World Trade Center

New York City

During his campaign for president, Governor George W. Bush exceeded expectations in terms of his command of foreign policy. Central to that achievement was Condoleezza Rice, the former Stanford University provost and professor of foreign policy, who had tutored and guided the candidate for two years.[1] In the course of his debate against Vice President Al Gore on October 12, 2001, Bush said he opposed "unchecked" military interventions by the U.S., favored less reliance on IMF bailouts and UN peacekeeping operations as measures of international stabilization, and thought the U.S. should "push hard" for a missile defense. As Robert Novak commented after the debate, "while endorsing much of President Clinton's foreign policy, he [Bush] did effectively stake out a position against Clinton 'nation-building' — as in Haiti and Somalia. Bush's performance contradicted the Gore campaign's attack on him as a 'bungler' and a 'bumbler.'"[2] Part of the strategy of exceeding expectations was to downplay the importance of the issue, and in this Bush succeeded as well.

In his State of the Union address on February 27, 2001, President Bush hardly mentioned foreign policy. His speech was devoted instead to domestic policy — education, health care, energy policy, and tax relief. When he raised the subject of terrorism, it was only to call attention to the virtue of missile defense as the way to neutralize terrorism.[3] National polls showed that foreign and defense issues ranked well behind domestic concerns, particularly given the fact that the economy was slowing down.

Bush, as many analysts commented at the time, brought a corporate style to the White House. He delegated deliberation and details to subordinates, preferring to concentrate on broad initiatives and messages. Responsibility for foreign and defense policy in the new administration was franchised to the titans of his father's administration, led by Secretary of State Colin Powell, Vice President Dick Cheney, and

Undersecretary of Defense Paul Wolfowitz. To this formidable array of talent and experience was added another longtime Bush collaborator, Donald Rumsfeld, who was appointed secretary of defense, a job he had held a generation earlier (1975–77) during the Ford administration. Dr. Rice remained, however, the pivotal person because of her frequent contact with the president (the press reported that she often saw him six times a day) as well as the trust he placed in her. In addition to the president's favor, her strength was her poise and precision in internal deliberation and public comment. Her deficiency was a lack of experience in crisis situations.

The other area where the incoming administration had "heavyweights" was energy. Donald Evans, the secretary of commerce, was CEO of one of the largest independent oil and gas firms in the United States, Texas-based Tom Brown, Inc. Spencer Abraham, the secretary of energy, had served as the energy industry's biggest ally in the Senate, where he had expended every effort to repeal the federal tax on gasoline. Vice President Cheney, who had resigned his post as CEO of the oil services giant Halliburton (and collected $22 million going out the door) before joining the Republican ticket, was one of the most successful dealmakers in the oil and gas industry during the 1990s. While serving on the board of Chevron, he had put together a $20 billion Chevron-led joint venture in 1993 to tap Caspian Sea oil and pipe it nine hundred miles to the Black Sea for transport to the world. Another oil chieftain was Condi Rice, who had served on the Chevron board for ten years before resigning to serve in Bush's presidential campaign. Dr. Rice was sufficiently well-regarded by Chevron that in 1999 the company had christened a 136,000-ton oil tanker in her name, the *Condoleezza Rice*. (In 2001, at the White House's insistence, Chevron renamed the tanker the *Altair Voyager,* according to the *San Francisco Chronicle*.)[4]

Neither Cheney nor Rice, however, was the most powerful personality in the new administration's "kitchen cabinet" on energy. That figure was Kenneth L. Lay, the energy tycoon whose friendship with Bush went back a good twenty-five years. After Bush won the election, many insiders believed that Lay would be appointed treasury secretary. He clearly had earned it. No one, with the exception of Karl Rove, had

been so instrumental in Bush's election. Lay had moved enormous
money, both through the $100,000-per-member "Pioneer's Club," of
which he was the founder, and through millions of dollars of energy
money channeled into the Republican Party.

Bush called Lay "Kenny boy," and it signaled to Bush's lieutenants
that this was a personal, not just political, relationship. The two had
worked together both in and out of office. During his father's first year
in office, "Bush Jr.," as he was then referred to, called Rodofo Terrango,
the Argentine minister of public works, and asked him to award a
contract worth hundreds of millions of dollars to Enron.[5] Terrango
thought the approach inappropriate, but Enron got in the door. Later,
as governor of Texas, whether it was a ballpark deal in Houston or a
cracking plant in Port Arthur, Bush remained on call. Lay, for example,
wrote him in April 1997 that Enron was putting together a $2 billion
joint venture in Uzbekistan, one that "can bring significant opportunities to Texas." He needed Governor Bush to speak with Ambassador
Sadyq Safaev, the former foreign minister of Uzbekistan and its then
ambassador in Washington.[6] Bush, as always, complied.

Lay was a man of marvelous audacity. When energy shortages first
hit San Diego in the summer of 2000, energy companies, led by Enron,
moved to exploit them, using phantom sales, falsifying records, and
moving bought energy in and out of the state to bypass price controls.[7]
As electricity blackouts swept over California, with electricity prices increasing by a factor of 800 percent, Enron's revenues soared, increasing
in the last quarter of 2000 by 300 percent from the same quarter in
1999.[8] Bush was meanwhile blaming the Democrats for a "botched
deregulation scheme" in California. From Lay's standpoint, the game
couldn't get better than this. His personal profit over the previous three
years was $112 million, according to the Consortium of Independent
News.

The California energy crisis was thought to be the beginning of a
nationwide one. Accordingly, in a speech given in Michigan in September 2000, Governor Bush outlined his energy proposals, among
them the loosening of price regulations in the energy industry, a soft-
ening of environmental standards, and, above all, the finding and cap-
turing of new fields of oil and gas. A week after taking the oath of

office, President Bush called for a new energy policy and asked the vice president to head up the task force charged with achieving it. Enron, which had served as something of a shadow government for Bush for President (providing a slew of consulting contracts, corporate jets, and offices in several places in the country), put several of its key executives and directors in the new administration.[9] Foreign policy might be franchised to his father's friends, but energy policy would be a wholly owned enterprise in Bush II.

Cheney's task force began meeting in secret in the first week of February 2001 and reviewing and exchanging communications (29,000 documents in total) on the strict basis of need to know. Naturally enough, Lay and his lobbyists were all over the process. When asked just what one of their meetings was about, Cheney confined himself to saying that they were old friends and had once put together a ballpark deal: "I'm flattered that he decided to meet with me."[10] What Lay wanted from Cheney was apparent in a memo he sent him discussing their exchange: "The administration should reject any attempt to re-regulate wholesale power markets by adopting price caps or returning to archaic methods of determining the cost-base of wholesale power."[11] This meant California.

The General Accounting Office, the investigative arm of the Congress, requested that the task force release its list of participants and consultants. Cheney's office at first promised to comply, but then refused. The GAO, for the first time in its eighty-one-year history, sued the executive branch in federal court.[12]

Why the secrecy surrounding the energy task force? First, there was the factor of political embarrassment, given Enron's collapse and the skein of investigations and indictments that followed. Rove, among others, had attended task force meetings while he still held Enron stock.[13] But the larger danger for the administration was that the National Security Council had become involved in plans to secure control over new and existing oil fields. Rice and Cheney had interceded with the government of India over Enron's Dahbol Energy project. Journalists in India had produced evidence that Enron had bribed Indian officials to approve the construction of the project, a $2.3 billion price tag. Once the plant was built, Enron sold power back to the government at grossly inflated prices. The newly elected government in India declared that, since the entire deal was vitiated by corruption, it was backing out. But Rice and Cheney pushed hard, linking other national security issues (such as settlement of the Indo-Pakistani dispute in Kashmir) to their demand that the Indian government stick to the deal. What was good for Enron was good for the Bush administration. On May 18, 2001, the president signed two executive orders, implementing the task force's recommendations.[14]

National security, in the judgment of the energy task force, required the "capture of new and existing oil and gas fields." Just what this meant is now evident from the so-called Vaughn Index (which lists documents withheld by the Energy Department). Under court order, the administration released the 16,000-item index of documents, if not the documents themselves.[15] Studded throughout are subjects relating to "National Energy Security and International Affairs," "National Security Opportunities in Venezuela," and the like. Among documents released in July 2003 were maps of Iraqi oil fields and an evaluation of "foreign suitors for Iraqi oil-field contracts." The task force was contemplating the means to get around UN sanctions and the oil embargo. One route was to remove the sanctions and "privatize" oil production. The other was to attack Iraq, a contingency that was activated shortly after the Bush administration took office. According to then–Treasury Secretary Paul O'Neill, at two National Security Council meetings during the administration's first two weeks in office, detailed plans were discussed and approved to take down Saddam and secure Iraq's oil wealth.[16]

"Regardless of whether we say so publicly," said Anthony Cordesman, a brilliant foreign policy analyst known to be close to Wolfowitz and Rumsfeld, a man who held the Arleigh Burke Chair in Strategy at the Center for Strategic and International Studies in D.C., "we will go to war because Saddam sits at the center of a region with more than 60 percent of the world's oil reserves." This extraordinary admission, made in April 2001, paralleled the study of the James A. Baker Institute of Public Policy at Rice University. In February 2001, the Cheney task force had commissioned the Baker Institute to study and make recommendations for an international energy policy. The report, also issued in April 2001, is titled, "Strategic Energy Policy Challenges for the 21st

Century." Among the advisers listed in the document are Kenneth Lay of Enron; Luis Giusti, of the Shell Oil board of directors; John Manz, regional president of British Petroleum; David O'Reilly, CEO of ChevronTexaco; and Sheikh Suad al-Nasser Sabah (formerly Kuwait's oil minister), along with the usual complement of Council of Foreign Relations types. The Baker report set forth an alarming scenario:

> The United States remains a prisoner of its energy dilemma. Iraq remains a destabilizing influence to the flow of oil to international markets for the Middle East. Saddam Hussein has also demonstrated a willingness to threaten to use the oil weapon and to use his own export program to manipulate oil markets. Therefore the U.S. should conduct an immediate policy review toward Iraq including military, energy, economic and political/diplomatic assessments.[17]

The assertion was, of course, absurd. How could Saddam Hussein use his "oil weapon" to manipulate world markets when, under UN sanctions, Iraq could make only a controlled quantum of sales? Absurd or not, this recommendation was repeated in the National Energy Policy, albeit more diplomatically. "The [Persian] Gulf will be a primary focus of U.S. international energy policy," the plan stated, noting that it might be necessary to overcome foreign resistance in order to gain access to new supplies. In other words, access to oil was cause for war.

The beginning of the end of Colin Powell as the commanding figure in Bush's foreign policy was his opposition to the get-the-oil-or-go-to-war option. He had argued for a strengthening and sharpening of sanctions against Iraq in February 2001, but two Wolfowitz disciples, Tony Cordesman and Richard Perle, ridiculed "smart sanctions" in Senate testimony in March 2001. "We've got to stop preaching and issuing strong statements and not backing them up militarily," Cordesman said. "We need to define what Iraqi action would lead us to launch a military action, and then if [Saddam Hussein] does that, we need to strike."[18] This became the basis for the administration's policy.

On Iran, Powell advocated increased normalization for reasons of peace in the region and to strengthen Iranian moderates. Oil executives aligned with the administration, however, were looking for a mega-oil deal if relations improved, according to the two National Security

Council officials.[19] When the Iranians refused to put oil on the agenda, the Bush administration terminated the normalization option. Six months later, the president identified Iran in his State of the Union address to Congress as part of an "axis of evil."

Venezuela was yet another case of the oil-or-else option. During the first months of 2001, Venezuela was paralyzed by strikes and protests against left-wing president Hugo Chavez. Powell initially prevailed on the White House to stay out of the fray. Then Chavez made it clear that he would use Venezuela's oil power to reinvigorate the OPEC cartel, traveling to Iran, Iraq, and Libya to discuss market intervention to reduce world supply. At that point, the Bush administration became involved in the plot to overthrow the Venezuelan president, a plot that backfired when mass protests in favor of Chavez brought him back to power in April 2002. The incoming chairman of the Senate Foreign Relations Committee, Senator Richard Lugar (R-Ind.), was so indignant about the role of Otto Reich (the Bush nominee for assistant secretary of state for western hemisphere affairs) in the coup attempt that he told the White House in December 2002 not to bother sending Reich's name to the Senate Foreign Relations Committee.[20]

The Powell doctrine, which had defined and driven the conservative internationalism of Bush's father, had now been superseded by Wolfowitz's concept of oil preemption. Nine years before, in the "Defense Planning Guidance" draft authored by Wolfowitz (and dismissed as unacceptable by the elder Bush), the first item for "unilateral action" is "access to vital raw materials, primarily Persian Gulf oil."[21] Wolfowitz, supported now by Cheney and Rumsfeld, had replaced Powell as the conceptual chieftain of foreign policy.

Two of the states thought to be key to the "capture of new and existing oil and gas fields" were Afghanistan and Saudi Arabia. Both were sponsors of Al-Qaeda — we knew that — but both, in the view of the Bush administration, could play important roles in securing new oil and gas concessions. Oil came first.

The Clinton administration, in a series of clumsy approaches and transparent maneuvers in 1996 and 1997, had attempted to romance the Taliban in the cause of oil. It had proven to be a fool's errand.[22] What little attraction remained for the black-turbaned tyrants was shattered once and for all by the 1998 embassy bombings. The U.S. intelligence community had then concluded that every terrorist attack could be traced to Al-Qaeda's state-within-a-state in Afghanistan. After the *Cole* attack in October 2000, the Clinton administration deliberated plans to kill bin Laden. National Security Adviser Sandy Berger and his counterterrorism chief, Dick Clarke, were persuaded they had the instrument to do it — the forty-nine-foot drone called the Predator, which in the course of its twelve missions into Afghanistan spotted and took pictures of bin Laden (or so CIA analysts concluded) on three occasions.[23]

There were questions, however. The *Cole* attack, despite O'Neill's breakthroughs in Yemen that pointed at Al-Qaeda, could not conclusively be credited to bin Laden and his organization. The CIA, moreover, didn't want responsibility for the Predator, questioning whether the Hellfire missile on the aircraft was powerful enough to get the job done. What about fanatical retribution by Al-Qaeda against CIA personnel worldwide? There was also the proscription against the assassination of foreign leaders, even though this was internally being termed as "an attack on Al-Qaeda."[24]

In briefings with the incoming Bush appointees, the Clinton officials stressed the priority of the Al-Qaeda threat. "You're going to spend more time during your four years on terrorism generally and Al-Qaeda specifically than any issue," Berger assured Rice during their meeting. Rice said nothing. Powell got the same message at the State Department. General Don Kerrick, Berger's deputy, who served the Bush administration during its first months, put his concern in writing regarding the Al-Qaeda threat. "We are going to be struck again." There was no response.[25]

Part of the problem may have been Clinton himself. No one doubted his immense understanding of the terrorism issue. In his State of the Union address in January 2000, he had extemporaneously signaled the likelihood of an attack and identified terrorism as *the* issue of grave urgency for Americans in the coming decade. But because of his association with the issue of counterterrorism—because he had, in the view of many, "wagged the dog" in the 1998 cruise missile attack in Afghanistan that had occurred at the height of the Lewinsky affair — the Bush leadership downgraded the importance of terrorism. Clinton's final inglorious act — the midnight pardons — only sealed their deep disregard for him and anything with which he was associated.

The new administration was also receiving warnings from independent and authoritative sources. The Commission on National Security/21st Century, chaired by former senators Gary Hart and Warren Rudman, had predicted that "America will be attacked by terrorists using weapons of mass destruction and Americans will die on American soil, possibly in large numbers." That assessment was repeated in several statements in the commission's final report to President Bush on January 31, 2001, with the recommendation that he immediately create a national homeland security agency to prevent and respond to such attacks. Former senator Hart crisscrossed the country, making dozens of speeches and TV appearances, warning of a terrorist attack on American soil. In addition to a deep understanding of intelligence and defense matters derived from his years on the Hill, Hart had used his years in the political wilderness (after the Donna Rice affair) constructively. He had written books of trenchant acuity about public policy and civic culture and had even studied for a doctorate at Oxford University. What enabled him to speak out clearly and authoritatively, however, was more basic — he hadn't sold out.

In February 2001, the CIA confirmed that Al-Qaeda was behind the attack on the *Cole*. The National Security Council's Dick Clarke formally recommended that the U.S. arm Ahmed Shah Massoud, the Tajik warlord still in battle against the Taliban, as well as the Uzbek leader Rashid Dostum. The purpose was to eliminate bin Laden's habitat by taking down the Taliban. Again, the CIA was not so sure. Dr. Rice herself reserved a polite contempt for these Clinton-sourced proposals. According to the *Washington Post*, Rice felt that the Clinton administration's handling of counterterrorism policy was "empty rhetoric that made us look feckless."[26] The national security adviser ordered a full review of U.S. counterterrorism policy in April 2001. By September 2001 this review was neither complete nor its policy changes in place.

The Bush administration rejected Clarke's covert action proposal and tried a new tack, one consistent with the driving purpose of its foreign policy — the "capture of new and existing oil and gas fields." As Tony Cordesman had recommended (in capital letters, no less) to the

Cheney task force: "Today's Rogues Had Damn Well Become Tomorrow's Suppliers." One set of rogues who were thought to be tomorrow's suppliers was the Taliban. The U.S. government "Energy Information Fact Sheet" summarized the prospect: "Afghanistan's significance from an energy standpoint stems from its geographic position as a potential transit route for oil and natural gas exports from Central Asia to the Arabian Sea. This potential includes proposed multi-billion dollar oil and gas export pipelines through Afghanistan, although these plans have now been thrown into serious question."[27]

What had thrown those plans into serious question was, first, the state of civil war in the country, and, second, the Clinton administration's executive order issued in 1999 forbidding Americans from transacting with the Taliban. In 1998, the U.S. oil giant Unocal had put together a consortium to build a pipeline called CentGas, whose other principal partner was the Saudi firm Delta Oil Company. The forty-eight-inch-diameter pipeline was to extend 790 miles from the Afghanistan-Turkmenistan border through Afghanistan via Herat and Kandahar and cross into Pakistan near Quetta. In on the deal was Halliburton Energy Services, which, while not in the consortium, got a $30 million contract from Turkmenistan for exploration and appraisal of the oil and gas fields. "This major new award will expand and solidify the Halliburton Energy Services presence in the Eastern Caspian," commented HES president Zeke Zeringue, "and position the company well for both upstream and downstream projects which are rapidly developing in this emerging market."[28] After Clinton ordered the cruise missile attacks against Al-Qaeda camps in August 1998, Unocal put the project on hold.

Although the Taliban relaunched pipeline negotiations in the summer of 2000, the Clinton administration called for new international sanctions against the Taliban and refused to participate. Internally, the administration discussed plans to assassinate bin Laden.[29] On December 12, 2000, the UN Security Council passed a resolution imposing the American-proposed sanctions and freezing aid to Kabul.

The Bush volte-face in trying to reach out to the Taliban was first evident in a communication from U.S. ambassador to the United Nations Nancy Soderberg, who stated on February 12, 2001, that the

United States would develop "a continuing dialogue" with the Taliban and would look to the UN to lead that endeavor. A short time later, a Taliban delegation, led by Sayde Hashimi, an adviser to Mullah Omar, arrived in Washington for talks. Coordinating the delegation was Laila Helms, related by marriage to former CIA director Richard Helms. The turbaned officials had lengthy meetings with CIA officials and the State Department Bureau of Intelligence and Research. (Both agencies have rejected requests under the Freedom of Information Act to release the memoranda of the discussions.)

The point person for the Bush administration in Taliban negotiations was Assistant Secretary of State for South Asian Affairs Christina Rocca, a former CIA agent who had coordinated relations between the Agency and the mujahideen leaders during the war against the Soviet Union in the 1980s. Overseeing the exchanges was Deputy Secretary of State Richard Armitage, who had consulted for Unocal at the time when it was launching the Afghani pipeline. At the National Security Council, the key figure was Zalmay Khalilzad, a native-born Afghani who had also worked for Unocal. Khalilzad, a protégé of Paul Wolfowitz during the first Bush administration, acted as a sort of ambassador-at-large for the Taliban. He had done the advance work for the Taliban visit to Houston in December 1997. "The American oil executives reportedly wined and dined them [the Taliban delegation] and took them on a shopping tour."[30] Khalilzad wrote an op-ed piece during this period in the *Washington Post* about the need for reconciliation. "The Taliban do not practice the anti-US style fundamentalism practiced by Iran. We [the U.S.] should be willing to offer recognition and humanitarian assistance and to promote international economic reconstruction. It is time for the United States to re-engage."[31]* Negotiations went

---

*Journalist Hamid Mir was the last journalist to interview bin Laden, shortly before U.S. bombing began in October 2001. Bin Laden asked Mir about the status of Zalmay Khalilzad. Mir said he did not know. Bin Laden predicted that after the war, "Khalilzad would call the shots in Kabul and the Northern Alliance would get nothing." In December 2001, President Bush appointed Khalilzad U.S. special envoy to Afghanistan. He retained his post on the National Security Council and as special assistant to the president. In December 2002, Afghan president Hamid Karzai, who had also worked for Unocal, signed the three-country agreement to build the $3.2 billion gas pipeline by a consortium led by Unocal. Khalilzad, the former emissary of the Taliban, stated in August 2002 that "the Taliban are the embodiment of evil."

forward between representatives of the Taliban, the United States, Russia, Iran, and Pakistan in Berlin during the summer of 2001. As two French authors, Jean-Charles Brisard and Guillaume Dasquié, have written, these talks were different from the previous "6 + 2 meetings," as they were called. The negotiators were all former diplomats without official portfolios, thereby maintaining official deniability. The Bush administration was represented by two former ambassadors — Robert Oakley, who was well-known to the Taliban from his days representing Unocal in Peshawar, and Thomas Simons, who had served as American ambassador in Islamabad. "The objective was to convince the Taliban that once a broad-based government of national unity was installed and the pipeline was in the works, there would be billions of dollars in commission — of which the Taliban, with their own resources, would take a cut."[32] In late June, as a sweetener, the Bush administration authorized a $43 million payment to the Taliban for drug eradication, although nothing was being eradicated.

But the secret talks went nowhere, and the Bush administration negotiators became openly frustrated. They spoke to the other representatives about using a "military option" to get rid of the Taliban and eliminate bin Laden. According to former Pakistani foreign secretary Niaz Naik, who was attending the session, Christina Rocca bluntly communicated to her Taliban counterpart, "Either you accept our offer of a carpet of gold, or we bury you under a carpet of bombs."[33] This was the doctrine of preemption in a metaphoric nutshell — gold or bombs. By early August 2001, three Special Forces A-teams got the preliminary order to get ready to depart for the K2 base in Uzbekistan from which they would be dropped into northern Afghanistan. Mike Spann was among them.

The whole "unofficial" quality of the exchanges between the Taliban and the former ambassadors probably violated the executive order signed by President Clinton on July 6, 1999, which expressly prohibited "any transaction by any United States person . . . that evades or avoids . . . any of the prohibitions set forth in this order."[34] When the United States government charged John Walker Lindh with a felony violation of this order (to which he ultimately pleaded guilty), his attorneys, informed of the previous contacts by the Bush administration, raised the defense of "selective prosecution." During the same month that Lindh signed up to fight with the Taliban, negotiators for the Bush administration were trying to work out the pipeline deal with the government in Kabul. Washington had even made a $43 million drug war payment in June 2001 to sweeten the deal. Just who in fact had committed treason, John Walker Lindh or the Bush administration?

In late July 2001, French intelligence analyst Jean-Charles Brisard met with John O'Neill at the Oak Bar in New York's Plaza Hotel. The purpose of the meeting was to discuss Brisard's lengthy report on "The Economic Network of the bin Laden Family," which he had given O'Neill a month earlier in Paris. After drinks they went from the Plaza Hotel to the China Club, a multifloor bar and discotheque frequented by R&B aficionados and *salseros*. (O'Neill, in addition to other pursuits, was a skilled dancer who was proud to have once won a dance competition on *American Bandstand*.) In the course of the evening, recounted in Brisard's and Dasquié's later book, O'Neill is quoted as saying, "All the answers, all the clues allowing us to dismantle Osama bin Laden's organization can be found in Saudi Arabia." The reason why the U.S. could get nothing out of Saudi Arabia is "corporate oil interests."[35]

Brisard's 6,000-word report analyzed in some detail a company called the Carlyle Group, one of whose equity investors was the bin Laden Group (a $5 billion book value conglomerate).[36] Before he ran for governor, George W. Bush had served on the board of one of Carlyle's companies, Caterair, a Texas-based airline food caterer. Bush's father, George H. W. Bush, was one of Carlyle's "senior advisers" and, as such, had made several trips to Saudi Arabia after leaving the presidency. Carlyle had (and continues to have) several long-term contracts of interest to the Saudi royal family. One of those is the training of the Saudi Arabian National Guard, an elite unit sworn to protect the monarchy. Acting as a "merchant bank," Carlyle has placed several hundred million dollars in Saudi equity in its various enterprises. Acting as a "defense contractor" (Carlyle ranks eleventh in size among defense companies), Carlyle buys and "flips" companies in need of just one huge contract. This is called "access capitalism." Currently in its portfolio is United Defense, a company that produces the controversial Crusader, a forty-two-ton self-propelled howitzer that moves and operates like a tank. Despite a dismal record in battle, the Crusader (price tag to date, $11 billion) lives on, thanks to the Carlyle Group.

Two of Donald Rumsfeld's close friends, former secretary of state and White House chief of staff (under Reagan) James Baker, and former secretary of defense (under Reagan as well) Frank Carlucci, are directors in the Carlyle Group. Carlucci is its former chairman. Was it less than irony that at 9 A.M. on September 11, when the second hijacked airliner smashed into the South Tower, Baker and Carlucci should be hosting, in the plushest ballroom of the Ritz-Carlton Hotel in D.C., Carlyle's annual investor conference, which included representatives of the bin Laden family?[37]

Feeding at the trough of Saudi largesse and inside-traded defense deals is hardly novel in Washington. Having, however, "a vast, interlocking, global network of businesses and investment professionals," as Carlyle describes itself, whose principals act as a shadow government in the name of exponential profit, in which two presidents are tied by blood and by an old-boy network, is unexampled in American history. In his spirited and much-needed book *Sleeping with the Devil,* Robert Baer writes of a dual result to the "Pavlovian" conditioning of the Washington elite — "an almost pathological unwillingness on the part of U.S. government agencies to stare reality in the face, coupled with a massive money grab by those who do see that the House of Sa'ud is on its last wobbly legs."[38] This sellout and resulting bureaucratized blindness would not be possible without shared bipartisan greed. The Democrats may get less time at the trough than the Republicans, but satiating them is a critical part of the Saudi strategy. Why else would the Democrats maintain such a deafening silence before the cascading evidence of Saudi complicity in Al-Qaeda and the plot that produced 9/11? Baer captures the blinkered sense of reality in the form of an unstated commandment in Washington, "Don't ask, don't tell, don't know. Above all, speak no evil. . . ."

In February 2001, on the basis of new leads emanating from the *Cole* investigation, CIA director George Tenet ordered the Counterterrorism Center "to form a strategic analysis group to help put context into threat reporting and to think out of the box."[39] O'Neill, who the year before would have run such a strategic analysis group, was not included, even though no one remotely had his range and depth of information and judgment. One of the "mastermind suspects" his investigation had identified was Khalid al-Mihdhar.[40]

Through an intercept from an Al-Qaeda safe house in Sanaa, the FBI learned in advance of the now-famous Al-Qaeda summit in Kuala Lumpur that took place on January 3–8, 2000.[41] What neither O'Neill nor other FBI and National Security Council counterterrorist leaders knew, however, was that the CIA later received (from Malaysian intelligence) photographs of the five attendees, as well as all of al-Mihdhar's vital information — his full name, passport number, passport photograph, and his multiple-entry visa to the United States. The CIA also knew that al-Mihdhar's Al-Qaeda comrade Nawaf al-Hazmi had entered the United States on January 15, 2000, via Los Angeles. The National Security Agency also independently possessed information linking al-Hazmi to Al-Qaeda, but neither the CIA nor the NSA put the names of either one, much less both, on the terrorism watch list, the TIPOFF database.

Senator Richard Shelby (R.-Al) later summarized the extraordinary breakdown:

> By this point [March 2000], both al-Mihdhar and al-Hazmi — both terrorists known to the CIA — were living in San Diego under their true names. They signed these names on their rental agreement, both used their real names in taking flight school training in May 2000, and al-Mihdhar even used his real name in obtaining a motor vehicle identification card from the State of California. In July 2000, al-Hazmi even applied to the INS for an extension of his visa, using both his real name and current address in San Diego. . . .
>
> The CIA's failure to watchlist al-Mihdhar and al-Hazmi became even more alarming and inexplicable in January 2001, when the CIA discovered that the Malaysia meeting had also been attended by a suspect in the USS *Cole* bombing. This presumably made the two terrorists even more interesting to the CIA — their known

presence in the U.S. even more dangerous, by confirming their linkages to Al-Qa'ida operational cells — but the CIA still did not bother to inform TIPOFF.[42]

In Los Angeles, in the days following their arrival in January 2000, the two Al-Qaeda lieutenants established contact with a Saudi citizen, Omar al-Bayoumi, the subject of a 1999 FBI investigation because of his links to violent Islamic extremism. Al-Bayoumi claimed to be a student, but the FBI's informants thought otherwise. One called him a "Saudi intelligence agent," a conclusion consistent with the fact that he went into the Saudi consulate for a meeting shortly before picking up al-Hazmi and al-Mihdhar at a restaurant. Al-Bayoumi drove the ringleader-hijackers from L.A. to San Diego, where they stayed in his luxury apartment for several days. He then cosigned for their own apartment, paying the security deposit and the first month's rent. He also arranged for their lessons at the San Diego flight school.[43]

During this time, al-Bayoumi was moving significant amounts of money to individuals and institutions known to be violently radical. He gave $400,000 to a mosque in San Diego and was supporting several individuals who had been subjects in previous FBI investigations. There was a curious source to some of the money he was getting — Princess Haifa bint Faisal, daughter of the late King Faisal and wife of Prince Bandar, the Saudi ambassador to the United States. Beginning in early 2000, Princess Haifa — or someone acting in her name — sent approximately $3,500 every month to Manal Bajadir, the wife of al-Bayoumi, and $2,000 every month to the wife of Osama Bassnan, a colleague of al-Bayoumi who was also in touch with al-Mihdhar and al-Hazmi. When British newspapers broke the story, Saudi officials hotly denied the connection. "To think that my government uses the bank account of the ambassadress to pay informants is both ludicrous and insulting," said Turki al-Faisal, the former chief of Saudi intelligence. But two things seemed clear: first, that the Saudis were dangerously compromised, and second, that American law enforcement and intelligence officials did less than the minimum to cut out the cancer. Al-Mihdhar, along with Mohammed Atta, is now regarded as one of the two critical leaders of the 9/11 attack.

★ ★ ★

Back in San Diego in the first months of 2001, the FBI's "highly reliable" counterterrorist informant (name to date embargoed) was in touch with both of the future hijackers. It is highly probable that the informant was also in touch with Hani Hanjour, the eventual pilot of the airliner that crashed into the Pentagon. During the first months of the congressional investigation, the FBI claimed the informant was no more than an observer, that he was "duped." Later the Bureau backed away from this characterization of the informant's role and admitted that there were serious inconsistencies in many of his statements. When the joint congressional committee formally requested to interview the informant, the Bush administration "objected." When the committee sought to serve a subpoena and deposition notice on the informant, "the Administration also would not agree."

On June 11, 2001, two of O'Neill's top Yemen investigating agents met with a CIA analyst and an FBI intelligence operations specialist in New York. The meeting was tense. The CIA analyst passed the photographs of the Al-Qaeda lieutenants taken in Malaysia. "Do you know any of these guys?" he reportedly said. One of the FBI agents then asked, "Why are you looking at this guy?" The CIA official refused to say.[44] The two FBI agents in New York became angry, one asking, "What the fuck is going on here?"[45] They identified al-Mihdhar, but the CIA official told them nothing about his presence in the U.S. or that of his comrade al-Hazmi.[46] Two days later al-Mihdhar applied for a new visa in Jeddah. On July 4, he was back in the U.S.

The plot was on. In the third week of August, the CIA's Counterterrorism Center realized it had made a terrible mistake in letting al-Mihdhar, "a major league killer who orchestrated the *Cole* attack," back into the U.S. The CTC alerted the full panoply of federal law enforcement about the need to find him and detain him and al-Hazmi. The New York FBI office was accordingly notified, but then received a "back-off from FBI headquarters" in a communication extraordinary in its stupidity. According to Senator Shelby, "FBI headquarters prohibited FBI criminal investigators in New York from participating in the search for these terrorists and refused even to tell them what little was known about the two men at the time. As one of the New York agents was told, "information will be passed over the wall [to New York]" only if "information is developed indicating the existence of a substantial federal crime."[47] A New York–based agent replied, "Someday someone will die and the public will not understand."[48] Asked in July 2003 if he believed that the order to "back off" had anything to do with the vendetta against John O'Neill, the special agent replied, "Of course it did."[49]

O'Neill spoke with his friend Chris Isham about his intuition that there was something coming — "a lot of warnings, a lot of red flags . . . yet he felt he was frozen out . . . so it was a real source of anguish for him."[50] Later that month, the FBI renewed its internal investigation into O'Neill's lost briefcase, even though this investigation had been concluded months before by the Justice Department. O'Neill was distraught. Then a *New York Times* reporter started working on a story about the incident, now two years old.[51] They were going to take him out "with a thousand cuts," O'Neill told his friend John Miller. "It is time to end the bloodletting."[52] He applied for a job as director of security at the World Trade Center and got it shortly thereafter.

On his last day at work on August 22, after thirty-one years with the FBI, O'Neill called Fran Townsend at around 6 P.M. "What in the world are you still doing there on your last day?" she asked him. O'Neill told her that he was still working on his "final act in the FBI." Townsend was curious: "OK. What is it?" O'Neill replied, "I just signed the authorization to send the agents back into Yemen. I wasn't leaving here until I did it because I promised we'd send them back."[53] He had promised Lou Gunn, the father of a sailor who had been killed in the *Cole* bombing, and wrote him an e-mail just before he left his office for the last time. "The FBI will be back in Yemen with full resources by early September if all goes well. . . . I have put my all into the investigation and truly believe that significant progress has been made. Unknown to you and your families, I have cried with your loss."[54]

O'Neill had done his passionate best. In Yemen he had opened the major leads that should have led to the disruption of the 9/11 plot, if only he had remained in the loop. He *would* have connected the dots and he *would* have gone straight to the top — as he had in the millennium investigation — to stop the World Trade Center assault.

By July 2001, warnings from the intelligence community had taken on an urgent tone. In a briefing prepared by the CIA for senior government officials, including the national security adviser, there was the conclusion that "based on a review of all-source reporting over the last five months, we believe that UBL [Usama bin Laden] will launch a significant terrorist attack against U.S. and/or Israeli interests in the coming weeks. The attack will be spectacular and designed to inflict mass casualties against U.S. facilities or interests."[55] On August 6, Rice flew to the president's ranch in Crawford, Texas, to brief him. Among the most significant subjects discussed in their exchange were terrorist threats. In the President's Daily Briefing for August 6 that Rice carried with her, there was the headline, "Bin Laden Determined to Strike in U.S."[56] In the briefing, there were specific references to "FBI judgments about patterns of activity consistent with preparation for hijackings" by Al-Qaeda and equally specific intelligence that members of the Saudi Arabia government as well as private Saudi individuals were "bankrolling" Al-Qaeda operatives.[57] Subsequent to his session with Rice in Crawford on August 6, the president received a briefing by a CIA official about the possibility of terrorist attacks using hijacked planes.

How seriously were these warnings of an Al-Qaeda attack taken by senior Bush administration officials in the summer of 2001? They were specific and threatening enough for Attorney John Ashcroft to decide, according to a CBS News report on July 26, 2001, "to travel only by private jet and not commercial airliners because of 'threat assessment.'"[58] Such an advisory continued to be in effect for high-ranking U.S. officials into September. According to *Newsweek,* "a group of top Pentagon officials suddenly canceled travel plans for the next morning, apparently because of security concerns." The day of the cancellation was September 10, 2001. Why could the Bush administration have not provided the same level of protection for the American people? An urgent travel advisory, for example, or heightened security measures at airports? It is no accident that the administration has roadblocked every prospective independent investigation into 9/11, embargoed and "sanitized" relevant documents, "harassed" (in words of former New Jersey governor Thomas H. Kean, the Republican chairman of the 9/11

Commission) all manner of witnesses, and resolutely refused to allow Rice (not to mention Cheney, Ashcroft, or Powell) to testify, much less under oath. There is much to hide, and it is damning.[59]

On the evening of September 10, O'Neill was out on the town, picking up with different friends as he went from Windows on the World to table one at Elaine's and then, leading the charge, to the China Club for some dancing. "We're due in for something big," he told Jerry Hauer as they chatted at Elaine's about the terrorism threat. He got home at about 4 A.M. and his girlfriend, Valerie James, was furious at him for not showing up at 10:30 P.M. as he had promised. The next morning he apologized. "Babe, please forgive me. I really fucked up and I'm sorry." Valerie replied, "I do forgive you."[60]

The FBI later found the five pages of instructions the hijackers had been instructed to read the night before and the morning of their attack. "If God grants any of you a slaughter, you should perform it as an offering on behalf of your father and mother, for they are owed by you." Another prayer read: "Oh, Lord, block their vision from in front of them, so that they may not see." Still another: "When the confrontation begins, strike like champions who do not want to go back to this world."

The next morning, O'Neill was in his office on the thirty-fifth floor in the North Tower at 8:46 A.M. when American Airlines Flight 11 crashed into it. He made his way to the outside of the building and watched the first of dozens of people start to jump from the upper floors. He called his girlfriend and said, "Val, it's horrible. There are body parts everywhere." At 9:03 A.M., another airliner banked into the South Tower, causing a roaring fireball that instantaneously destroyed four floors.

O'Neill joined the first of the police and firefighters in establishing a command center in the North Tower lobby. There was great chaos and confusion. All of a sudden FBI agent Wesley Wong saw O'Neill across the lobby in his dark blue pinstriped suit, talking on the phone and checking his Palm Pilot and beeper. Then O'Neill saw him and walked over. "Did they hit the Pentagon?" he asked his old friend. Wong checked with the operation center at headquarters and said yes. O'Neill began walking away, talking on the phone, and Wong (who had missed O'Neill's going-away party) called after him, "Hey John. I owe you lunch." O'Neill smiled a bit: "Yeah, give me a call when things settle down. It'll be on me. I have an expense account." He walked away, making his way through the crowd, heading for the South Tower "as calm and as in charge as he always had been," Wong remembered. A half-hour later, in a hail of steel and mortar and human beings, the South Tower collapsed, killing O'Neill and hundreds of others.[61]

When we look at two events *after* 9/11, we see the mirror image of what went wrong at the executive level — a pattern of structured corruption and deliberate concealment — that made the operational interdiction of the 9/11 plot impossible. The House and Senate joint investigating committee did a credible job of sorting through the evidence of the intelligence and law enforcement breakdown, despite sustained resistance from the Bush administration and the supine irrelevance of the Democratic "leadership." Beyond the report's 738 pages detailing human lapses and the abject incompetence of the CIA and the FBI, the Bush administration's decision to excise some twenty-eight pages from the released report demonstrates a cruel reality: that in the "war on terrorism" the U.S. itself is compromised.

According to former Senate Intelligence Committee chairman Bob Graham (D-Fla.), the twenty-eight pages detail that "the foreign government [Saudi Arabia] was much more directly involved in not only the financing, but the provision of support — transportation, housing, and introduction to a network which gave support to the terrorists." In the course of this coordination, there were "scores" of contacts between Saudi intelligence operatives in the United States and the Al-Qaeda hijackers. The Saudi agents, according to Senator Graham, "were being directed by persons of significant responsibility within the [Saudi] government."[62] A high-ranking staffer on the Senate Foreign Relations Committee commented off-the-record that the Bush administration blocked the release of this information because it did not want to be forced to ask the Saudi government to extradite the Saudi agents associated with the Al-Qaeda hijackers.[63] But why?

In the mirror image of what went wrong and what *is* wrong in America's failed effort to defend itself against terrorism, we see a grotesque and treacherous element at work in American government, one that relates to the insatiable and all-preemptive allegiance to oil and to the money derived from it.

Two days after the cataclysm, in a country still reeling from the terrorist attacks, and with firefighters and rescue workers still sorting through the hell of Ground Zero, something else occurred that revealed Washington's pernicious compromise with the Saudis. According to the *New York Times,* "an elaborate but hurried evacuation [took place] within a week of the hijackings in which private planes picked up Saudis from ten cities around the country."[64] The evacuation of 140 Saudi citizens, with clearance from the Bush administration, touched off near-chaos for air traffic control authorities, who were enforcing the ban on all nonmilitary aircraft for reasons of national security. The *Tampa Tribune* broke the first story, entitled "Phantom Flight from Florida," detailing the airlifting of the son of the Saudi defense minister, Prince Sultan bin Abdul Aziz (later named in a civil suit by the surviving families for his alleged role in the financing of terrorist groups).

Members of the bin Laden family, with the approval of the administration, were also spirited out of the country. At least one of the bin Ladens who made their escape, Abdullah, had been under FBI investigation for his relationship with the World Assembly of Muslim Youth, a suspected terrorist financing organization. Foreign news organizations such as the BBC ran the story, revealing leaked FBI documents for good measure.[65] But no major newspapers or networks in the U.S., engaged as they were in self-censorship, went near the scandal. In late September, the *New York Times* did run a brief article that repeated the administration's alibi that the airlift was purely humanitarian.[66] Even columnist William Safire, Bush's old friend, felt compelled to blast the administration. When Prince Bandar, the Saudi ambassador to the United States, said "Jump," Safire wrote, the response of the administration was, "How high?"[67] The Bush administration later insisted that the departing Saudis had been questioned prior to leaving American soil, but Dale Watson, the FBI's head of counterterrorism at the time, contradicted this.[68] In fact, at Logan Airport (the assembly point whence the bin Ladens flew out of the country), FBI agents had protested their inability to board the outgoing plane before it took off.

Finally, they were permitted to board for a brief period before takeoff. In an interview in July 2003, one of the special agents was still seething almost two years later: "What the fuck is that oath for?"[69] He was referring to the presidential oath. According to that same FBI agent, one of those on board the airlift had already been identified as a Saudi intelligence official who had financed and provided cover for at least two of the Al-Qaeda hijackers.

While thousands were being detained and interrogated, over one hundred nationals from the state that had financially sponsored Al-Qaeda, a state from which fifteen of the nineteen terrorist-hijackers held passports, escaped unscathed and unquestioned. The difference? Those individuals benefited from a "special relationship." On the same day the White House authorized the airlift — September 13, 2001 — the Special Forces and the CIA SPECAT who were attached to those units got the go-order for war in Afghanistan. Mike Spann called a probate attorney in Manassas. He needed a will.

7

RENDEZVOUS
September–November 2001

November 24–25, 2001

Basement, pink building

Qala-e Janghi fortress

On September 4, 2001, the inner core of the National Security Council, the so-called Principals Committee, met to consider action against Al-Qaeda. Dick Clarke, the National Security Council counterterrorism chief, was pushing for the "executive elimination" of bin Laden and covert action to destroy the Taliban. The recommended instrument to assassinate bin Laden was the much-discussed, much-tested Predator drone armed with its Hellfire missile. The covert means Clarke was advocating to take down the Taliban was to arm the Northern Alliance and mobilize Uzbek fighters led by General Dostum.[1]

With respect to those objectives, however, the meeting went nowhere. When National Security Adviser Rice raised the issue of the Predator, she asked a question supposedly resolved nine months before: "Do we want it?" The response, with the military again raising the question of the Hellfire missile's "kill probability," was effectively no. CIA director George Tenet declared that it would be a terrible mistake for him to fire such a weapon. It would only happen, he said, over his dead body.[2] Clarke's recommendation for covert action against the Taliban was watered down to the continuation of what was already going on, namely "reconnaissance." The nondecision of the "Principals Committee" meant that no action would be taken either to kill bin Laden (which would have required the president's go-ahead) or to take down the Taliban.

On the same day as the Principals met, Pakistani ISI director-general Mahmoud Ahmad arrived in Washington to brief the administration on relations with the Taliban and the effort to capture, or otherwise eliminate, bin Laden. On the morning of September 11, General Ahmad met with heads of the House and Senate intelligence committees (Representative Porter Goss and Senator Bob Graham, respectively) over breakfast. After the attacks, he was hurried to State Department to confer with Deputy Secretary of State Richard Armitage.

Two days later, the United States, acting on a tip from Indian intelligence, "sought [Ahmad's] removal [from the ISI] after confirming the fact that $100,000 was wired to WTC hijacker Mohammed Atta from Pakistan by Ahmad Umar Sheikh on the instructions of ISI Lt. General Ahmad."[3] Although Ahmad was immediately removed from his position back in Islamabad, the Bush administration made no effort to have him arrested or extradited for indictment as an accomplice. There were too many fingerprints on him in Washington.[4]

The Pakistani dictators and their henchmen had a long history of making fools out of American administrations. General Zia's maneuver to get the U.S. in 1979 to invest in the mujahideen's fight against the Russians in Afghanistan had not only sustained his ferocious rule and the creation of a class of military archcriminals, but had allowed Pakistan to develop "the Islamic H-bomb." As Zbigniew Brzezinski would later remind us, perhaps that high price was worth it in terms of toppling the Soviet Union. But a generation later, the U.S. was still colluding with the Pakistani Frankenstein. After 9/11, the Bush administration consecrated yet another compromised and scheming man, General Pervez Musharraf, as "our new ally in the war against terrorism," in the words of President Bush.

For the prosecution of the war in Afghanistan, the Bush administration clearly needed Pakistan's tacit to active support in denying Al-Qaeda sanctuary and in permitting the U.S. to execute attacks along the Pakistani frontier. What was not necessary — again — was the degree to which Washington embraced the brutal regime in Islamabad. The alliance poisoned relations with India, the great power of the subcontinent, and emboldened Musharraf to go to the brink of war over Kashmir. And what about bin Laden? Two years later, he was still roaming around somewhere in the Pakistani hinterland. When terrorism expert Yossef Bodansky was asked why Pakistan would not hunt him down, he replied that bin Laden was Pakistan's "Get Out of Jail Free" card. "Every time we complain about the heroin production, they say 'Look, we're helping you with bin Laden,' and we backpedal. When we complain about Pakistan sponsoring terrorism in Kashmir, they invoke bin Laden, and we backpedal."[5]

The Bush administration's military plan of action against Al-

Qaeda and the Taliban in Afghanistan was brilliantly conceived and executed. Military and intelligence disunion gave way to a sudden synergy of forces. As one Bush official put it, "the difference between the activity before 9/11 and after 9/11 is the difference between a mule and an 8-cylinder Chevy."[6] General Hugh Shelton, chairman of the Joint Chiefs of Staff, who previously had demanded a "firewall" between the CIA and the U.S. armed forces (the official U.S. military policy), endorsed the post-9/11 plan put forward by Secretary Rumsfeld and Director Tenet to launch a Special Forces war spearheaded by the CIA.[7] Small squads (so-called A-teams, uniting CIA paramilitaries with Special Forces) would link up with local Northern Alliance forces and attack the Taliban army. As the two sides engaged, the A-teams would call in precision-guided bombardment of Taliban positions. In the second week of September, President Bush signed off on the Tenet-Rumsfeld plan, whose running price tag was over $1 billion.

The CIA's two years of clandestine infiltration into Afghanistan paid off hugely in the October–December 2001 operations. The Special Activities Division now knew how to get its agents into Afghanistan undetected and to keep them that way. It had working relationships with three of the Northern Alliance generals, including Dostum. The Afghan operation turned out to be a rare achievement in U.S. warmaking. The most sophisticated image and signal intelligence had been melded with the most basic human intelligence to form a seamless strategy of attack. The military result was devastating. The first CIA paramilitary unit infiltrated into Afghanistan on September 27, 2001, and the first Special Forces A-team went in on October 6. The United States began bombing on October 7.

On October 5, Mike and Shannon Spann, along with four-month-old Jake, went down to Old Town Manassas to a law office, so that Mike could sign his last will and testament. He was straightforward about the process and traded smiles with Shannon while they waited for the attorney, Elizabeth Munro von Keller.[8] Three days later, Mike was gone to the war zone.

He flew in first to the CIA–Special Forces base called "K2" in Uzbekistan and spent three days there being briefed. His mission was to establish a ground relationship with the forces of General Dostum and to select night landing zones and safe houses for the Green Beret TIGER 02 A-team that would follow and link up with him. Shortly before Mike's eight-man SAD team split up to infiltrate into Afghanistan, they took a photograph in front of an aircraft. Mike is pictured on the far right of the picture with his AK-47 held at port arms.

Mike Spann was dropped into Afghanistan from an MH-47 helicopter, probably on the night of October 11, along with two other paramilitaries. They set down somewhere in the Tingi Pass near a town called Shulgareh. Spann and his comrades were carrying hundreds of thousands of dollars to enable Dostum to recruit and equip a force. Some three days later, they had linked up with the Uzbek general, who was accompanied by a squad of poorly armed men on horseback. Dostum was a block of a man, six feet tall and a good 240 pounds, with a visage like the Popeye character Bluto. He was in his mid-fifties with a swarthy mustache and bristly salt-and-pepper hair.[9] According to one source, Spann's main job after handing off a large sum of cash to Dostum was to reconnoiter safe houses and night landing sites.[10]

On October 19, the twelve-man A-team TIGER 02 landed at night about forty-five miles south of Mazar-e Sharif. Spann, moving mostly by foot and sometimes on horseback, made his way south to meet up with them. According to his father, there were problems that caused Mike to retreat into the mountains to evade detection.[11] About five days later, the TIGER A-team linked up with Spann, and thereafter Dostum, who rode up this time with a far larger and better-armed retinue of troops on horseback. TIGER's mission left much up to improvisation: "Find and support Dostum, stay with him and help. Go with him wherever he goes — if he wants to take over Kabul, go. If he wants to take over the whole fucking country, that's fine too. If he starts mass executions on the way, call HQ and advise, maybe exfil [leave the country] if you can't rein him in."[12]

TIGER 02's first objective was to take the city of Mazar-e Sharif. Dostum, Spann, and the Special Forces A-team soon encountered dug-in Taliban brigades, some with armor and artillery. The American–Northern Alliance manner of attack bridged two centuries. Dostum and his forces would mass in ravines or behind ridges mounted on their horses as the Americans moved forward into recon positions to laser in

Taliban positions with their electronic binoculars. As Dostum and his men prepared for a cavalry charge, TIGER 02 would call in laser-guided 500- to 2,000-pound bombs directly on Taliban positions. As the bombs were exploding with precision accuracy, the Northern Alliance cavalry would be galloping directly at the Taliban lines. The result of this extraordinary coordination was rout after rout by the allied forces. Spann, with his wide variety of skills, soon became a highly respected comrade on the TIGER team. Outside of battle, he helped direct the flow of intelligence to guide the mission. When he had guard duty at night, he liked to do push-ups in between reading the Bible. On a phone call home, he told his daughters that he kept two mice in his rucksack as pets.

Mazar was liberated on November 9. At this point, northern Afghanistan was awash with refugees and fleeing Taliban, some looking to make a stand. In the city of Mazar, some 500 foreign al-Ansar fighters decided to hold out in a large madrassa, shooting emissaries sent to arrange their surrender. TIGER called in airstrikes that proved so accurate that one bomb followed the previous one through a hole it had blown in the school's roof. More than 450 foreign Taliban were killed. It was a sign of things to come.

In mid-November the A-team was given a new mission on another front and was separated from its comrade Mike Spann, who linked up shortly thereafter with veteran CIA case officer and linguist Dave Tyson. Their mission was to evaluate and interrogate the hundreds of prisoners in and around Mazar-e Sharif, in search of Al-Qaeda.

John Walker Lindh's fight with the Taliban ended before it even began. If we accept his version of events (and the government did not contest him on this point), he never fired a shot. Instead, as American A-team Texas 11 attacked with General Mohammad Daoud's Northern Alliance forces, the F-18 and B-52 bombing runs broke the Taliban lines. Lindh, with his al-Ansar comrades, fled south on foot, pursued by Northern Alliance units. Freezing and exhausted, Lindh reached Kunduz to find some 5,000 Taliban holding out in a city surrounded by Northern Alliance forces who were poised to attack.

General Dostum, who had made it a point to offer amnesty to the Taliban in exchange for surrender, pressed the Taliban commander,

Mullah Feisal, to give in before they were all killed. Their negotiations led to an unruly and unresolved surrender. The Taliban thought that by contributing $500,000 to Dostum and giving up without a fight, their forces would be taken to Herat and released. Possibly under pressure from the United States, Dostum either did not agree to this or went back on the deal. There was a third possibility set forth in Mark Kukis's account — namely, that the release only applied to Afghan Taliban, not foreign fighters.[13] Whatever the case, Lindh and his al-Ansar comrades *thought* they would be released after surrender, and this may have sparked the decision to rise up.

When Lindh and the rest of the 537 Taliban prisoners reached the outskirts of Mazar-e Sharif, they were ordered off the trucks to be searched. As Northern Alliance commander Haji Raof remembered, "Some of them were scared. Some of them were angry. Some of them were ready to fight."[14] There was a brief standoff before most of the Taliban dropped their weapons by the side of the road and got back into the trucks. Some, however, kept their weapons, mostly grenades stashed in the loose folds of their *kalmar shaweez*. The trucks arrived at Qala-e Janghi toward late afternoon and drove into the interior courtyard. As the prisoners climbed down, they were searched haphazardly. One of them suddenly ran toward two Northern Alliance commanders, detonating a grenade that killed them both and blew the attacker in two.[15] The prisoners were then immediately herded into the basement of a pink building in the interior of another part of the huge courtyard. Sometime after midnight a Northern Alliance soldier retaliated for the earlier attack by dropping a grenade down an air shaft, killing three or four of the prisoners and wounding a good dozen more. John Walker Lindh, who was in another of the basement's seven rooms, escaped unscathed.

Shawki Mohammed, a Northern Alliance commander interviewed for this book, reports that he and his guards could hear talking from below coming up from the stairwell. Most of the conversation, he remembered, was in Arabic, not in any of the languages Afghans could comprehend — Urdu or Dari (which share a common ancestry with Farsi).[16] Some of those prisoners, no doubt, were discussing a plan to attack their captors and seize the fortress. And what about John Walker

Lindh? What did he hear, and, if he heard anything about the coming attack, how did he respond?

Contacted by this author on June 21, 2003, by phone, Abd al-Haribi, a Pakistani Taliban then living in Quetta, Baluchistan, who was in that basement and was later captured by American forces and transferred to Guantánamo for interrogation, before being released in June 2003, remembered that everyone knew there would be an uprising. "Then we argued about if we were released . . . if it was not good to fight." Al-Haribi said he told this to his American captors. Some prisoners, he said, especially those with weapons, said they would attack. Some stayed silent. When he was asked why they remained silent, he said, "Because either they were scared or they were ready to fight." And the American John Walker Lindh? "I do not know what he wanted to do." But did he know about the plan? "Everybody knew that it would happen."[17]

Mike Spann arrived at the fortress that morning with his partner to see what intelligence they could get from the prisoners. He had mentioned the mission to his father in an e-mail. "We've gotten some prisoners from Kunduz — some guys with good information," he wrote. Spann continued to keep a journal that he planned to give Shannon when he got back. In the white truck that he drove over that morning to Qala-e Janghi and parked in the courtyard, he brought the journal with him. Despite the fact that the truck was later bombarded and largely incinerated, parts of the journal somehow survived. Among the entries was this one from Mike to Shannon: "One thing has troubled me. I'm not afraid of dying, but I have had a terrible fear of not being with you and our son. I think about holding you and touching you. I also think about holding that round boy of ours. . . . It would be cool to have a slow dance with you to 'Always and Forever.'"[18]

8

The United States of America

v. John Walker Lindh

October 4, 2002

Albert V. Bryan federal courthouse

Alexandria, Virginia

If Frank Lindh did one thing right after his son's capture, it was to call San Francisco trial attorney James Brosnahan at his home on Sunday afternoon, December 2, and ask him to represent John Walker Lindh. At first Brosnahan wasn't sure he wanted to, but then he invited the older Lindh to stop by his office the next day. On Monday morning Brosnahan called his partner, George C. Harris, to discuss the idea.[1] The two attorneys had a long history of litigating high-profile cases, particularly against the U.S. government. Brosnahan liked Frank Lindh, but thought his son's statements in the CNN interview that aired over the weekend were damaging. He also was unwilling to represent Lindh if he was a violent fanatic, but Frank Lindh assured him that his son was a sincere person incapable of violence. Brosnahan accordingly signed on and that afternoon sent letters to the secretaries of state and defense as well as the attorney general, advising them that he represented the captured Lindh.

On paper, Jim Brosnahan was one of the most accomplished trial lawyers in the country. He had 120 jury trials under his belt in a wide array of legal fields — from high-tech to tax to antitrust. He had authored legal articles and treatises on a raft of subjects and had served on more than a dozen governing boards of social and educational justice organizations. The normal mode of behavior for an attorney of that achievement, particularly at the age of sixty-nine, was to cruise along on a wave of collegial accolades, huge partnerships fees, and rainmaking endeavors that would further gild the firm and himself. But that was not Jim Brosnahan. He seemed to relish the man-killing harness of trial work, often throwing himself into cases with hundreds of thousands of dollars of cost and not a penny of recompense. In 1985 he had decamped to Tucson to defend a group of church leaders who had given "sanctuary" to brutalized Central Americans. For a period of eight years in the 1990s, he had stopped the U.S. and British governments from extraditing alleged IRA escapee Kevin Barry Artt. Brosnahan's philosophy of representation was summarized in a trial program he taught. It was called "Against All Odds in Trial Advocacy." This was a man built for legal warfare.

Senior Republicans in Washington, D.C., who knew Brosnahan tended to fear him. When asked to describe the trial attorney, a former Republican majority counsel of the Senate Judiciary Committee replied, "He's a cross between a pit bull and a junkyard dog." Certain Republicans felt that in the Iran/Contra investigation, which had led to a skein of indictments and resignations of Reagan administration officials, Brosnahan, as one of the attorneys for the independent counsel, had crossed the line. In 1992 he and Harris had joined independent counsel Lawrence Walsh in the final phase of the Iran/Contra investigation and written a 7,000-word indictment of former defense secretary Caspar Weinberger for perjury and obstruction. Among other things, Weinberger was alleged to have covered up a $25 million illegal arms purchase by Saudi ambassador Prince Bandar.

By September 1992, President Bush had vented publicly about the matter and especially its timing. "I have nothing to explain. I've given every bit of evidence I have to these thousands of investigators. And nobody has suggested that I've done anything wrong at all."[2] If Weinberger went down, it was felt, he might take the president and Weinberger's former deputy, General Colin Powell, then chairman of the Joint Chiefs of Staff, with him. Weinberger was indicted on the Friday before the Tuesday general election. Republican Washington was in a state of rage.

After Bush's defeat by Bill Clinton, Senator Bob Dole called publicly for Brosnahan to be fired for "manipulating the prosecution." Walsh refused. Then on Christmas Eve, Bush pardoned Weinberger and five other indicted former officials.[3] The war was over, but bitter memories remained.[4] The senior Bush, who generally refrained from press comments about issues affecting his son's administration, made an exception in the case of John Walker Lindh — and it is fair to surmise that it had something to do with Jim Brosnahan. On ABC News on December 16, 2001, the former president said Lindh had committed treason. "I thought of a unique penalty," he said. "Make him leave his hair the way it is and his face as dirty as it is and let him go wandering around the country and see what kind of sympathy he would get. . . . I am so sick of these Marin hot-tubbers."[5]

The former president wasn't alone. Threats to Brosnahan's firm, Morrison & Foerster, a distinguished San Francisco institution founded in 1892, with more than a thousand attorneys worldwide, were regarded as sufficiently serious for the firm to state publicly that Brosnahan and company were on their own in defending Lindh.[6] Even the *New York Times* got swept up in the fury against the American Taliban. "For Many, Verdict's In for Taliban Volunteer (and Skip the Trial)," the headline on December 7 read.

In addition to his trusted partner, George Harris, Brosnahan recruited thirty-seven-year-old Tony West for the defense team. West, a cum laude graduate of Harvard and president of the *Stanford Law Review,* was a gifted expositor who brought experience from the Justice Department in national law enforcement policy as well as in criminal prosecution as a former assistant United States attorney in the Northern District of California. Associate Raj Chatterjee signed on to do the necessary spadework of research and drafting.

West would soon find out that Brosnahan was not only not allergic to pressure but seemed to thrive on it. In the course of an exchange on speakerphone, Brosnahan, sensing that someone had tapped into the transmission and was listening in, spoke into the phone receiver, "I hope at some point you'll remember the reason why you got into government work in the first place. In the meantime, fuck off." In an interview in the summer of 2003, West, an African-American, explained why he was inspired to work with Brosnahan. When William H. Rehnquist had pretty much sewn up U.S. Senate confirmation in 1986 to be chief justice of the Supreme Court, Brosnahan, a former assistant United States attorney in Phoenix from 1961 to 1963, gave testimony before the Senate Judiciary Committee as to why Rehnquist might be unfit for the appointment. He detailed numerous complaints that had taken place on election day in 1962 when Rehnquist, spearheading a voter vigilante group called "Eagle Eye," had tried to run off Hispanic and African-Americans as they entered the polls in south Phoenix.[7]

With John Ashcroft in command, the government strategy was to keep Brosnahan at bay while it put together its case against Lindh. The key was to get a full confession that neither the twenty-year-old nor his attorneys could later walk away from. Accordingly, the government ignored Brosnahan's communications and made sure no letters from Lindh's parents reached their son. Deputy Defense Secretary Paul Wolfowitz announced on December 18, 2001, that Lindh was being "treated consistent with the Geneva protections of prisoners of war." When a reporter asked why the letters of his parents had not been delivered, something the Geneva Convention required, Wolfowitz amended his statement: "He's not legally a prisoner of war."[8]

After the CNN interview on December 1, 2001, Lindh had been half carried to a van that took him and his Green Beret detail back to Dostum's guesthouse. The next morning Lindh was removed to the Turkish school from which the SAS had left at top speed a week before for Qala-e Janghi to rescue Mike Spann.[9] According to the account of Mark Kukis, Lindh was visited by the Red Cross's Simon Brooks, who found him dignified, even eloquent, regarding his situation.[10] The next day, December 3, he was put into seclusion and interrogated by U.S. Army and Defense Intelligence Agency officers about his knowledge of Al-Qaeda training, battlefield tactics, leadership, and the scene at Qala-e Janghi.

Among the Special Forces who were guarding Lindh, there was mounting anger at their prisoner. Someone blindfolded Lindh and wrote "SHITHEAD" on the blindfold. There were taunts. Cocked pistols were put to his head. Soldiers took several photographs of Lindh, including some with guards in them. In one there was a piece of cardboard held over Lindh's head with the written notation "Cunt Face." By the time Lindh was shackled again for the trip to Camp Rhino, a U.S. base south of Kandahar, he was a sobbing, pleading mess.[11] The shrapnel in his leg had come out, but the bullet wound in his thigh, left untreated, was causing a fever.

At Camp Rhino, Lindh, now under Marine guard, was placed naked and blindfolded on a stretcher and lashed to it with duct tape. He was then put in a metal shipping container. One night the Special Forces sergeant came by to deliver some of Lindh's effects to the guard.

He remembered that it was very cold in the room where Lindh was being held and he could hear him shaking inside the container. "I felt sick
for some reason," he later said in interview.[12] This was not the standard
of humanity Mike Spann had died for. When Lindh had to urinate, the
metal box was raised upright so the urine would flow out the bottom.
Holes were punched out of the metal siding for air. He was fed intermittently — about a thousand calories a day. He often talked to himself,
either out of delusion or delirium. Although much of the evidence regarding the circumstances of Lindh's treatment was later destroyed in an
effort to cover up the abuse, a Navy medic made a note of the statement
of a Marine officer that the U.S. military viewed sleep deprivation,
cold, and hunger as legitimate tools of interrogation.[13] The medic was
concerned enough about the prisoner to write up a diagnosis of his
condition. He warned his superiors that "suicide is a concern."

It was in this condition that Lindh was taken out of the box,
dressed in a hospital gown, and escorted to a tent where FBI special
agent Christopher Reimann was waiting for him. Shortly before
Reimann was scheduled to interrogate the prisoner, the FBI notified
the Justice Department that the agent would question Lindh without
presence of counsel. A trial attorney at Justice, John De Pue, was not
sure if this was proper and referred it to the Professional Responsibility
Advisory Office. A thirty-year-old attorney, Jesselyn Radack, a Brown
University and Yale Law School graduate, researched the matter and
replied that it would be unethical, even illegal, to do so. It would be "a
pre-indictment, custodial overt interview," Radack wrote. Additionally,
Lindh's father had retained a lawyer for his son. No way.[14] But in
Afghanistan the treatment of Lindh had taken on a cruel and unusual
life of its own.

Despite the concerns expressed at the Justice Department, the FBI
allowed Reimann to interrogate Lindh. He showed the prisoner his FBI
badge and read him his Miranda rights, adding about his right to an attorney, "Of course, there are no attorneys here." (Later, using logic
worthy of a Soviet setting, U.S. attorney Paul McNulty stated that what
this *really* meant was that since there were no attorneys available, he
didn't have to talk if he didn't want to.) Reimann then invited Lindh to

state verbally that he was waiving his rights and then to sign a document formally waiving them and consenting to be interrogated. With his handcuffs still on, Lindh signed the waiver.

For several hours over a two-day period, Reimann questioned Lindh. The interrogation was not tape-recorded, nor was a second agent present, as the Bureau normally requires.[15] Further, Lindh never read or signed the interrogation document.[16] It is doubtful that Reimann acted either incompetently or extraprocedurally, but rather under orders. On the arrest warrant and affidavit of evidence, Reimann's name never appears. Rather a third-party agent, Anne E. Asbury, was called in to swear to the veracity of it all — a permissible practice but, under the circumstances, emblematic of concealment and coercion.[17]

When Justice Department attorney Radack learned that the interrogation had taken place without an attorney, she was amazed. "The interview may have to be sealed or only used for national security purposes," not for a criminal case, she advised De Pue, who e-mailed her back, "Ugh."[18] Radack added that the residual problem for the government in bypassing Lindh's right to counsel was that the interrogation might be seen by the court as "a coerced confession."[19]

One reason the FBI and Ashcroft were pushing so hard was because they were initially planning to try Lindh for treason, a crime punishable by death. By mid-December more competent heads prevailed. The standard of proof for the only crime set forth in the Constitution was high, as one might expect from men, namely the founding fathers, who had committed treason themselves against the Crown. To get a conviction, the government needed either two witnesses or a confession in open court that the accused had aided the enemy in time of war. In the 225-year history of the United States, there had only been thirty cases brought for treason. In the first, against Aaron Burr in 1807, Chief Justice John Marshall had acquitted the former vice president. Even though Burr, in his plot to make himself the emperor of Mexico, had planned war against the United States, Marshall reasoned, he had never "levied" it. Some consideration was also given to trying Lindh as an "enemy combatant," but to do so the government would have had to strip him of his citizenship first.

On January 15, 2002, Attorney General Ashcroft held the first of his several press conferences about the "American Taliban." "John Walker," Ashcroft said, "chose to join terrorists who wanted to kill Americans, and he chose to waive his right to an attorney, both orally and in writing, before he was questioned by the FBI." If the tactic was to keep the defense in the dark and railroad a strong result in a friendly court, what Ashcroft was doing was not smart. Like a talkative coach working out his strategy in the press the week before the game, Ashcroft was dropping too many hints about what was really going on. And Brosnahan, an old pro, was watching.

Within the Justice Department, there were doubts being expressed in writing about the quality of the government's case. One attorney wrote, "At present we have no knowledge that he did anything other than join the Taliban." What happened to that candid soul is not known, but as for Radack, she was quickly silenced. Even though the year before she had been given a bonus for her excellence, she now received a highly negative job performance rating and was advised to get out of the Justice Department — otherwise her performance rating would be made a permanent feature of her record. Having no alternative, she resigned and found a job in a private firm.[20]

Attorney General Ashcroft, in another of his unguarded comments about the Lindh case, said that the defendant's rights, both legal and otherwise, had been "scrupulously honored" — an Orwellian representation if there ever was one. By the third week of December, Lindh's abuse had become a controversial subject among his captors. Navy personnel aboard the USS *Peleliu,* to which Lindh was airlifted in the second week of December, were shocked at the sight of the naked, wounded man in the metal container. Lindh was taken out of the container, the slug was removed from his thigh, and he was put on a normal diet. When FBI agents flew onto the *Peleliu* to advise Navy officers about the "Ashcroft doctrine" (which holds that national security concerns outweigh the rights of the accused), they encountered open hostility from certain commanding officers, two of whom were later subpoenaed as witnesses by the defense in preparation for the trial.

Then there was another fumble. President Bush alluded to Lindh's improved treatment aboard the ship by saying, "I suspect he's finding his berth a little better than it was when he was placed in the prison in Afghanistan. And, you know, we've heard — the administration has heard from his lawyer . . ." In Ashcroft's world, Lindh didn't have a lawyer.

The government's strategy, according to an internal memorandum prepared for the head of Justice's criminal division, Michael Chertoff, was to prove a "timeline of terror" — to link Lindh's intent with his actions.[21]

1. Hostility towards the United States;

2. Training in two terrorist organizations that are in a state of war against the United States;

3. Foreknowledge of and recruitment for suicide missions against U.S. nationals;

4. Fighting against U.S. forces (post-9/11) with the Taliban army; and

5. Conspiracy to join other Taliban prisoners in the uprising at Qala-e Janghi and attacking Johnny Micheal Spann shortly after the attack began.

The third week of January, Lindh was flown back to the United States in advance of his arraignment in federal court in Alexandria, Virginia. The government had chosen its venue well: the jurors would be sitting nine miles from the devastated Pentagon and the federal judge who would be presiding was T. S. Ellis III, a bright, opinionated Reagan appointee, who had matriculated at Princeton and Harvard and had been appointed in 1987, the year Iran/Contra had ignited. Ellis's court was known as the "Rocket Docket" for its speedy verdicts. By this time, alerted to the fact that they could see their son, Frank and Marilyn Lindh as well as attorneys Brosnahan, Harris, and West flew to D.C. and, early in the morning on January 24, went over to the federal courthouse to meet the defendant.

His parents saw John first, shaven, in a green prison outfit, and there was a tearful reunion. Then Brosnahan and his partners walked into the holding pen to confer with Lindh. "Boy, am I glad to see you guys," was John's first comment. "I've been waiting to see you guys for a long time."[22] Minutes later, Lindh was escorted into the packed court, where U.S. magistrate W. Curtis Sewell advised him that he would be charged with conspiring to kill Americans and aid terrorist groups.

In court, Brosnahan immediately raised the issue. "For fifty-four days the United States government has kept John Lindh away from a lawyer." U.S. attorney Paul McNulty demurred. "Mr. Walker had signed a statement waiving his right to a counsel when he spoke to the FBI."[23]

On February 5, 2002, Attorney General Ashcroft held another press conference, in which he announced that the government would charge Lindh with "conspiracy to kill nationals of the United States" and with providing "material support to Al-Qaeda." Lindh's allegiance to "fanatics and terrorists" never faltered, Ashcroft noted, "even with the knowledge that they had murdered thousands of his countrymen." Ashcroft released the ten-count indictment, which carried a potential punishment of three life sentences plus an additional ninety years in prison. Included in the charges was a violation of the 1999 executive order proscribing contact and transactions with the Taliban.

The FBI affidavit was a 4,000-word redaction of Special Agent Reimann's interrogation of Lindh on December 9 and 10, 2001. It was the heart of the prosecution's case. Among the allegations critical to the government's case was the contention that in his interview at the Dar ul-Anan headquarters in Kabul, "Walker was told that the Arab group is Usama bin Laden's al-Qaeda group and that, because Walker's HUM [Harkat ul-Mujahideen] training was insufficient for their purposes, Walker would have to attend an al-Qaeda camp for additional and extensive military training. Walker further stated that he knew at the time that bin Laden and al-Qaeda were against America and the government of Saudi Arabia and that al-Qaeda's purpose was to fight Americans."

Another important allegation in the affidavit was set forth as follows:

> Within several weeks of his arrival there, in or about early June 2001, Walker learned from one of his instructors that Bin Laden had sent people to the United States to carry out several suicide operations. . . . Walker also stated that during his training at Al-Farooq, he met with Abu Mohammad Al-Misri, an Egyptian whom Walker understood to be the general manager of the training

camps. Al-Misri asked Walker, as well as other foreigners at the camp whether he was interested in traveling outside Afghanistan to conduct operations against the United State and certain Israeli targets. Walker declined the offer and chose instead to go to the front lines and fight.

Finally, the affidavit alleged that Lindh (or Walker, as he is referred to in the document) stayed with his Taliban fighting unit after learning of the terrorist attacks on 9/11. "Walker stated that, on September 11 or 12, he learned about the terrorist attacks in Washington and New York by radio. According to Walker, it was his and his comrades' understanding at the time that Bin Laden had ordered the attacks and that additional attacks would follow."[24]

In the affidavit, there is a full description of the circumstances leading up to the prisoners' attack against Spann, Tyson, and their other captors, but no specific allegation as to Lindh's role in that attack. By this time, the Qala-e Janghi survivors had been transferred to the Marine base at Guantánamo Bay, Cuba, where a team of interrogators was trying to obtain testimony implicating Lindh in the uprising.

At a hearing to determine eligibility for bail on February 7, 2002, the government successfully argued that releasing Lindh on bail might result in his flight from justice. In its well-argued brief, the government sought to demonstrate that through Lindh's e-mails to his parents he had "repeatedly expressed what can only be termed a hostility to his country of birth and citizenship." The magistrate agreed with the government, ruling that Lindh was ineligible for bail. It was a small but crucial mass media victory for the prosecution. The e-mails were quoted and reprinted all over the country, demonstrating to prospective jurors that in his heart John Walker Lindh hated the United States.[25]

At the bail hearing, Lindh's defense team got its first look at the opposing side. The nominal chief of the prosecution was forty-four-year-old U.S. attorney Paul J. McNulty, a politically astute protégé of two Republican titans, former House majority leader Dick Armey and Attorney General Ashcroft. McNulty's legal pedigree wasn't sterling (Capital University Law School in Columbus, Ohio) and he'd never seen the inside of a trial court except for press ops on opening day. But as Richard Cullen, one of McNulty's predecessors as U.S. attorney and later attorney general of Virginia, had put it, "what makes Paul so popular is his likeable personality as well as his ability to get along with Democrats."[26] McNulty had served as the Republican staff spokesman during the Clinton impeachment, somehow remaining on cordial terms with the Democrats — no mean feat. Brought up Catholic, Democrat, and liberal, he had progressively seen the fundamentalist Christian, Republican light, and by 2000 was as prayerfully patriotic as his close friend, Attorney General Ashcroft. At his best, McNulty was a political fixer, and this would prove important in the outcome of the case against John Walker Lindh.[27]

To try the case, the government brought in two heavyweights, Randy I. Bellows and David N. Kelley, both with extensive trial experience in national security and terrorism cases. Bellows, a Florida Gator and a graduate of Harvard Law School, had served as lead counsel in the prosecution of Robert Hanssen for espionage, as well as in other high-profile cases. He wrote and argued eloquently and had a string of public-sector awards to show for it.[28] It said something about Bellows that out of Harvard, instead of cashing in at some brass-plate firm, he had gone to work in Washington as a public interest attorney at the Center for Law and Social Policy. Then he had joined the equally unremunerative D.C. public defender's office.[29] After a stint at Justice in the criminal division, he had moved on to the U.S. attorney's office in 1989, where he became, in the words of one of his colleagues, "our best horse, our thoroughbred."[30]

Public-sector attorneys in D.C. generally have a choice on politically charged cases: either play one side of the two-party game, or duck. Bellows did neither. From May 1999 to May 2000, he had led an attorney general-mandated review of the government's handling of the Wen Ho Lee espionage case. Based on the FBI's investigation, the House Republican leadership had made Lee's case, involving the alleged stealing of nuclear secrets by the sixty-year-old scientist, into a cause célèbre, emblematic of treasonous negligence by the Clinton administration.[31] Bellows's investigation, which resulted in an eight-hundred-page report, instead proved treasonous negligence by the FBI and the

Department of Energy. The narrative, backed by thousands of documents and interviews, as well as a damning use of italics, was nothing less than scalding:

> Given its slap-dash quality, its flawed rationales, its complete mis-characterization of the predicate, and its queer mash of intense review of some pertinent records and complete ignorance of other venues of compromise, once Wen Ho Lee was "tagged" with the patina of suspicion, the AI [Administrative Inquiry] was all but over. He would be *it*.[32]

FBI director Louis Freeh, who had spent the better part of a year convicting Lee in the press, demanded that the report be sealed on the basis of national security.[33] Two chapters (160-odd pages) were, however, released. Bellows's conclusions about the deficiencies of the FBI fulfilled one of the more candid admissions that Freeh had made on Capitol Hill. "We are potentially," he had told the members of the House Judiciary Subcommittee on Crime, "the most dangerous agency in the country."[34] Years later, in the course of confidential interviews with FBI agents for this book, mere mention of the name "Bellows" would occasion profane acrimony.[35] To put it simply, Bellows was *the* best federal prosecutor in the country in national security cases, but he was not, either ethically or professionally, a company man.

The other lead prosecutor, David N. Kelley, was the former chief of the terrorism and organized crime unit in the U.S. attorney's office for the Southern District of New York. Kelley's unit was the best of its kind in the nation, thanks in part to the investigative strength of Kelley's friend and collaborator in the millennium interdiction and the USS *Cole* investigation, John O'Neill.[36] Kelley was New York tough, having worked as a cop in the city while putting himself through New York Law School. After 9/11, he had come to Washington to co-chair the investigation into the terrorism attacks, working with some sixty other attorneys in the FBI's new state-of-the-art command post, the Strategic Information Operations Center. The read on Kelley was that he was meticulous and relentless.[37]

On February 15, Lindh pleaded not guilty to the charges against him. Judge Ellis set trial for August 26, overruling Harris's request that the trial be delayed until November, given the 9/11 anniversary. Brosnahan called the government's case "weak," questioning the reliability of "a hearsay affidavit based on a coerced confession" after several weeks of brutal treatment and physical privation. The battle was on. Outside the court, the Spanns let fly. Shannon told the press that she was sorry that Lindh would not be facing the death penalty, and Johnny added, "Tell them, America will not tolerate traitors."

Brosnahan and Harris could tell that the government was scrambling to put together its case. There were revealing little changes between the complaint and the indictment (which legally superseded the complaint.)[38] But they knew that, given the friendly judge and jury, all the government really needed was an average case. For the defense, it was all uphill.

One encouraging factor for the defense was Lindh himself, who proved attentive and lucid in the long hours he and his attorneys would spend in the little jailhouse conference room. His accounts of what had happened never varied. Brosnahan decided that at trial he would put him on the stand. Given the raw hatred Lindh inspired, this seemed like a highly risky proposition, but what could they do? Everything, it seemed, depended on Lindh's believability.[39]

In addition to sending two San Francisco private investigators to retrace Lindh's odyssey to Yemen and the Indian subcontinent, the defense team retained two other experts, Dr. Tamara Sonn, an Islamic scholar who was the Kenan Professor of Religion and Humanities at William and Mary College, and Rohan Gunaratna, among the top international experts on terrorism.[40]

Sonn's charge was to ascertain what sort of a Muslim Lindh was. Had he gone to do jihad out of religious duty or political hatred or both? If the defense could show that it was reasonable for a young Muslim to want to defend Islam from attack — as opposed to engaging in bin Laden's blood scourge — the jury might encounter a reasonable doubt as to the purpose of his strange journey. Dr. Sonn, a PhD from the University of Chicago, who is fluent in Arabic and deeply read in Islam, confined herself, in an interview with the author, to a description of her role and academic background.[41] Under the "Special Administrative Orders," whose effect is to gag attorneys and witnesses in the case, she withheld any account of her exchanges with Lindh. Others, however, were willing to paraphrase her account of her interview with the defendant.

Sonn found Lindh to be a sincere Muslim, but a political naïf. He had a sort of street-level idealism for jihad — "Muslims were being attacked in many places" and "the Taliban was trying to create a pure Islamic state." It wasn't enough, Lindh said, for a sincere Muslim "just to do *salat*" (daily prayers). The reason he had quit Harkat ul-Mujahideen, he told Sonn, was because it wasn't really trying to save Kashmiri Muslims; it was just serving Pakistani political designs. He had hoped that the Taliban would be better, he said.

But what about the Taliban's condemnation of the Shiites or its treatment of women? Sonn asked. Lindh said he didn't know much about that and would need to study it. "I wondered," Sonn told Jane Mayer. "How could he *not* know?"[42] Indeed. We know of his contempt for Shia, and it is difficult to believe that in the course of his months in Afghanistan he did not learn of the extraordinary repression of women by the Taliban.

With regard to bin Laden's mission to attack America and its allied regimes in the Middle East, Lindh evidenced a peculiarly — or was it deliberately? — blinkered recognition of what was really going on. What did he think about bin Laden's fatwas calling on Muslims to kill Jews and Americans? Sonn asked. "Osama Bin Laden can't issue a fatwa," he retorted. Only religious authorities could do so, he told her. But that wasn't really the question, was it?

In the course of his interviews with Sonn and Gunaratna, Lindh described his encounters with bin Laden in deprecatory terms. On at least three occasions, bin Laden had visited al-Farooq and lectured to the al-Ansar trainees. According to Lindh (and his account to the two defense experts conformed with his interrogation with the FBI), bin Laden had spoken of the war against the Soviets, the local situation, and political issues. But what about the entire thrust of the Al-Qaeda cause — war against the United States? Killing Americans and Jews? It is difficult to believe that in the cause of inspiring the young men preparing for jihad, there would have been no mention of the "great infidel" itself — the United States.

Lindh informed both Sonn and Gunaratna that he had actually dozed off in at least one of the lectures. "To tell you the truth, he was really boring," he told Sonn. Lindh claimed that he was "offended" by bin Laden's "glorifying himself" and by the way everybody lined up to shake or kiss his hand. On bin Laden's third visit to the al-Farooq camp, Lindh was one of a small group that met with the Al-Qaeda leader. Despite what everyone describes as Lindh's exceptionally detailed memory about every other aspect of his journey, he didn't remember much of the meeting, or so he said, only that bin Laden thanked him for being there.

Perhaps we can accept that Lindh found bin Laden uninspiring, or even offputting, for the above reasons. What is more difficult to believe are sentiments demonstrating his ignorance of bin Laden's bloody purpose, or his claim that he had never even heard the words "Al-Qaeda" at the camp. The trainers at the camp were Al-Qaeda, the Arab section of al-Ansar was funded by Al-Qaeda, Osama was the revered leader of Al-Qaeda, but Lindh had never heard of Al-Qaeda?

The contrast between his responses in his CNN interview on December 1, 2001, and his subsequent responses weeks and months later is noteworthy. In answer to CNN reporter Robert Pelton's question about the al-Ansar brigade in the CNN interview, Lindh said, "So the Arab section [Lindh's] of al-Ansar is funded by Osama bin Laden. Also the training camps that the Arabs train in before they come to the front line are all funded by Osama bin Laden." Pelton asked if Lindh's goal was to be martyred. "I tell you, to be honest," Lindh replied, "every single one of us, without any exaggeration, every single one of us was 100 percent sure that we would all be *shahid,* be martyred."[43] At the end of the interview, Pelton asked him if he thought jihad was "a good cause." Lindh's response was "definitely."

Beyond the FBI's extractive interview, conducted in coercive circumstances at variance with the Bureau's own standards, or the interesting and relevant exchanges between Lindh and the defense experts, the CNN interview demonstrates Lindh's clear intent to be a martyr in the cause of jihad.

The primary purpose of the al-Farooq camp, at the time Lindh was there, was to train the foreign al-Ansar legion as an assault force for the Taliban army. When Lindh, under questioning, said he was sent to join "al-Ansar," the government put "Al-Qaeda" in the transcripts either out of ignorance or tactic. Gunaratna among others pointed out that Lindh's training as a soldier in al-Ansar was military, for the purpose of serving the Taliban, not terrorist, for the purpose of serving Al-Qaeda. True enough.

But toward the end of Lindh's training, by all accounts, he was approached to perform suicide missions. The man, who was then working as a trainer at al-Farooq, was Abu Mohammed al-Misri (also known as "Saleh"), an Al-Qaeda operative who was then under indictment for the 1998 embassy bombings in East Africa. He took Lindh into a room alone and sat down next to him. Would he do "martyrdom missions," al-Misri asked Lindh, against U.S. and Israeli targets? Lindh said he answered no. "I came to Afghanistan to fight against the Northern Alliance." Lindh's defense team would argue that this demonstrated his refusal to become a terrorist in the cause of attacking the United States. But Lindh's recollection also indicated that he undoubtedly understood that the most prized purpose of jihad for those who commanded and financed the al-Farooq camp was to kill U.S. and Israeli civilians. Unlike his decision to quit Harkat ul-Mujahideen when he discovered that its purposes were not what he had joined for, in this instance, John Walker Lindh stayed. He *didn't* quit. Instead he boarded a truck bound for Kandahar, carrying his AKM rifle and grenades, along with some 150 other al-Ansar mujahideen. After falling sick and convalescing for a few days, he took a bus to the front line of the war against the Northern Alliance. It was September 6.

As David Fecheimer discovered in his fact-finding trip to Afghanistan, Lindh's recollection of just where his foxhole was located in Takhar Province near the Tajik border was uncannily precise, even if his memory of his conversation with bin Laden wasn't. The foxhole was located near the abandoned village of Chichkeh in a place that Fecheimer said resembled "the end of the world."[44] The Taliban was planning a final assault to put an end to Ahmed Shah Massoud's resistance in the Panjshir Valley. Massoud himself was assassinated by two Al-Qaeda operatives posing as journalists on September 9. As Lindh's al-Ansar unit readied itself for attack along the northern front, Al-

Qaeda attacked the World Trade Center and the Pentagon. Later that day of September 11, Lindh learned about the attacks from someone who had heard about them on the radio.

Brosnahan knew that his team needed a break of some kind, a turnover maybe, to stop the government's momentum. Combing through what classified documents the government was sharing in a secure vault called the Secure Classified Information Facility, George Harris saw something that caught his attention. There were two summaries of the transcript of Lindh's December 3 interrogation, but they were different. One of them quoted him as saying, "Lindh was disillusioned and wanted to leave his Taliban unit, but could not do so for fear of death."[45] The second version omitted reference to any such statement. A few days later, Team Lindh filed a brief citing the conflicting documents and questioning the integrity of the government's evidence. The defense demanded immediate access to all relevant government interviews and investigation records and access to Taliban prisoners held at Guantánamo Bay as well as the "confidential U.S. witness 1" (Spann's partner, Dave Tyson).

On April 1, in the course of a four-hour hearing, the prosecution suffered two major setbacks. Where was the evidence in paragraph 12, Brosnahan asked, that "in or about June and July 2001, as part of his Al-Qaeda training, Lindh participated in terrorist training courses?"

Special assistant U.S. attorney David Kelley seemed to freeze for an instant, conceding that they didn't have any such evidence. "It's not what you learn there. It's how you use it."[46] Brosnahan pressed him. But where was the evidence that Lindh tried to kill American citizens? Kelley replied, "At the moment, I am not aware of it." This was a staggering concession. Judge Ellis was able to get the prosecution back off the ropes by rejecting the defense motion that the government specify the Americans Lindh conspired to murder. He did so with a stinging rejoinder: "Do you think Mohammed Atta knew the names of the people in the World Trade Center?" Raising his voice and pointing his finger at Brosnahan, he added, "Do you think any terrorist cares who they kill?" Brosnahan just stared at him and let the silence sink in.

Harris raised the issue again a few moments later. "The defendant contests that he ever intended to be part of a conspiracy to kill civilians or Americans." Judge Ellis interrupted him: "Well, what was he doing out there then?" Realizing he had gone too far, Ellis then offered a retraction: "You don't have to answer that. It was an inappropriate question."

Brosnahan asked that the court require the government to identify the names of military personnel who had questioned Lindh. "That's too broad," Ellis responded, rejecting the request. "I would assume not everyone Mr. Lindh grunted at falls into that category." The judge, by this time, was losing his composure. When the defense asked for access to Taliban and Al-Qaeda prisoners who might be witnesses, Ellis also rejected the request, adding derisively, "I presume there are people at Guantánamo Mr. Lindh knows."

Twenty minutes later, Brosnahan was up again questioning the prosecution's allegation in the FBI affidavit and arrest warrant regarding Lindh's alleged role in the killing of Johnny Micheal Spann. Where's the evidence for that? he asked. Ellis appeared ready to interject when Assistant U.S. attorney John S. Davis made an incredible admission. "There is no evidence at this time and no allegation of personal involvement in that overt act in this conspiracy." Even Ellis, according to a court reporter, sat back when he heard this one.[47]

Brosnahan, old prizefighter that he was, quickly moved in. "What *is* the conspiracy that my client is alleged to have been in? We don't know who was supposed to be murdered. . . . We don't know the names of any co-conspirators." He looked at the judge, then across the way at the prosecution. "It's not fair." Ellis seemed embarrassed. He then instructed the prosecutors to contact "Dave" (Tyson) and other witnesses to find out if they would agree to "voluntary" interviews with the defense. As to compelling them to do so, Ellis said, he would consider that in the hearing on May 31.

Outside the courtroom, with the press massed around him, Brosnahan tossed out a bomb — the picture of the naked, blindfolded Lindh lashed with duct tape to a stretcher, his bullet wound untreated. "The government had said that they treated John Lindh the same as wounded American soldiers. The picture might indicate to the casual observer that that was not the case." Brosnahan, who looks and sounds on the news tape like a slow-talking small-town doctor, walked away.

The prosecution scrambled fast and produced a brief a few days later. Lindh was not tortured, it argued. "Were the facilities at Camp Rhino ideal? Of course not," Randy Bellows wrote. "But the United States Marine Corps had not plucked John Walker Lindh out of the California suburb where he used to live and dropped him into a metal container in the middle of Afghanistan. While the Navy physician who was treating him had to sleep on a concrete floor in a sleeping bag in a room with a hole in the wall and a hole in the ceiling, Lindh slept on a stretcher in a container that protected him from the elements."

But, Brosnahan asked in court, was the photo real or not? And would the prosecution invite the Navy physician who had lain on the floor in order to permit Lindh sole use of the metal container to testify? Or was a subpoena required? Ellis had had enough of this and instructed the prosecution to draft an order instructing all relevant agencies of government — the FBI, the armed forces, the CIA, the State Department — to desist from destroying evidence, but instead to preserve it.[48] The directive went through the government like an electrical current, reaching its highest precincts. It was time, in the impolite phrase, to cover your ass.

The Pentagon under duress released a fresh set of abusive photos before other, possibly less patriotic, Americans did. They showed Special Forces soldiers sporting obscene communications in front of the prostrate Lindh. Secretary Rumsfeld ordered General Tommy Franks to investigate and to discipline the men.[49] The government's predicament was the one Senator Sam Ervin had noted in Watergate, quoting Sir Walter Scott: "When first we practice to deceive, oh, what a tangled web we weave." Let an attorney like Jim Brosnahan near a web of government deception and obstruction and look out. By mid-May, the defense had identified by name and rank seven sailors who would testify to Lindh's "disgraceful" condition when he was brought aboard the USS Peleliu. By late May that number included thirty officers and enlisted men who would be subpoenaed to testify at the July 15 suppression-of-evidence hearing. The prosecution had no choice but to agree.[50] The government didn't know whether these witnesses would be friendly or hostile, or if — dangerous moment — they would go for the defense of superior orders (i.e., "I was doing what I was ordered to do"). Bellows and Kelley now had to assume that Brosnahan would charge obstruction and would go as high as he could. Secretary Rumsfeld was known to be deeply unhappy with the whole situation.[51]

The "Ashcroft doctrine" then blew up in Ashcroft's face. Judge Ellis asked Justice for copies of all the internal e-mails regarding expressed concerns about the impropriety of the FBI interrogation of Lindh the previous December. Somebody went and doctored the file before turning it over to Ellis, but Bellows advised Jesselyn Radack, the attorney who had sent the warnings, that only two e-mails of the complete file had been sent to the judge. Radack went and electronically retrieved the other ten or so more e-mails.[52] In June the e-mails were leaked to *Newsweek*. Justice slapped a criminal investigation on Radack, even though research for this book reveals that it was actually an aggrieved FBI agent who had done the leaking.[53] Judge Ellis then made himself look like a Keystone Cop by ruling that the e-mails were "privileged" — this after the entire city of Washington, D.C., had read them. According to the seventeen people interviewed for this chapter, it was the integrity of the prosecutors, especially Bellows and Kelley, that left the door open for the defense to reveal the government's ethical misadventure. The prosecution insisted, at least after early March, on fair disclosure in discovery and, as was evident at the pretrial hearing on April 1, would not mislead the court about indictments that lacked evidence.

Brosnahan's next front was Guantánamo. In early March, down in the SCIF, West and Harris read through thirteen heavily sanitized summaries of interviews of Al-Qaeda and Taliban prisoners. According to Harris, some of the testimony they saw actually exculpated Lindh with regard to knowledge of any plan to rise up at Qala-e Janghi.[54] (Judge Ellis would concede the same at the sentencing in October 2002.) The defense then asked that Spann's partner be subpoenaed to testify at the pre-trial hearing scheduled for July 15 to detail his interrogation of Lindh. To get the Afghan intelligence videotape into evidence and show it to the jury, Tyson would need to authenticate it. Further, Tyson's stated threat to Lindh that "you're going to fucking die here" had a certain theatrical pregnancy to it.[55] Brosnahan knew that the CIA avoided trials like the plague, so the tactical effect of demanding to see Tyson would be to send the CIA packing.

Judge Ellis initially opposed Team Lindh's request for direct access to Taliban and Al-Qaeda prisoners at Guantánamo. In March he changed his position a bit, agreeing with the prosecution that Lindh's lawyers could provide written questions to the detainees. The questions would be "pre-screened and asked by a Department of Defense review team." The defense rejected this. Assistant U.S. attorney Davis said the government would give no ground. What would happen, he rhetorically asked the judge, if the prisoners at Camp X-Ray learned that there were lawyers there?[56] Ellis asked if the government could agree to a video hookup so that the defense could ascertain the credibility of the witnesses. Davis said he doubted it. This time Ellis let the government have it. "If that's the case, the government would not be able to proceed against this defendant," he said.

There were reasons other than national security to exclude enterprising attorneys from Camp X-Ray. The place was Kafkaesque. Beyond matters of inhumanity such as prisoners crouched in six-by-six-foot wire mesh cages in the open sun, there was a substantial breakdown in prison order. Suicide attempts were constant, as were hunger strikes. American military authorities at the camp were having difficulty pacifying the prisoners, having mixed mad dog Chechen types (who attacked other prisoners when they weren't bashing their own heads on steel bars) with other more docile prisoners. The military wardens had tried to stabilize the situation with counselors and time for daily prayers, but their best tool was shooting up the prisoners with huge doses of tranquilizers.[57] By May 2002 the main "national security" objective was the avoidance of national and international shame.

By September 2003, the military was losing control of the situation at Guantánamo, arresting U.S. Army captain James J. Yee, who had been serving as Islamic chaplain for the prisoners, on suspected espionage. Two weeks later, military police arrested U.S. Air Force senior airman Ahmad al-Halabi, who had been serving as a translator at Guantánamo, on thirty-two criminal charges, including spying and "unlawfully delivering baklava pastries to detainees."[58] If convicted, he and Captain Yee faced execution by firing squad. It was a case of institutional farce preceding human tragedy.

Perusing the briefs, transcripts, press accounts, and reminiscences of the principals, it was as if Brosnahan and company were moving up the hill, mounting an attack every two weeks or so against the government's high-ground position. At times these assaults were done in the traditional manner of submitting briefs. At others, Brosnahan and Harris would open up in the hearings in court, or afterward in press commentary. They were taking ground. Beyond their skill and experience, they had the advantage of having nothing to lose. What became evident in late spring was that the government did.

One flanking effort that surprised and concerned the prosecution was a defense move in April to lay the groundwork for an attack on the credibility of FBI special agent Christopher Reimann, who had interrogated Lindh in the second week of December in Camp Rhino. Since Reimann had seen fit to advise Lindh that "there are no lawyers here" and to forgo the Bureau's practice of bringing along a second agent as corroborating witness, he was vulnerable. The brutalized condition of Lindh at the time of the interrogation only made it worse — and the confession was the evidentiary centerpiece of the government's case.[59]

Reimann, the defense found out, had so badly botched an interrogation in December 1995 that the FBI, after having arrested and charged three Cuban immigrants for stockpiling assault rifles to kill Fidel Castro, had dropped the charges. One of the accused, Rene Cruz, reported that Reimann had treated him "like an animal."[60]

On June 17, Team Lindh mounted a broad constitutional challenge, asking Judge Ellis to dismiss the indictments on several grounds. Lindh, Harris told the court, had a constitutional right to associate with the Taliban. Ellis dismissed this contention outright. "The First Amendment guarantee of freedom of association is not a pass to provide terrorists with resources and services," he said. Brosnahan said Lindh couldn't get a fair trial in northern Virginia, given its proximity to the attacked Pentagon, but this challenge went nowhere as well. "The issue," Harris said, "is whether under the statutes the government can proceed with guilt by association rather than individual culpability." Davis cleanly batted this one down. "The case is not about association, but about acts of violence with groups bent on violence."

Toward the end of the hearing, Brosnahan made a final argument that looked like a throwaway, but may well have been an antipersonnel device aimed at a higher target. Lindh, he said, was being "selectively prosecuted" under the 1999 executive order (count 9 of the indictment) when "other corporations and individuals" were also transacting with the Taliban. Either charge everyone who broke the law, he said, or dismiss count 9 against Lindh. Ellis spurned the argument as baseless and threw it out.

If the "selective prosecution" argument didn't register in court, it did within the State Department. According to one source, the State Department's legal adviser was asked for an informal opinion as to the legal vulnerability of the government given the secret oil negotiations with the Taliban by the ex-U.S. ambassadors.[61] Another concern was the Bush administration's $43 million "good behavior" drug-war payment to the Taliban in June, which happened to coincide with John Walker Lindh's arrival in Kabul to join the Taliban army. Whatever the legality of these actions, they would not pass the smell test if they went public.

To complicate matters further for the government, the blockade of information and investigation relating to 9/11 suddenly began to break down. Under remitting pressure from the surviving families of 9/11, and with a critical bipartisan assist led by Senator John McCain in Congress, the Bush administration agreed to form an independent commission to investigate the disaster.[62] When the president put forward the name of former secretary of state Henry Kissinger to head the commission, the families reacted by demanding to see a list of his clients. After weeks of delay, Kissinger elected to keep his list of clients secret and resigned the appointment.[63] Eventually, Thomas H. Kean, the former Republican governor of New Jersey, was nominated by Bush to head the commission.

In April and May of 2002, there were shocking revelations about 9/11 that indicated extreme negligence by the Bush administration in the weeks before the attacks. Colleen Rowley, a twenty-three-year FBI veteran from Minneapolis, advised the Senate Intelligence Committee that FBI headquarters "deliberately sabotaged" the investigation of the so-called 20th hijacker, Zaccarias Moussaoui, in August 2001. Despite the fact that the FBI field office had a file five inches thick indicative of a wider plot, Rowley's request to the special supervisory agent in D.C.

to seize Moussaoui's laptop computer (which would have connected the dots of the conspiracy) was rejected. FBI director Mueller and National Security Adviser Condoleezza Rice had maintained that the intelligence community warnings had been general, not specific, as to the use of airliners as weapons. But Rowley unveiled a high-priority cable dated August 21 from the Minneapolis field office: "[It's] imperative that the [U.S. Secret Service] be apprised of this threat potential indicated by the evidence. . . . If (Moussaoui) seizes an aircraft flying from Heathrow to NYC, it will have fuel on board to reach D.C." Then there was a CIA memorandum that had gone forward to Rice's shop at NSC in August, citing "suspect 747 airline attackers" and "suspect airline suicide attackers."[64] Leaders on both sides of the aisle in Congress demanded an explanation.

After CBS News broke the story that the president had been informed on at least two occasions about the Al-Qaeda threats preceding 9/11, White House spokesman Ari Fleischer conceded that, even so, Bush had not "received information about the use of airplanes as missiles by suicide bombers." Fleischer, under sharp questioning, distanced himself from his earlier contention that the administration had received "no warnings" at all.[65] Vice President Cheney called the suggestions that the president knew about the attacks in advance "incendiary" and questioned the patriotism of both Democrats and Republicans who did so. "Such commentary is thoroughly irresponsible and totally unworthy of national leaders in a time of war," Cheney said. In June 2002 the Pentagon reviewed its first strategic scenario for the invasion of Iraq.

But the lie would not hold. "As the capital wakes up almost daily to disclosures about intelligence warnings before September 11," Elisabeth Bumiller of the *New York Times* wrote, "the White House has abruptly switched its strategy of mounting ferocious partisan assaults on Democrats to one of self-inoculation — admitting past mistakes and preparing for more bad news to come."[66] The worst news of all for the Bush administration was the fact that the intelligence committees in the Congress were reviewing classified information that Saudi agents, under the command and control of the Saudi government, had "scores of contacts" with the Al-Qaeda hijackers prior to the attacks; further, that one of those agents, Osama Bassan, who had moved over $100,000 in funds from the wife of Saudi ambassador to the U.S., Prince Bandar, had flown to Houston in April 2002 and accepted a suitcase full of money from Saudi crown prince Abdullah, who was visiting the president himself. Despite his intimacy with two of the hijackers, Bassan was never questioned about his role in the plot, but was instead deported from the United States on November 17, 2002.[67]

By June 2002, the Bush administration was gazing into an abyss of scandal that smacked of treason. Bush and his top policy advisers had gotten the fullest of intelligence warnings about an Al-Qaeda attack in July and August 2001, but aside from advising Ashcroft and certain Pentagon officials not to use commercial airliners had failed to protect the American people. The airlift of Saudi officials, at least one of whom had trafficked directly with the hijackers, only further signaled the corrupt nexus of profit and power. As if there were any doubt as to what was really going on, the administration fought tooth and nail to cover up the Saudi role in the 9/11 attacks, first with the intelligence committees of the Congress and then with the American people. In the prosecution of John Walker Lindh, according to a former chief counsel of the Senate Judiciary Committee, the administration began weighing the risks of a drawn-out trial in which the defense team would be hammering holes in certain corrupt arrangements leading up to 9/11.

As the suppression-of-evidence hearing (a sort of mini-trial about what evidence can be submitted in trial itself), scheduled to start the morning of July 15, approached, the administration grew more worried and concerned. Thirty officers and enlisted men from three branches of the military were flown in to Washington to testify. Brosnahan, to borrow the "junkyard dog" analogy used by a senior Republican, was now roaming into unexpected corners of government, striking as if by pure instinct, and Donald Rumsfeld, for one, didn't like it. Bush himself made the decision in early July to terminate the prosecution.

CBS legal analyst Andrew Cohen thought the outcome of the suppression-of-evidence hearing was fairly certain — it would go the government's way.[68] On Friday, July 12, there was a brief hearing before Judge Ellis, at the conclusion of which Randy Bellows handed Jim Brosnahan a note. "We need to talk," Bellows said. Later that afternoon attorneys for the two sides gathered. The government was looking for a plea deal, one that the prosecution said had been cleared by the chain of command. It was now clear that the government wanted out.

For over a week, the plea deal had been discussed at the highest levels of the Bush administration. United States attorney Paul McNulty would later say that the prosecution team itself had initiated the concept within the government, but this seems doubtful. Generally speaking, ambitious men like McNulty do not make career-killing proposals. McNulty's subsequent commentary, conflated with the inevitable win–win stuff, reads like that of the good political soldier.[69] Those close to the case thought the command to "get rid of it" had come from the White House itself. There was a further irony in the "deadline" McNulty had internally set for the government to work out the plea deal: it looked like the government was afraid that if it prevailed in the suppression-of-evidence hearing, it would then be forced to go to trial.

Sitting around the plastic table in plastic chairs in the jailhouse conference room, Brosnahan, Harris, and West informed Lindh of the proposed deal. They weren't confident about winning in the suppression-of-evidence hearing. The best outcome at trial would be conviction with a forty-year sentence. Acquittal was not in the cards. They outlined the rudiments of their counteroffer to the government: drop all the terrorism counts, the conspiracy to kill U.S. nationals, and accept guilt of the single count of supplying services to the Taliban. That count, plus carrying the gun and grenades, would get him twenty years, which could be reduced to seventeen for good behavior. There was no parole possible.

"Wow," Lindh said. "That means I'll be as old as Tony when I get out." Everyone laughed. West took pains to show Lindh that despite his advancing age — thirty-seven — he had no gray hairs. Lindh agreed, saying he wanted the conditions of continuing his education in jail and traveling to Mecca to make his hajj upon release.[70]

The lawyers worked through the weekend on the plea agreement via fax, phone, and two brief face-to-face sessions. Even though the defense knew the government was determined to cinch the deal before Monday morning, Brosnahan insisted that they prepare simultaneously for mini-trial hearing while negotiating with the prosecution. At 2 A.M. Monday morning, July 15, the deal was done with Lindh's signature on it. The government dropped nine out of ten counts on condition that Lindh plead guilty on supplying services to the Taliban. Beyond that, and the carrying explosives add-on, the government imposed a battery of conditions regarding the terms of Lindh's incarceration and cooperation. One such condition was that the defendant retract all allegations of mistreatment by the U.S. military. Ellis accepted the plea agreement and Lindh pled guilty to having provided services as a soldier to the Taliban and carrying a rifle and two grenades.

Attorney General Ashcroft pronounced the outcome "a victory in the war on terrorism." This was abject nonsense; it was rather a humiliating defeat, one born of Ashcroft's own incompetent overreaching. The right-wing websites fairly scorched the administration with charges of cowardice and incompetence. Among the "breakthroughs" promised by the Patriot Act was to deliver terrorist convictions by opening up federal grand jury investigations to the military and intelligence communities. The result in *The United States of America v. John Walker Lindh,* however, was badly framed indictments based on badly gathered evidence. In the end, the would-be patriots had to go off with their tails tucked neatly between their legs.

On the *NewsHour with Jim Lehrer,* McNulty did his amiable best to explain the "very tough" sentence of seventeen years.[71] But why, *NewsHour* host Margaret Warner wanted to know, did the government drop all the terrorism counts? The reply is moderately priceless: "Well, dropping counts doesn't concede somehow that those counts could not have been proven or that they were not well substantiated." The government's case was very, very strong, McNulty said. "That's what motivated them [the defense] to seek a plea agreement."[72]

By August 2003, Ashcroft was back on the road, attacking librarians — yes, librarians — for their "anti-American" reaction toward the federal edict to know everybody's public library reading list. In September, the attorney general demanded that federal prosecutors *stop* plea bargains with criminal defendants, particularly in national security cases. Leniency had gone far enough, Ashcroft said in a speech in Cincinnati on September 22. "The direction I am giving our U.S. attorneys is direct and emphatic," he said. American patriots must hold the line.[73]

In Winfield, Johnny Spann was stunned when he got the news of the plea bargain. He drove to Birmingham, took a flight to D.C., and went straight to the U.S attorney's office in Alexandria. "How could you do this?" he asked McNulty. "You *can't* do this!" McNulty, no longer quite so amiable, dealt with him coldly. Bellows was different, Spann remembered a year later, sitting at home on his couch with a pile of old photos of Mike in front of him. "Randy Bellows looked hurt. And he looked like he wanted to tell me something."[74]

Perhaps Bellows just wanted to say how sorry he was. Perhaps there was something else he felt like saying. Contacted in September 2003, Bellows, now a judge on the Fairfax (Virginia) circuit court bench, said his position did not afford him the liberty of comment. He referred the author back to the U.S. attorney's office where he had worked for thirteen years.

What happened on that terrible morning in Qala-e Janghi deserved an adversarial airing in court. It still does. The best evidence suggests the following: after the grenade attack killed the Northern Alliance guard, three hundred or so prisoners began streaming out of the entry to the pink building, overwhelming four other guards and grabbing their rifles.[75] The audio reveals that an AK-47 began firing within four seconds of the grenade attack. This was Mike Spann's. He advanced toward the entryway, at first firing single shots, several of which found targets, and then a short burst which found more. A little more than one minute after the first grenade explosion, he had expended his clip. Those who converged on him were the escaping cavalcade coming out of the pink building, not the prisoners, bound and kneeling on the ground. Most of those simply lay flat. John Walker Lindh, however, got to his feet and ran a short distance before being hit by a ricocheting bullet. Who fired this bullet from which direction is not ascertainable.

As the foreign Taliban bore down on Spann, he made no effort to run but instead shot two or three more of his attackers with his 9 mm. before using it to club them. He was soon enveloped by a screaming mass of prisoners. One witness reported seeing him tackled and fall on his right side, at which point he was variously pummeled, kicked, and even bitten to unconsciousness by his attackers.[76]

His partner, Dave Tyson, by his own account, fought back, first with an AK-47 he had seized from a guard and then with his 9 mm. No witnesses interviewed or consulted for this book could place him on the scene once the fighting began, however. Tyson was next seen on the ARD-TV videotape sprinting toward the guard tower holding his 9 mm by the barrel instead of the grip.[77]

Consistent with Mike's wishes, his father, Johnny, had the casket opened and examined his son's body himself. The fatal shots were fired into Mike Spann's head near the temples, exiting the back of his head.[78] It is probable that he was executed by the foreign Taliban not long after they had taken over that part of the courtyard. About a half-hour after Mike Spann was overcome, an SAS squad on the first rescue detail reached Qala-e Janghi from the nearby Turkish school. As noted, one of the SAS troopers made his way to the top of the parapet and, spotting Spann lying in the courtyard, fired two rounds on either side of him. There was no movement.

Johnny Spann initially subscribed to the Special Forces conclusion that Mike, still alive, had been dragged into the basement of the pink house, tortured in the form of breaking both his legs, and executed thereafter.[79] Subsequently, on the basis of a year's research, he reached a different conclusion consistent with the above account. Johnny Spann remains the most credible and informed source regarding the circumstances of his son's death.

What about John Walker Lindh's knowledge or ignorance of the plan to attack the Northern Alliance captors? First, he said that he knew that some of his fellow prisoners were armed. Second, he stated in the CNN interview that "some of the brothers were tense." Beyond this, there are conflicting accounts. From Guantánamo, there were over a dozen interrogations done by the U.S. military of prisoners who had been captured at the fortress in the days after the uprising, none of which the author was able to declassify for this book. Accordingly, we must rely on the conclusion of Judge Ellis, who did review those interrogations. Ellis stated in court that "the government did not have evidence that linked this defendant to the murder of Mr. Spann."[80]

Other primary research done in 2002 and 2003 revealed, however, that Lindh *did* have prior knowledge of the uprising. We have recounted

the testimony of Abd al-Haribi, one of three Pakistani prisoners released from Guantánamo in June 2003. Al-Haribi said that he had told
U.S. military interrogators that everyone in the basement had known
that something was going to happen.[81] Subsequent to his interrogation,
al-Haribi tried to commit suicide and had, by his own admission, a nervous breakdown thereafter.

There is also the account of Mark Kukis, the reporter who re-
traced Lindh's steps. In May 2002, Kukis interviewed two Pakistani Taliban held by Dostum's forces in a prison in Sherberghan. The Pakistanis,
Enamul Hak and Wahid Ahmad, had been left behind by the American
military, either because of their physical condition or their lack of intelligence value. According to Kukis, they both said that "the group in
the basement was split, with seemingly everyone aware that at least
some in their ranks were considering staging an attack. If Hak and Ahmad are to be believed, then Lindh knew of the revolt, a foresight that
would make him culpable in Spann's death."[82]

Is this enough to charge and try Lindh for conspiracy to murder?
Surely it is. Under the United States Code, Title 18, Section 371, courts
have interpreted conspiracy to mean "a mutual understanding" between
two or more persons to do something that, if actually carried out, would
amount to another federal crime. Each person must "willfully become
a member of such conspiracy," but "because the essence of a conspiracy
offense is the making of the agreement itself (followed by commission
of the overt act), it is not necessary for the Government to prove that the
conspirators actually succeeded in accomplishing their unlawful plan."
That Lindh got up and ran is immaterial to his guilt or innocence. What
counts is, what did he know and was he willfully a part of it? Whether, in
the light of the conflicting testimony, he could be proven to have such a
quality of knowledge beyond a reasonable doubt is a matter of conjecture.

The sentencing of John Walker Lindh took place on October 4,
2002, in Alexandria at the graceful Albert V. Bryan federal courthouse
on the square. The courtroom was packed. Although Judge Ellis retained the option of changing the sentence, it was soon clear that he
had no intention of doing so. He offered his own conclusions about the
case and then invited the defendant to speak.

Slender as ever and slumped over a bit, Lindh stood at Ellis's prompting. In a husky and halting voice, with Brosnahan standing to his right and occasionally patting him on the back when he lost his composure, he read his statement. He began by thanking God, the court, his family, the crew on the USS *Peleliu,* and the American people. "I understand why so many Americans were angry when I was first discovered in Afghanistan. I realize that many still are, and I hope that with time and understanding those feelings will change." He spoke of his travels abroad to study Islam and Arabic and how he ended up as a foot soldier for the Taliban.

> I went to Afghanistan because I believed it was my religious duty to assist my fellow Muslims militarily in their jihad against the Northern Alliance. Because the term jihad had been commonly misunderstood, I would like to take a few minutes to explain the meaning of the term. In the Arabic language, jihad literally means struggle. In Islamic terminology — in Islamic terminology, jihad refers to the spending of one's utmost exertion in the service of God. I have never understood jihad to mean anti-Americanism or terrorism. I condemn terrorism on every level. . . .
>
> I went to Afghanistan because I believed there was no way to alleviate the suffering of the Afghan people, aside from military action. I did not go to fight against America and I never did. . . . Since returning to the United States, I have learned more about the Taliban, such as reports of the Taliban's repression of women, which I did not see or hear of while I was in Afghanistan, and which I believe is strongly condemned by Islam. I have also become aware of the relationship between the leaders of the Taliban and Osama bin Laden's organization. Bin Laden's terrorist attacks are completely against Islam, completely contrary to the conventions of jihad, and without any justification whatsoever. His grievances, whatever they may be, cannot be addressed by acts of injustice and violence against innocent people in America. . . .
>
> I made a mistake by joining the Taliban. I want the court to know and I want the American people to know that had I realized then what I know now about the Taliban, I would never have joined them. When I began my studies in Islam, I had the ambition of one day teaching, writing and translating Arabic texts into English. I still have these ambitions and I hope to pursue my studies in Islam, the Arabic language, world history, linguistics, sociology and English literature. I hope to use this knowledge to serve Islam and

the interests of Muslims around the world to the full extent of my
capability. And to conclude, I would like to thank the court again
for giving me this opportunity to speak.

Lindh walked away from the podium and sat down. He had made
an intelligent and graceful apologia, but one that had not mentioned his
encounter with Mike Spann. Judge Ellis, who had signed an order the
day before permitting Johnny Spann to speak, invited him forward.
Spann looked tired and anguished. At first, he spoke about the 9/11 attack, but then, sounding surprisingly like his son Mike, he posed questions that went to the heart of the matter.

> Mr. Lindh, the way I understand it, has admitted that he fought on
> the front lines of Takhar. Are we supposed to believe that any kind
> of an army would let somebody come and be a member of their
> army and be on the front lines, but never fire his weapon? That's a
> little bit hard to believe. . . .
>
> We know that when they surrendered in Kunduz, that they
> were carried down through Mazar-e Sharif on trucks and carried
> down to Qala-e Janghi fortress. We also know — I don't think
> there's a doubt in anyone's mind, we saw it on TV, where John
> Walker Lindh appeared the next day. So we know that he was there
> the night before. We know that he, in fact, spent the night in the
> pink house. . . . And the reports are different but I am assuming that
> there were some four-hundred-plus prisoners in that building. Are
> we to believe that a person could spend the night in a building, that
> small of a building with four-hundred-plus prisoners — and a third
> of them never have been searched, a third of them still have their
> weapons, they still have their grenades under their head gear, un-
> derneath their slouchy clothes — are we to believe that those
> people spent the night there and they didn't talk about that?
> "We've got weapons. We've still got guns"? That's a little hard for
> me to believe too. And it's a little hard for the American people that
> talked to me to believe.
>
> I thought that it was the responsibility of Americans that if you
> knew that there was something going to happen — and I realize
> that what you have already said, that evidently the court believes
> that Mr. Lindh didn't know there was going to be an uprising. It's
> hard for me to believe that.

Ellis interrupted Spann at this point. "Let me be clear about that," he said. "The government has no evidence of that."

"I understand," Spann replied.

"And your suspicions," the judge continued, "the inferences you draw from the facts are not enough to warrant a jury conviction, even if they are shared by wide segments of the American public. But I understand all your suspicions and I assure you that I had them too. I assure you that I looked for that evidence. But I share, everyone shares, those suspicions."

"I feel like it is not a just punishment," Spann said. "Some of the things that Mr. Lindh said a while ago about, if he didn't want to fight against Americans, where was he when the uprising started? Did he do anything to help Mike? Did he drag Mike inside the pink house with him? Did he take him anywhere to try to help him? Did he not know that Mike was an American?"

Those questions should have been asked in trial, but because of the government's incompetence and its political agenda, they were not. In addition to that legal reason to go to trial, there was a moral reason as well. Before a jury Lindh should have been asked what he had known and why he had remained silent. Didn't he realize at long last that, in Mike Spann's words, "the people you're with are terrorists"? Why could he not have said then what he said a year later, when he stood up before the court and claimed, "Terrorism is never justified, and has proven extremely damaging to Muslims around the world. I have never supported terrorism in any form, and never would"? Had he found, through his lawyers, one more route of escape, this time from life imprisonment?

It was as if John Walker Lindh's moment of truth was *there,* squatting on that mat with Mike Spann questioning him in the Qala-e Janghi courtyard. And because of his cowardice or hatefulness, or some alloy of the two, he had let his chance pass by. The chance was to redeem himself and, in so doing, save further loss of life. Spann could have broken him, could have had Lindh tortured, but his humanity as much as his training would not have permitted him to do that.

And so Mike Spann's moment of truth came — and he'd had been preparing for it all his life. He stood as a Marine and as a man from

north Alabama was supposed to. He fought until it was not possible for
him to fight anymore. We should respect and remember that.

If the trial of John Walker Lindh had gone forward, as it should
have, we would also have seen Jim Brosnahan put the government itself
on trial, not just for the malicious tactics the defense team had already
brought to light but for the selective prosecution of his client. Who, in
fact, had been trafficking with the Taliban? Who, in fact, out of a
brazen greed had opened the door to Saudi double-dealing with Al-
Qaeda? Perhaps, as the body count mounted in the so-called war on
terrorism, that trial might have touched off a national debate about the
"collateral damage" we have so easily consigned as the patriotic right of
government. The death of Mike Spann, for example.

Whether John Walker Lindh got away with murder remains an
unanswered question. Whether the American government got away
with murder is increasingly in question.

Did the administration's policy of preemption, and specifically the
decision to seize oil-rich countries, lead to an even more systematic
sellout to the Saudi royal family, including giving its clandestine agents
in the U.S. the unrestricted ability to interact with Al-Qaeda terrorists?
Is this the reason why the twenty-eight pages that spell out the evidence
of offical Saudi complicity in 9/11 were excised by the Bush White
House from the public release of Congress's joint inquiry report?

Did the Bush administration's trafficking with the Taliban from
February to July 2001 for the purpose of constructing the gas pipeline
supersede, and thereby shelve, the proposed plan to assassinate Osama
bin Laden, as some former CIA officials now allege? Did the Bush administration cut John Walker Lindh a plea deal to conceal its own un-
clean hands?

The war to drive Al-Qaeda from Afghanistan, the one in which
Mike Spann died and John Walker Lindh survived, was justified and
necessary. Why has America not finished that war? Why instead, as
Afghanistan dissolves into civil violence, is the U.S. consorting again
with the criminal regime in Pakistan, a government that once created
the Taliban, supported Al-Qaeda, and in whose territory bin Laden
continues to roam freely?

In the course of the amnesiac decade of the 1990s, the American ruling class came to rely on a crass and ahistoric presumption that market growth and liberal democracy would "end" the cycles of history. Inherent in that presumption was that the United States could have it both ways regarding violently destructive groups in the world: that those in Washington could traffic with terrorist states for corporate and military advantage, and at the same time rely on those states to contain the terrorists with whom they themselves were associated.

To this presumption, the second Bush administration proposed an additionally foolish construct — preemption — which served not only to open the door wider to a terrorist strike within the United States prior to 9/11, but to redouble the march of folly in its wake. Today the U.S. is more unsafe at home, not less, and more exposed and detested in the world than ever before. We have squandered the great reservoir of international sympathy and support in the wake of the terrorist attacks and failed to observe what the founding fathers thought essential in their Declaration of Independence — "a decent respect to the opinions of mankind."

Tragedy, as Robert F. Kennedy once said regarding America's experience in Vietnam, can be used as "a tool for the living." Tragedy can bring us to our senses and lead us to a communion of moderation as human beings and the targeted use of power as a country. But the catastrophe of 9/11 has not provided our leaders with such a tool in our war against terrorism, but rather a self-replicating specter stimulated by our own worst fears and misguided actions.

In its first years as a republic, the United States faced a hysteria of similar proportion. In July 1798, after Congress had passed the Alien Act and the Sedition Act, the federal government began arresting "enemies of the state," both American and non-American, as it prepared for hostilities against France. In a letter to Thomas Jefferson, James Madison summarized the dilemma we encounter today in the war on terrorism: "The management of foreign relations appears to be the most susceptible to abuse of all the trusts committed to Government. . . . Perhaps it is a universal truth that the loss of liberty at home is to be charged to provisions against danger, real or pretended, abroad."

Today the pretended has become real. What hangs in the balance is the survival of the American republic and the integrity of its Constitution.

NOTES

Chapter 1 Murder: The Uprising at Qala-e Janghi Fortress

1. "Secret CIA Units Playing a Central Combat Role," *Washington Post,* 18 November 2001. "How the CIA Fights Its New War," *Time,* 5 November 2001, p. 21. "CIA Commandos Remain Covert," *Dallas Morning News,* 27 October 2002. This chapter is drawn from six confidential interviews (nos. 7, 8, 11, 16, 18, and 22) from sources in American intelligence services.

2. This account is based on the videotape of the scene from ARD-TV (Germany) as well as footage shot by Combat Films. The key reporters at the scene (hereafter cited) were Alex Perry of *Time* magazine, Arnim Stauth of ARD-TV, Dodge Billingsley of Combat Films, Alessio Vinci of CNN, and Jean-Paul Mari of the *Nouvel Observateur.*

3. Johnny Spann, the father of Micheal Spann, in interviews conducted with Afghan intelligence and Northern Alliance guards, provides this total. See Johnny Spann, untitled memo that deals with his visit to Qala-e Janghi, 8 December 2002.

4. Mohammed Atef, also known as Abu Hafez, was the senior military commander for Al-Qaeda and second-in-command. Seven others traveling with him were also killed. See "Confirmation de la mort de Mohammed Atef," *Confidentiel.net.* Dateline: Quetta, Pakistan, 17 November 2001. Mullah Najibullah, the Taliban leader in Spinboldak, confirmed the death. Also BBC News, 16 November 2001.

5. Quoted in Robin Moore, *The Hunt for Bin Laden: Task Force Dagger* (New York: Random House, 2003), p. 233.

6. Robin Moore details this exceptionally well in *The Hunt for Bin Laden,* chapter 1.

7. The author has not interviewed Tyson, who is currently in Tashkent, in this account. Tyson's linguistic proficiency is referred to in the article by Jean-Paul Mari, "Massacre à la citadelle," *Nouvel Observateur,* 31 January 2002, pp. 19–21.

8. This attack killed Nader Ali, chief of security for the Northern Alliance forces, and Sayed Asedullah Masrour, a Hazara commander.

9. This is the account of Alex Perry, "Inside Qala-e Janghi," *Time,* 21 December 2001, pp. 12–13.

10. This is French journalist Jean-Paul Mari's assertion, based on a senior Taliban source he interviewed. It conforms with other reports after the Dostum-Feisal negotiation. "Massacre à la citadelle," pp. 19–21.

11. The CIA paracommandos and Special Forces had also rejected the use of the Mazar-e Sharif airport for the incarceration of the prisoners. Mari, "Massacre à la citadelle," pp. 19–21.

12. American Special Forces were under the strictest orders to avoid situations in which prisoners were being tortured or executed. The only exception to this was the elimination of Al-Qaeda operatives. The several hundred executed Taliban left in trailers by the side of the road were thought by most foreign reporters to have been killed by Dostum's Uzbek troops. The bombing of the *madrassa* by American smart bombs was accomplished after some 400–500 Al-Qaeda–trained foreign fighters, holed up in the school, had refused to surrender and then executed the emissaries that Dostum had sent in to arrange their surrender. See "Massacre Warning for Afghan City," BBC News, 23 October 2001. Also "US Allies Deny 'Mazar Massacre,'" BBC News, 16 November 2001.

13. The author transcribed the tape, which was taken by Afghan intelligence.

14. As stated in "House of War: The Uprising at Mazar-e Sharif," *CNN Presents,* aired 3 August 2002. Pelton is the author, inter alia, of *The World's Most Dangerous Places* (New York: HarperResource, 2003).

15. Ted Gup has written a book of surpassing depth and poignancy about the people behind these stars, *The Book of Honor: The Secret Lives and Deaths of CIA Operatives* (New York: Anchor, 2000). With Spann's death, there are now seventy-nine stars.

16. Moore, in his book about the Special Forces in Afghanistan, correctly ascribes this account to Dostum's Uzbek soldiers. The story appeared as such four days later in a weekly newspaper in Mazar. This account may be dismissed outright since four witnesses have said that Spann fired both his AK-47 and 9 mm. From the audio portion of the videotape of the German camera crew, one can hear the extended clatter of automatic arms fire. There are thirty rounds in the magazine of an unmodified AK-47.

17. As stated in "House of War," *CNN Presents.*

18. This account draws on the eyewitness testimony of Mohammed Daoud, interviewed by both Jean-Paul Mari, days after the incident, and Johnny Spann, a little over a year later. It is also drawn from Lindh's contemporaneous testimony on December 1 (to reporters Colin Soloway and Robert Pelto). See Mari, "Massacre à la citadelle," pp. 19–21; Colin Soloway, "Tale of an American Talib," *Newsweek,* 18 December 2001, p. 7. Spann's account, dated December 8, 2002, also cites a Northern Alliance fighter on the scene as well as two doctors who lay on the ground before fleeing. Tyson has not been interviewed, although his somewhat garbled account over ARD-TV's sat phone to the U.S. embassy in Tashkent is featured on "House of War," *CNN Presents.*

19. As is evident in the ARD-TV videotape.

20. See Alex Perry's account as he stood alongside the Special Forces, "Inside Qala-e Janghi."

21. See Jean-Paul Mari's account in "Massacre à la citadelle," pp. 19–21: *"Merde! Arrêtons de déconner et allons-y! Dites à ces mecs d'arrêter de se gratter les couilles et de voler!"* (author's translation).

22. From the ARD-TV tape.

23. Moore, *The Hunt for Bin Laden,* p. 171.

24. Colin Soloway interviewed Lindh in the courtyard on the morning of December 1 and Robert Pelton Young did so on videotape in the Turkish-Afghan hospital in Sherberghan later that day.

25. The Special Forces maintained that Spann, though badly beaten, was still alive before being taken into the pink building, where he was tortured before being executed. It is more probable that he was not taken into the pink building but rather executed with two shots through the head in the courtyard. His body, once recovered, was flown to K2 (the Special Forces base camp in Uzbekistan). Confidential interviews 8, 11.

26. The best and most judicious evaluation of the warfare lessons learned in Afghanistan is Stephen Biddle, "What Really Happened in Afghanistan," *Foreign Affairs,* March/April 2003, vol. 82, no. 2.

27. The SAS does not release information on their dead and wounded.

28. Moore, *The Hunt for Bin Laden,* pp. 172–73.

29. Trapped in the courtyard for several very dangerous minutes, Billingsley and his cameraman, Damien Degueldre, captured part of this flight.

30. "House of War," *CNN Presents,* incorrectly reports Dostum's tour as occurring on Wednesday morning.

31. This is a paraphrase of Jean-Paul Mari's description: "*Hirsutes, puant, terriblement maigres, portant un blessé, marchant en boitant, en saignant, en gémissant de douleur. Et surtout, le regard, fou, perdu.*" "Massacre à la citadelle," pp. 19–21.

32. "American Taliban," *The Independent Weekly,* 30 January 2002, p. 8.

33. "Inside the Afghan War Machine," *National Geographic Adventure Magazine* (interview with Robert Pelton), 2 March 2002.

34. This exchange is contained in the audio online, "Finding John Walker Lindh," in ibid. Robin Moore, who had the full confidence of Tiger 02, the medic's A-team, reports that such an effort, at least in the sense of communication, was made by the Special Forces, through Dostum, to execute Lindh. *The Hunt for Bin Laden,* p. 179.

35. In his interview with CNN's Aaron Brown on December 19, 2001, Young told Brown that the Special Forces medic had taken care of Lindh "so he could stay alive . . . and so they could get more information out of him." Jane Mayer, in her first-rate account in the *New Yorker,* describes the injection as "a sedative painkiller." "Annals of Justice: Lost in the Jihad," 10 March 2003, pp. 27–43.

36. In another part of the interview, Lindh says it differently: "And when the guns started, everybody stood up and ran. And I was — the whole time just up against the wall." CNN.com, transcript of John Walker interview, 2 December 2001, p. 3.

37. The elements of the "conspiracy to murder U.S. Nationals" can be found at 18 U.S.C. sect. 2332(b). Also sect. 1111(a).

38. See, for example, "Midnight Confession: How CNN Captured John Walker," *Village Voice,* 2–8 January 2002, p. 15.

39. On September 23, 2001, Secretary of State Colin Powell said as much: "We will put before the world, the American people, a persuasive case." *New York Times,* 24 September 2001, p. 21.

40. *Newsweek,* 4 February 2002, p. 27.

41. Seymour Hersh, "Annals of National Security: What Went Wrong," *New Yorker,* 8 October 2001. Hersh writes: "Every one of Tenet's close friends told me, 'He's history.'"

42. "CIA Reports Officer Killed in Prison Uprising," *Washington Post,* 29 November 2001.

43. This is covered in chapter 6, "Preemption: 2000–2001."

44. *Wall Street Journal,* 27 September 2001, p. 19. The article predicted that the stock of the bin Laden Group would appreciate because of its equity position in Carlyle (with former secretary of state James Baker and former secretary of defense Frank Carlucci as principals), a merchant bank that would get huge war-on-terrorism contracts.

45. BBC News, 18 October 2001. Former CIA counterterrorism officer Vince Cannistraro confirmed this. He told Jane Mayer that there was "an interconnectedness among family members that frustrates and tantalizes American investigators." See "The House of Bin Laden," *New Yorker,* 12 November 2001, p. 37.

46. These comments are from an untitled and undated compendium on the Internet.

47. Sean O'Neill (1967–2001) was the author's cousin. James O'Neill (1928–2002) was his uncle.

Chapter 2   Blowback: How America Enabled the Rise of Terrorism

1. Alexis de Tocqueville, *Democracy in America* (New York: Everyman's Library, 1994 reprint), vol. 2, chapter 7.

2. Nobel Symposium 95, "The Intervention in Afghanistan and the Fall of Détente," Lysbu, 17–20 September 1995. The Norwegian Nobel Institute, Oslo, 1996.

3. Selig Harrison, "The Shah, not the Kremlin, Touched Off the Afghan Coup," *Washington Post,* 13 May 1979, p. 17.

4. Confidential interview 27 (a U.S. military attaché, Defense Intelligence Agency, who served in Afghanistan in the 1970s). Confidential interview 6 (a senior policymaker in the State Department in the Carter administration).

5. Colin Powell (with Joseph E. Persico), *My American Journey* (New York: Random House, 1995), p. 242.

6. Stephen Kinzer, *All the Shah's Men: An American Coup and the Roots of Middle Eastern Terror* (New York: John Wiley & Sons, 2003), p. x.

7. Ibid., p. 37.

8. This is from declassified Politburo documents published in the *Washington Post,* 15 November 1992, p. 17.

9. Department of State Report, 16 August 1979. Vol. 30.

10. Vincent Javert, "Avec Zbigniew Brzezinski," *Nouvel Observateur*, 15–21 January 1998.

11. As quoted in Artyom Borovik, *The Hidden War* (New York: Grove, 1990), p. 5.

12. Ibid., pp. 10–11.

13. Nobel Symposium 95, "The Intervention in Afghanistan and the Fall of Détente," Lysbu, 17–20 September 1995. The Norwegian Nobel Institute, Oslo 1996, p. 81.

14. Memo appended in John K. Cooley, *Unholy Wars: Afghanistan, America and International Terrorism* (London: Pluto Press, 1999), p. 247.

15. Jimmy Carter, *Keeping Faith: Memoirs of a President* (New York: Bantam Doubleday, 1982), p. 248.

16. *Washington Post,* 3 January 1980, p. 21. *Newsweek,* 18 January 1981, pp.14–16.

17. It is now obvious from declassified Soviet documents that the major, and possibly exclusive, reason why the Soviet Union invaded Afghanistan was to keep it from slipping into the hands of the U.S. and endangering Russia's southern Muslim border. This is what Soviet officials concluded in 1979 and presented at the Oslo conference in 1995.

18. Carter, *Keeping Faith*, pp. 471–74.

19. Ibid., p. 143.

20. "There was a seesawing relationship between Carter and his two principal foreign-affairs specialists, Cyrus Vance, the secretary of state, and Zbigniew Brzezinski. Vance took a 'soft' line in foreign affairs, placing great faith in the value of negotiation and diplomacy, Brzezinski was the opposite, seeing the Soviets as presenting a constant challenge in a bipolar world and any crisis not dealt with firmly as a potential flash point for even greater trouble. When Carter gave a speech on foreign policy, each man sent him diametrically opposed drafts which he resolved by incorporating both into his speech." John Ranelagh, *The Agency: The Rise and Decline of the CIA* (London: Touchstone, 1987), p. 650.

21. Jeane J. Kirkpatrick, *Dictatorships and Double Standards: Rationalism and Reason in Politics* (New York: Simon and Schuster, 1982), p. 37.

22. The author, while a graduate student in international relations at the School of Advanced International Studies in 1975, spent two hours in a colloquy with Brzezinski on October 10, 1975. Dr. Robert E. Osgood, the SAIS dean, hosted the discussion.

23. In interview with the author in December 1975, W. Averell Harriman, former American ambassador to the Soviet Union, criticized Brzezinski as "totally anti-Soviet." Harriman unsuccessfully lobbied President-elect Carter to pass up Brzezinski for national security adviser.

24. Col. Charles A. Beckwith and Donald Knox, *Delta Force: The U.S. Counter-Terrorist Unit and the Iranian Hostage Rescue Mission* (London: Avon, 1984), p. 221.

25. U.S. Vietnam tactics are described in the obituary of General Creighton Abrams, *New York Times,* July 13, 2003, p. 16. Also Shelby L. Stanton, *The Rise and Fall of an American Army: U.S. Ground Forces in Vietnam, 1965–1975* (New York: Dell, 1987); Timothy J. Lomperis, *The War Everyone Lost — And Won* (Washington, D.C.: Congressional Quarterly Press, 1993).

26. Alexander Coburn and Jeffrey St. Clair, *Whiteout: The CIA, Drugs and the Press* (London: Verso, 1998). There was the report of booby-trapped toys, but these had been "psyops" by the mujahideen. Then there was the report of chemical warfare by the Soviets in the form of "yellow rain," but this turned out to be, as the *Guardian* reported, "one part bee feces, plus many parts State Department disinformation mixed with media gullibility." Rather reported that the AK-47s carried by the mujahideen were captured from fallen Russian soldiers, pp. 255–56.

27. Quoted in Mary Anne Weaver, *Pakistan: In the Shadow of Jihad and Afghanistan* (New York: Farrar, Straus and Giroux), p. 80.

28. Milt Bearden, "Black Ops: The Departments of Disinformation," *Washington Post,* 20 July 2003, p. 20.

29. CIA Field Report, 30 October 1979.

30. Interview with Alfred McCoy "Causes and Cures: National Teleconference on the Narcotics Epidemic," 9 November 1999. McCoy has written the most authoritative account to date of this nexus in *The Politics of Heroin: CIA Complicity in the Global Drug Trade* (New York: Lawrence Hill & Co., 1991).

31. Cockburn and St. Clair, *Whiteout,* p. 260.

32. James Adams, *Trading in Death: The Modern Arms Race* (London: Hutchinson, 1990), pp. 66–68.

33. Tim Weiner, *Blank Check: The Pentagon's Black Budget* (New York: Warner, 1990), p. 253.

34. Robert D. Kaplan reports that Hekmatyar, a creation of Zia, was "loathed by all the other party leaders, fundamentalist and moderate alike." *Soldiers of God: With Islamic Warriors in Afghanistan and Pakistan* (New York: Random House, 1990), pp. 68–69. He reports the range of his killings on pp. 169–170. Hekmatyar's men ambushed and killed thirteen of Massoud's commanders as well as tortured

and murdered his friend Jan Mahmad. Michael Griffin, *Reaping the Whirlwind: The Taliban Movement in Afghanistan* (London: Pluto Press, 2001), pp. 22–23.

35. The ISI liked him because, as a loyal ISI agent, he governed the three million Pashtun refugees in Pakistan with a bloody fist. Departing from the usual safe verbiage of the diplomat, Robert Neumann, a former U.S. ambassador to Afghanistan, echoed a widespread conviction: "Hekmatyar is a nut, an extremist and a very violent man. He was built up by Pakistan. Unfortunately, our government went along with the Pakistanis. We were supplying the money but they [the Pakistani officials] were making the policy."

36. Barnett Rubin, *The Search for Peace in Afghanistan: From Buffer State to Failed State* (New Haven: Yale University Press, 1995), p. 94.

37. Kaplan, *Soldiers of God,* p. 171.

38. Quoted in Bobovik, *The Hidden War,* p. 251.

39. Vincent Javert, "Avec Zbigniew Brzezinski," *Nouvel Observateur,* 15–21 January 1998.

40. See Weaver, *Pakistan,* p. 87.

41. Philip J. Caputo, *A Rumor of War* (New York: Henry Holt, 1977), p. xxi.

42. Paul M. Kennedy, *The Rise and Fall of the Great Powers: Economic Change and Military Conflict from 1500 to 2000* (New York: Random House, 1988).

43. The bombing killed 220 Marines, 18 sailors, and 3 U.S. Army servicemen.

44. Powell, *My American Journey,* pp. 291–92.

45. Quoted in Max Boot, *The Savage Wars of Peace* (New York; Basic, 2002), pp. 318–19, from Powell, *My American Journey.*

46. Powell, *My American Journey,* pp. 302–3.

47. Quoted in Boot, *The Savage Wars of Peace,* p. 319.

48. In reaction to the Marine Corps barracks bombing, Congressman John McCain (R-Ariz), a freshman congressman who had spent six and one-half years of his life in prison in North Vietnam, quoted General Maxwell Taylor's standard for U.S. military intervention:

> First, the objectives of the involvement must be explainable to the man in the street in one or two sentences. Second, there must be clear support by the Congress for the involvement. Third, there must be a reasonable expectation of success. Fourth, we must have the support of our allies for our objectives. And finally, there must be a clear U.S. national interest at stake.

Like the Powell doctrine, the essence of Taylor's conclusion is that the case for war must be compelling, clearly communicated, and have the support of the Congress and America's allies. Otherwise, don't do it.

49. Quoted in Richard J. Barnet, *Roots of War* (New York: Scribner, 1971), p. 132.

50. Powell, *My American Journey,* p. 98.

51. Chester Cooper, *The Lost Crusade: America in Vietnam* (New York: Dodd, Mead, 1970), p. 422. Another lesson from Vietnam pertained to the limits of counterinsurgency (the training and equipping of native forces to resist insurgency) made popular in the Kennedy administration. The first experiment, in which the CIA directed a counterinsurgent invasion in the Bay of Pigs using military and ex-military as advisers, ended ignominiously. In Vietnam, the Agency did no better, inserting some 500 Vietnamese agents into North Vietnam, all of whom were either killed or "turned." In June 1961, in three National Security Action Memoranda (NSAMs), Kennedy transferred unconventional warfare to the Pentagon. By this time, U.S. Army Special Forces (the Green Berets) were recruiting and training Vietnam's ethnic minorities in the western highlands and forming them into Civilian Irregular Defense Groups (CIDGs) to fight the Viet Cong. The Special Forces on their own went deep into North Vietnam and Cambodia in successful search-and-rescue missions. This "low-intensity warfare," in which the Green Berets lived with and integrated themselves with the locals, many of whom were aborigine, made distinct headway in 1962 and 1963. Then, with Kennedy's death and the expansion of the war, came a new commander, General William Westmoreland. "Westy," a decorated veteran of World War II, used a formula he knew well: attack with large forces and heavy armor and, through firepower, annihilate the enemy. This had worked well against the Wehrmacht, but it went nowhere in Vietnam, where the enemy would melt away before large forces attempting to "search-and-destroy" them. The covert war went on, commanded by the "Studies and Observation Group" (SOG), but the regular Army's high command didn't believe in it, and the CIA progressively pulled out of it. The CIA's station in Saigon, which was supposed to contribute three dozen "first string" intelligence officers to SOG, only seconded thirteen in 1964 and nine in 1965. The Agency was looking to run its own projects. One such project, spearheaded by the CIA and South Vietnamese security forces, was designed to break the Communist military and intelligence apparatus in South Vietnam. It was called the Phoenix Program.

As always, numbers sustained the ends — and covered up the means. Phoenix's director, former Saigon CIA station chief (and later CIA director) William Colby, was able to report that some 26,000 Viet Cong cadres were killed and another 33,000 captured. In fact, Phoenix was a poorly disguised assassination program that occasioned several congressional investigations. Bart Osborn, a U.S. Army

Intelligence officer, in testimony before Congress in 1972, described the Phoenix Program:

> I never knew in the course of all of these operations any detainee to live through his interrogation. They all died. There was never any reasonable establishment of the fact that any one of those individuals was, in fact, cooperating with the VC, but they all died and the majority were either tortured to death or things like thrown out of helicopters.

The Special Forces' marriage with the paramilitaries of the CIA's Directorate of Operations began — for better or worse — in Vietnam. Special Forces required the Agency's ground intelligence to launch many of its operations, and the CIA operatives needed the military's skill and command-and-control. For all the necessity of intermeshing personnel, intelligence, and operations, there was much incompatibility, however. In the memory of then Major Patrick Lang, agency operatives would often abandon field when the shooting started.

The CIA actively countenanced assassination, which was not a normal combat procedure for the Special Forces. In the spring of 1969, a Special Forces intelligence-collection detachment called "B-57" (part of Project Gamma) encountered evidence that one of their South Vietnamese allied personnel was trafficking in information and weapons sales with the North Vietnamese. At the CIA's encouragement, the man was executed after a lengthy interrogation. When this came to the attention of the regular Army high command, General Abrams ordered several Special Forces personnel, including Colonel Robert B. Rheault, to be court-martialed for murder. In the subsequent investigation, citing national security concerns, the Agency took a hike. Fortunately for the Green Berets involved, a recon team some months later killed a North Vietnamese officer, whose large leather satchel contained a list of agents, double agents, and spies. The executed double agent's name was on the list. The investigation was discontinued.

In Laos, the CIA joint-ventured with the locals — and achieved disaster. Because of its long border with Vietnam, the country was judged critical to the U.S. containment enterprise. The Ho Chi Minh Trail, the conduit of North Vietnam's infiltration of troops and weapons into South Vietnam, ran for 125 kilometers through Laos. The "neutralization" agreement reached between the U.S. and the Soviet Union in Geneva in 1963 supposedly kept the cold war from polarizing the poor, abysmally governed country, but the secret war went on. In the face of Communist Pathet Lao expansion, the CIA put together, at a cost of $300 million a year, "L'Armée Clandestine," a force of 30,000 militia under the tutelage of General Vang Pao. It became obvious within a matter of months that General Pao's interest in fighting Communists was incidental to his dedication to becoming a drug lord.

For Ted Shackley, CIA station chief in Vientiane, the use of irregular resources in black operations had not been a problem in previous posts. Operating out of a CIA base known as JM/WAVE from 1961 through 1963, he had overseen a series of assassination sorties against Fidel Castro, sorties that had employed Mafia henchmen, such as "Colonel" Johnny Roselli, to train snipers. As would later occur in Aghanistan and Central America, the Agency, in order to achieve some degree of command-and-control over the anti-Communist rabble, effectively franchised a guaranteed growth industry to its client — drugs.

Through a CIA front called "Air America," American pilots began ferrying not only the Laotian militia but opium bricks. Thanks to USAID's construction of 150 landing strips in the mountains of Laos, the opium trade spiraled. Ron Rickenbach, the head of the AID in the area, later admitted: "I was on the air strips. My people were in charge of supplying the aircraft. I was in the areas where the opium was grown. I personally witnessed it being placed on Air America planes. We didn't create the opium product. But our presence accelerated it dramatically."

By 1971, the situation was out of control. Neither of America's client regimes in Vietnam or Laos cared to fight, but they did share a corrupt dependency on their powerful patron. The use of drugs by American troops was spreading like a cancer, with one government agency actually assisting in the transport of opium, whose derivative, heroin, had already addicted between 40,000 and 80,000 U.S. troops in Vietnam.

Years before, a great general of World War II, Douglas MacArthur, had warned President Kennedy and his superb men about the dangerous frontier of containment in Asia. "The chickens are coming home to roost," MacArthur had said, "and you're in the chicken house." The war was going nowhere. After a decade of stoking the fires of anti-Communist phobia, now fortified by their own self-inflicted idiocies ("better to be dead than Red" or "America doesn't die for a tie"), the ruling class was committing a form of homicide, which, out of pride and military-industrial momentum, they could neither reform nor reverse.

After the war, the U.S. military entered into a chamber of disgrace. The performance of most units — especially the Special Forces — had been laudable. But the political objectives of the war, wrong in concept and contradicted in operation, left no chance for victory. Some, like Ronald Reagan, rhetorically imagined that "if we had only given our military permission to win," it would have worked out victoriously. But that particular caricature bumped up against the old reality, that under Democratic and Republican presidents and under various commanding generals, a land war — or a nuclear war — with China could not be hazarded. The American left faulted President Nixon and his national security adviser Dr. Kissinger for the manner in which they washed their hands of Vietnam, but what else could they do? Together Nixon and Kissinger struck a brilliant blow for peace in the opening to China, which in one stunning act of diplomacy accomplished what all the bloody little (and not-so-little) wars, and all the anti-Communist hectoring with its endless budgets, had failed to do: split the Communist world, definitively and irreparably, in two.

After the Vietnam War, the Special Forces dwindled down to a mere fraction of their original size. The paramilitary wing of the CIA was disbanded; virtually all the leaders in the Directorate of Operations, which commanded that wing, were forcibly retired. The reconstitution of those forces, which took place in the middle 1980s, was based on a far more sophisticated concept of training and deployment than before. Intelligence, integrated into the mission from the start, was used to drive the execution of the mission. The paramilitaries recruited by the CIA would themselves be veterans of elite combat units. When Mike Spann reported in at CIA headquarters in February 1999, he benefited from an immeasurable advantage in his training in unconventional warfare: all his trainers in every thing from hand-to-hand combat, to "halo" (high-altitude low-opening) drops, to sniping were Special Forces veterans of Vietnam.

52. Fred C. Ikle, *Every War Must End* (New York: Columbia University Press, 1991). Ikle was the undersecretary of defense for policy during the Reagan administration.

53. This is the paraphrase used in the PBS *Frontline* interview with William Kristol, "The War Behind Closed Doors," 14 January, 2003.

54. George H. W. Bush and Brent Scowcroft, *A World Transformed* (New York: Vintage, 1999), p. 391.

55. Ibid., p. 531.

56. "The War Behind Closed Doors."

57. "Colin Powell: Odd Man Out," *Time,* 10 September 2001, pp. 13–18.

58. Thucydides, *The Peloponnesian War,* book 3:37–38, 44 ed. Gregory Crane, the Perseus Digital Library, Tufts University.

59. David E. Sangar, "Rice Faults Past Administrations on Terror," *New York Times,* 31 October 2003, p. 14.

60. Condoleezza Rice, "Promoting the National Interest," *Foreign Affairs,* January/February 2000, vol. 79, no. 1, p. 49.

61. Confidential interviews 7 and 22.

62. Bin Laden, quoted in ABC News interview (conducted by John Miller), 28 May 1998.

63. Boot, *The Savage Wars of Peace,* p. 322.

64. Dana Priest, *The Mission: Waging War and Keeping Peace with America's Military* (New York: W. W. Norton, 2003), p. 23.

65. Tom Clancy with General Carl Stiner (ret.) and Tony Kolz, *Shadow Warriors: Inside the Special Forces* (New York: Berkley, 2002), p. 471.

66. In their book *Shadow Warriors,* Stiner and Clancy in Appendix I provide an excellent summary of the U.S. Special Operations Command in terms of its history and evolution.

67. The paramilitary wing of the CIA, in terms of training and deployment, is discussed in greater depth in chapter 4, "Soldier: The Making of Mike Spann."

68. Priest, *The Mission.*

69. Powell presented the plan. See Powell, *My American Journey,* p. 565.

70. John P. Murtha, *From Vietnam to 9/11: On the Frontlines of National Security* (University Park: Pennsylvania State Press, 2003), p. 148.

71. Ibid., p. 157.

72. Powell, *My American Journey,* p. 584.

73. So bin Laden later claimed, and experts such as Rohan Gunaratna agreed. Rohan Gunaratna, *Inside Al-Qaeda: Global Network of Terror* (New York: Columbia University Press, 2002), p. 157.

74. See Richard Mahoney, "La Emboscada de Historia," *El Comercio,* 3 March 2003, p. 20.

75. Mark Bowden, *Black Hawk Down: A Story of Modern War* (New York: Atlantic Monthly Press,1999).

76. Ibid., p. 111.

77. Murtha, *From Vietnam to 9/11,* p. 161.

78. Ted Galen Carpenter, *Bad Neighbor Policy: Washington's Futile War on Drugs* (New York: Palgrave Macmillan, 2003), pp. 1–2.

79. Powell, *My American Journey,* pp. 576–77.

80. His account is superlative. Richard Holbrooke, *To End a War* (New York: Modern Library, 1999).

81. Joseph Nye, *The Paradox of American Power* (New York: Oxford University Press, 2002).

82. Richard N. Haass, "The Squandered Presidency: Demanding More from the Commander in Chief," *Foreign Affairs,* May/June 2000, pp. 31–49.

83. Interview, Richard F. Celeste, U.S. ambassador to India, 1999–2001.

84. Cooley, *Unholy Wars,* p. 193.

85. Quoted in the *Congressional Record,* 7 October 1994, Hon. Peter Deutsch, p. 314.

86. Ahmed Rashid, *Taliban* (New Haven: Yale University Press, 2000), pp. 184–87.

87. The regime of Prime Minister Benazir Bhutto (1988–89) was an exception to this.

88. Quoted in Roger Faligot and Remi Kauffer, *Les Maîtres Espions* (Paris: Gallimard, 1998), p. 231.

Chapter 3 Counterterrorist: The Crusade of John O'Neill

1. Daniel Benjamin and Steven Simon, *The Age of Sacred Terror* (New York: Random House, 2002), pp. 22–24.

2. Interview: Clarke.

3. See Lawrence Wright, "Profiles: The Counter-Terrorist," *New Yorker,* 14 January 2002, pp. 27–46.

4. Interview: Clarke.

5. Ibid.

6. Wright, "The Counter-Terrorist," *New Yorker,* 14 January 2002.

7. Interview: Jadish Singh, Bureau of State Security.

8. Remarks of John P. O'Neill, Explosives Detection Symposium and Aviation Security Technology Conference, 8 November 1996.

9. Wright, "The Counter-Terrorist."

10. In June 2001 thirteen members of Saudi Hizbollah, a group with links to Iranian intelligence agents, were indicted for the attack.

11. Interview: Clarke.

12. *Frontline* interview: Frances Townsend. Freeh denied the story.

13. In *War in a Time of Peace,* David Halberstam would later depict the hesitant, incremental qualities of executive indecision in the Clinton administration.

14. The concept of "stealth imperialism" is in Chalmers Johnson, *Blowback: The Costs and Consequences of American Empire* (New York: Henry Holt, 2000), p. 65.

15. Executive Summary, "Personal Accountability for Force Protection at Khobar Towers," William S. Cohen, 31 July 1997.

16. Cooley, *Unholy Wars,* p. 237.

17. *Frontline* interview: Robert "Bear" Bryant, then deputy director of the FBI.

18. The other girlfriend remained in D.C. until 1999. She was Anna di Battista.

19. Interview: Lorraine di Taranto.

20. Wright, "The Counter-Terrorist."

21. Interview: Townsend.

22. Part of the interview can be seen on PBS *Frontline,* "The Man Who Knew."

23. Two of O'Neill's fellow special agents in the New York office confirmed this point, and, in so doing, requested confidentiality.

24. ABC News, "Preparing for Terror?" 3 March 2003.

25. The author viewed O'Neill's notes on an "eyes-only" basis.

26. Interview: Clarke.

27. Interview: Isham.

28. Interview: Wesley Wong, special agent, FBI.

29. John Miller's account, published in *Esquire,* 1 February 1999, is excerpted and reprinted in *Frontline,* www.pbs.org.

30. Interview: Dr. Fahdi Babukar, professor of Arabic.

31. "Greetings, America. My name is Osama bin Laden," *Frontline*'s reprint of Miller's account of the interview.

32. In their history of the Special Forces, Tom Clancy and General Carl Stiner devote three paragraphs in 500 pages to Somalia, emphasizing the humanitarian successes of getting food to the interior of the country. Max Boot, in his analysis of "the savage wars of peace," blames the withdrawal of large-force heavily armed Marine units as the reason for the disaster. Boot, *The Savage Wars of Peace,* pp. 334–35.

33. Interview: Fran Townsend, PBS, 30 May 2002. Interview: Robert M. Bryant, PBS, 2 July 2002. Bryant, the deputy director of the FBI, who was out of town at the time, refused in interview to identify Pickard — saying only that he had nothing to do with it.

34. Interview: Townsend.

35. James Risen, "To Bomb Sudan Plant, or Not: A Year Later, Debate Still Rankles," *New York Times,* 27 October 1999, p. 3. Seymour Hersh's account is

more damning: "Annals of National Security: The Missiles of August," *New Yorker*, 12 October 1998, pp. 34–41.

36. Peter L. Bergen, *Holy War, Inc.: Inside the Secret World of Osama bin Laden* (New York: Touchstone, 2001), pp. 122–25.

37. *Times (of India)*, 21 September 2001.

38. Benjamin Barber, *Jihad vs. McWorld* (New York: Ballantine, 2001), p. 222.

39. Nicholas Lemann reviews alternative theories about terrorism in Lemann, "What Terrorists Want," *New Yorker*, 29 October 2001.

40. Dore Gold, *Hatred's Kingdom: How Saudi Arabia Supports the New Global Terrorism* (Washington, D.C.: Regnery, 2003).

41. ABC News, 21 May 2003.

42. Interview: Clarke.

43. I am grateful to the FBI special agents in the New York office who worked the case as well as two of the members of the NYPD detail assisting the FBI during the millennium investigation.

44. Interview: Townsend.

45. The read on Al-Qaeda is that the number of suicidal assets it can muster is extensive, but the lieutenants that are deployed to command those sorties are rare and valued.

46. Interview: Clint Guenther.

47. CNN News, "Revised Timeline Raises New Questions about USS Cole Security," 20 October 2000.

48. Quoted in CNN, "Last Four Bodies from USS Cole Come Home as Investigation Continues," 22 October 2000.

49. "Remote Yemen May Be Key to Terrorist's Past and Future," *New York Times*, 5 November 2000.

50. Cited in ibid.

51. Quoted in Bergen, *Holy War, Inc.*, p. 194.

52. Interview: Barry Mawn.

53. Interview: Valerie James.

54. Interview: Chris Isham.

55. The interagency group on which O'Neill and Clarke sat recommended just that to the National Security Council. Interview: Richard Clarke.

56. Confidential interview 11 (a former FBI assistant director).

57 *Washington Post,* January 31, 2001, as cited in Bergen, *Holy War, Inc.,* p. 187.

58. Interview: Frances Townsend.

59. John Miller and Michael Stone with Chris Mitchell, *The Cell: Inside the 9/11 Plot, and Why the FBI and the CIA Failed to Stop It* (New York: Hyperion, 2002), p. 261.

60. Wright, "The Counter-Terrorist."

61. "Cole Inquiry Provokes Bitter U.S. Dispute," *New York Times,* 12 November 2000.

62. Wright, "The Counter-Terrorist."

63. *New York Times,* 5 November 2000.

64. Interview: James.

65. Her statement in the Sunday *Times* is quoted in "A Chronology of John O'Neill's Life and FBI Career."

66. Interview: Townsend.

67. Interview: Mawn .

68. Interview: Townsend. In her interview Townsend points out that the whole issue of classified material — from the then U.S. ambassador to Israel to Wen Ho Lee's alleged transgression — was very hot.

69. Interview: Townsend.

70. Confidential interview 38 (an NSC staffer specializing in counterterrorism who continued on in the Bush administration).

71. Fran Townsend reads this note in her interview.

Chapter 4   Soldier: The Making of Mike Spann

1. Interview: Odene May.

2. Interview: Joe Hubbert. Hubbert, who now owns and runs the Boar's Butt restaurant, rated as one of the best of its kind in northwestern Alabama, was a star college football player and then a professional wrestler.

3. According to his pilot log book, Mike soloed for the first time on June 30, 1986.

4. Warren Strobel, "CIA Agent Killed Remembered for Having 'Heart of Gold,' " Knight-Ridder, 2 December 2001.

5. Interview: Bill West.

6. "The Heritage of Marion County, Alabama," *Almanac of Alabama* (Tuscaloosa: University of Alabama Press, 1983), p. 2.

7. See Dodd and Dodd, "Winston: An Antebellum History of the Hill Country of Northern Alabama," in Carl Elliott, ed., *Annals of Northwest Alabama* (Tuscaloosa: privately published, 1971), vol. 4.

8. Wesley S. Thompson, *The Free State of Winston: A History of Winston County, Alabama* (Winfield, Ala.: Pareil Press, 1968).

9. Ibid., pp. 68–75.

10. Interview: Randy Brown. Brown serves as the president of the Sons of Confederate Veterans.

11. James Michael Hill, *Celtic Warfare, 1595–1763* (Edinburgh, UK: John Donald, 1986).

12. See Larry Stephens, *Mossbacks and Bushwhackers: Domestic Terrorism in Civil War Alabama* (Carrolton, Ga.: Battle Flag Press, 2001).

13. The author interviewed three officers who served with Mike Spann — Major Tray Ardese, Lt. Col. Justin Orabona, and Captain Michael Tapen — as well as seven enlisted men.

14. This information is from the ledgers and miscellaneous publications collected by the Winfield Public Library.

15. Michael Beschloss, "Carl Elliott, Sr.," in Caroline Kennedy, ed., *Profiles in Courage for Our Time* (New York: Hyperion, 2003).

16. Carl Elliott, Sr., ed., *Annals of Northwest Alabama,* vols. 1–5 (Tuscaloosa: privately published, 1971).

17. Winston S. Churchill to the House of Commons, October 28, 1943.

18. By Charles Edward Pollock (1853–1924).

19. Interview: Randy Sanders.

20. Interview: Tina Cantrell.

21. Interview: Jason Cantrell.

22. Andrew Tully, *CIA: The Inside Story* (New York: William Morrow, 1962), p. 266.

23. Tully's conclusion is worth full quotation, for it captures a certain moral schizophrenia in the justification for secret wars:

> But the argument still rages . . . [between] those who insist that in any such operation [to overthrow a government] use of United States armed forces is essential to insure success . . . [or] those who insist that a nation dedicated to morality and the rule of law cannot dispatch its soldiers and airmen to overthrow a foreign government, but may — in accordance with general international practice — give secret help to such an attempt by nationalists of the country in question.

24. Interview: James Wyers.

25. Paul Goodwin, *No Shining Armor: The Marines in Vietnam*. (New York: Ballantine, 1997).

26. Quoted in Ronald J. Brown, *A Few Good Men: A History of the Fighting Fifth Marines* (New York: Presidio, 2001), p. 84.

27. See Col. Joseph M. Alexander, USMC (Ret.), *The Battle History of the U.S. Marines: A Fellowship of Valor* (New York: Basic, 2000), p. 378.

28. Quoted in *The Globe* (Camp Lejeune's Marine newspaper), 7 October 1996.

29. *Marines: Official Magazine of the Marine Corps,* Almanac 1997.

30. Zinni is quoted in Priest, *The Mission,* pp. 64–65.

31. This account is based on the chapter, "Okinawa: Asia's Last Colony," in Chalmers Johnson, *Blowback,* pp. 41–64.

32. Johnson, *Blowback,* p. 55. The numbers are from FY 1998.

33. The rape occurred at knifepoint near Futenma Marine Corps Air Station. The vehicular homicide took place at Futenma in early January 1996 when a female Marine drove off the road and struck and killed a mother and her two daughters.

34. Interview: Jason Cantrell. Mike Spann's Auburn roommate was a personal reference for Mike's application to the FBI.

35. Spann had previously attended Church of Christ services at Camp Hansen.

36. Mike Spann to Aaron Catrett, 19 October 1999.

37. Interview: Michael Tapen.

38. *The Globe,* 28 October 1997.

39. See *The Globe,* 4 December 1996.

40. Interview: Tapen.

41. Interview: Lt. Col. Justin Orabona (Spann's first commander with UNITAS).

42. See Ronald H. Cole, "Operation Urgent Fury: The Planning and Execution of Joint Operations in Grenada, 12 October–3 November 1983," Office of the Joint Chiefs of Staff.

43. See "Army Is Devising Ways to Reorganize Its Forces," *New York Times*, 6 August 2003

44. Ross A. Parrish (Capt. USMC) to Johnny Spann, 21 April 2003.

45. Ross A. Parrish to Johnny Spann, 21 April 2003.

46. Once ordered, the arrangement admittedly turned a little tortuous. Sgt. Elzie was subjected to "separation" into "standby reserve." It was sort of a nondischarge discharge. See *The Globe*, 1 April 1993. The examples of bemedaled gay military heroes are ample. One unit well-known for its lifestyle (though that was not the word given them in World War II) was Carlson's Raiders, an extraordinarily brave assault force in the South Pacific. Their medals and commendations were only exceeded by their casualty rate.

47. Hackworth is quoted in "Defending America," 12 February 1997.

48. Cohen is quoted on CNN, 11 July 1997.

49. Clinton, despite a certain degree of infamy in the Corps, came twice to Lejeune during Mike Spann's time as a Marine. Perhaps it was emblematic of Marine discipline and honor of command that the president was received warmly and enthusiastically during his two visits (April 6, 1993, and December 23, 1996). Mike's buddy Captain Mike Tapen advanced the president's visit on behalf of General Charles Wilhelm, the commander of the Second Marine Expeditionary Force.

50. Ross A. Parrish to Johnny Spann, 21 April 2003.

51. Interview: Tapen.

52. See "Las Alas Largas del Cartel Azul," *El Tiempo* (de Bogotá), 11 November 1998. The "Blue Cartel" refers to the Colombian air force.

53. This defense contractor was DynCorp. See the *Nation*, 20 June 2000.

54. The author, who worked in human relief during the late 1990s in Colombia, visited a field clinic where young children were being treated. See also Martin Jelsma and Tom Blickman, TNI Briefing Paper, November 1998.

55. Priest, *The Mission*, p. 206.

56. See Horace Carter, *Buddy: Ernie Pyle, World War II's Most Beloved Typewriter Soldier* (North Carolina, 1982).

57. Interview: Johnny Spann.

58. J. M. Spann to Clandestine Service Trainee Division, 30 January 1998.

59. Spann's captain's salary was $45,000. His starting pay as a trainee in the Clandestine Service Division was $8,000 less than that, according to his father.

60. Interview: Johnny Spann.

61. Mike Charters to Micheal Spann, 21 August 1998.

62. Merritt's book is a well-presented manual of how and where to apply for work in the defense and intelligence areas.

63. Thomas, *The Very Best Men: Four Who Dared: The Early Years of the CIA* (New York: Simon & Schuster, 1995), p. 311.

64. Richard Mahoney, *Sons and Brothers: The Days of Jack and Bobby Kennedy,* pp. 228–30.

65. Robert Baer, *See No Evil: The True Story of a Ground Soldier in the CIA's War on Terrorism* (New York: Crown, 2002).

66. David Wise, "Why the Spooks Shouldn't Run Wars: The CIA's Paramilitary Role Has a History of Disaster," *Time,* 3 February 2003.

67. National Security Action Memorandum file, 1961, National Security Files, John F. Kennedy Presidential Library.

68. Mahoney, *Sons and Brothers,* p. 128.

69. Quoted in the *Dallas Morning News,* 27 October 1992.

70. Confidential interview 39. The Israelis and the British SAS deploy combat personnel who are fluent in foreign languages.

71. See Special Operations.com, Central Intelligence Agency, Special Activities Staff (SAS).

72. "The Plan" is detailed in Report of the U.S. Senate Select Committee on Intelligence and the U.S. House Permament Select Committee on Intelligence, "Joint Inquiry," December 2002, p. 231.

73. Three of Mike's friends, interviewed for this history, shared their recollections on this subject on condition of confidentiality.

74. Confidential interview 19 (one of Spann's fellow SAD officers who accompanied him to Afghanistan).

75. Interview: Johnny Spann.

76. Quoted in Edward Klein, "If Anything Happens to Me . . . ," *Parade,* 18 August 2002.

77. Ibid.

78. Special Operations.com. SAS.

79. Bob Woodward, "Secret CIA Units Playing a Central Combat Role," *Washington Post,* 18 November 2001.

80. This is based on an interview with an Indian ex–military intelligence officer. Confidential interview 17.

81. Interview: Johnny Spann.

82. Benjamin and Simon, *The Age of Sacred Terror,* pp. 344–345.

83. Quoted in Klein, "If Anything Happens to Me . . ."

Chapter 5   Jihadi: The Journey of John Walker Lindh

1. *Newsweek,* 17 December 2001, p. 28.

2. Interview: Hassan Qureshi.

3. *Time,* 29 September 2002.

4. The Martindale-Hubbell Law Directory, www.martindale.com.

5. A good introduction to Marin County can be found in Joanne Miller, *Best Places: Marin* (Seattle: Sasquatch, 2002).

6. The author spent two days in Marin County in August 2003, guided by his brother-in-law, San Francisco native and sometime Marinian Rick Whisman.

7. Joan Didion, *Slouching towards Bethlehem* (New York: Farrar, Straus and Giroux 1968), p. 18.

8. Confidential interview 43 (a former neighbor of the Lindh family who also lived on Laurel Avenue).

9. *Newsweek,* 17 December 2001.

10. Quoted in Harry Stein, "How the Father Figures," *Weekly Standard,* 28 January 2002.

11. *Time,* 29 September 2002.

12. *Newsweek,* 17 December 2001.

13. This translation is by Michael Sells. It can be found in Michael Sells, ed., *Approaching the Qur'an: The Early Revelations* (Ashland: White Cloud Press, 1999), p. 90.

14. Alex Haley, *The Autobiography of Malcolm X* (New York: African-American Images, 1989), pp. 339–40.

15. The author interviewed investigator David Fecheimer as well as two FBI agents who worked on the case.

16. Interview: Robertson Gaffney.

17. Quoted in *Time,* 29 September 2002.

18. Mr. Hyland is quoted in Margie Mason, "An American Taliban in Yemen: John Walker Lindh Bumbled His Way through the Mideast," Associated Press, 3 January 2002.

19. Interview: Fecheimer.

20. "Yemen Links to Al-Qaeda Gnaw at FBI in Cole Inquiry," *New York Times,* 26 November 2000.

21. Bergen, *Holy War, Inc.,* p. 179.

22. As reported in "Unofficial Communiqué," Yemen *Gateway,* 2000.

23. As expressed by Mohammedans, Yemen is divided between the Shafia Sunni and the Zaydi Shia.

24. Karen Armstrong, *Islam* (New York: Random House, 2000), pp. 128–39.

25. Bernard Lewis makes this point as well in "Annals of Religion: The Revolt of Islam," *New Yorker,* 19 November 2001.

26. As described in *Time,* 29 September 2002.

27. *Middle East International,* 18 March 1999. Al-Iman University was closed after 9/11 and purged of radical elements but was back in the news in May 2002 after a political assassination occurred on campus. *Al-Ahram Weekly,* 26 May 2002.

28. See the *Yemen Times,* September 1998–March 1999.

29. "Lindh Correspondence," images.latimes.com.

30. Quoted in Bergen, *Holy War, Inc.,* p. 56.

31. Quoted in Mark Kukis, *"My Heart Became Attached": The Strange Odyssey of John Walker Lindh* (Washington, D.C.: Brassey's, 2003), p. 28.

32. In an e-mail to his mother dated 1 March 2001. images.latimes.com.

33. Michelangelo Signorile, "Did Homophobia Corrupt John Walker?" 9 January 2002, www.wctimes.com.

34. Quoted in *Time,* December 29, 2001.

35. Bill Gertz, *Breakdown: How America's Intelligence Failure Led to 9/11* (New York: Basic, 2002), p. 57.

36. Dore Gold, *Hatred's Kingdom: How Saudi Arabia Supports the New Global Terrorism* (New York: Regency, 2003), p. 182.

37. *Time,* 29 September 2002.

38. See "Tablighi Jamaat under US Scanner," rediff.com, 14 July 2003.

39. This is the conclusion of the authoritative former member of the Cabinet Secretariat of the Indian government, B. Raman. "Dagestan: Focus on Pakistan's Tablighi Jamaat," undated.

40. See "Chowchilla, Ripe for Exploitation?" *Islamica Community,* undated. Also *New York Times,* 14 July 2003.

41. In his account of the odyssey of John Walker Lindh, Mark Kukis reports that Lindh traveled eight hours east of San Francisco with the missionaries. Kukis, "*My Heart Became Attached,*" pp. 35–36.

42. Interviews: George Harris and David Fecheimer.

43. Confidential interview 32. This is also the contention of Mohammed bin Salam, columnist for the *Yemen Times.*

44. The *Yemen Times,* January–October 2000, provides the source for much of the descriptive narrative.

45. See Yemen *Gateway,* 2000.

46. *Time,* "The Taliban Next Door," 10 January 2002.

47. *CityNews,* 7 September 2002.

48. Kukis, "*My Heart Became Attached,*" p. 48.

49. See Count Three (Providing Material Support and Resources to HUM), *United States of America v. John Walker Lindh,* Indictment, General Allegations, 15 February 2002.

50. Interview: Richard F. Celeste, U.S. ambassador to India, 1997–2000.

51. Interview: Fecheimer.

52. Mark Kukis sets the scene in "*My Heart Became Attached,*" pp. 91–94.

53. Affidavit in Support of a Criminal Complaint and an Arrest Warrant, *United States of America v. John Walker Lindh,* undated.

54. There are variations in Suleyman al-Faris's account of this conversation. They are discussed in the final chapter of this book.

Chapter 6   Preemption: 2000–2001

1. See "Transcript of Condoleezza Rice on Governor George W. Bush's foreign policy," *The Charlie Rose Show,* 12 October 2000.

2. Robert Novak, CNN, 12 October 2001. Allister Heath, "Recent Developments in U.S. Foreign Policy," European Foundation Working Paper 3, 1 November 2000.

3. "Address of the Hon. George W. Bush Before a Joint Session of the Congress on the State of the Union," 27 February 2001. Transcript online on CNN.

4. Untitled article, *Multinational Monitor,* vol. 22, no. 6, June 2001.

5. *La Nación,* 21 November 1994.

6. Kenneth L. Lay to the Honorable George W. Bush, 3 April 1997.

7. "The California Energy Crisis: A Brief Summary of Events," EETD *Newsletter,* September 2001.

8. *New York Times,* 11 May 2002.

9. Fourteen of the senior appointees owned stock in Enron (Special Assistant to the President Karl Rove and Undersecretary of State Charlotte Beers each reported up to $250,000 in Enron stock). The U.S. trade representative Robert Zoellick had served on the Enron advisory board, White House chief economic adviser Lawrence Lindsey had been a highly remunerated consultant, and the new secretary of the Army, Thomas E. White, Jr., was a former Enron executive.

10. Cheney is quoted in "Blackout: The New New Power Business — Power Politics," PBS *Frontline.*

11. Quoted in the *San Francisco Chronicle,* 30 January 2002.

12. See "Who Lobbied Bush on Energy?" CBS News, 25 May 2001. *USA Today,* 23 February 2002.

13. "Who Lobbied Bush on Energy?" CBS News, 19 July 2001.

14. "Presidential Documents," *Federal Register,* 22 May 2001.

15. The "Vaughn Index" can be viewed on the website of the Natural Resources Defense Council at www.nrdc.org.

16. "White House Energy Task Force Papers Reveal Iraqi Oil Maps," *WorldNet Daily,* 18 July 2003. Regarding Secretary O'Neill's revelations, see "Bush Sought 'Way' to Invade Iraq?" *60 Minutes,* 12 January 2004, www.cbsnews.com.

17. "Strategic Energy Policy Challenges for the 21st Century," James A. Baker Institute of Public Policy at Rice University, p. 81.

18. Quoted in the *Washington Times,* 3 March 2001.

19. See Benjamin and Simon, *The Age of Sacred Terror,* p. 330. "In foreign policy circles, word circulated that the new team wanted to break the deadlock with Tehran, and oil executives close to the incoming administration confidently asserted that Bush was committed to normalizing trade relations."

20. *Guardian,* 13 May 2002. CBS News, 23 December 2002.

21. Draft of "Defense Planning Guidance," reprinted in *Frontline,* "The War behind Closed Doors," 21 February 2002.

22. Ahmed Rashid, *Taliban,* pp. 165–92.

23. See Benjamin and Simon, *The Age of Sacred Terror,* pp. 321–323. Benjamin was then serving as director for counterterrorism on the NSC staff. Simon was the senior director of counterterrorism. Their version conforms with the author's interviews of NSC personnel.

24. The ban on assassinations dated back to President Gerald Ford's executive order in 1976. Two NSC directors, quoting Paul Pillar, a CIA official, explain the means of getting around the "ban" with admirable sophistry: "This does not imply an absolute and permanent ban on assassinations, however, since whatever is barred by executive order can, of course, be changed or suspended if the president of the day were to sign a new piece of paper — in this case, a covert action finding, or a memorandum of notification if there were an existing relevant finding." Benjamin and Simon, *The Age of Sacred Terror,* p. 285.

25. Ibid., pp. 334–36.

26. *Washington Post,* 20 January 2002. Until 1998, Rice's judgment was probably accurate, but not thereafter. By 1999, the various counterterrorism command points — the Counterterrorism Center at CIA, Station Alex, the NSC's Counterterrorism and Security Group (CSG) — were humming with an urgent synchronicity, as was evident in the millennium interdiction. Clarke commanded attention and resources as no one had before. At State, his colleague was the redoubtable former Green Beret Michael Sheehan, the special coordinator for counterterrorism. On the ground in New York or Yemen — or wherever — was the relentless O'Neill.

27. "Energy Information Fact Sheet, Afghanistan," Department of Energy, 18 December 2000.

28. Press Release, Halliburton Energy Services, 27 October 1997.

29. Rashid, *Taliban*, p. 182.

30. *Boston Herald*, 10 December 2001.

31. Quoted in *Drillbits and Tailings*, 31 January 2002.

32. Quoted in Brisard and Dasquié, *Forbidden Truth: U.S.-Taliban Secret Oil Diplomacy and the Failed Hunt for Bin Laden* (New York: Thunder's Mouth Press, 2002), pp. 41–42.

33. See BBC News, 18 September 2001.

34. Executive Order unnumbered, "Blocking Property and Prohibiting Transactions with the Taliban," 6 July 1999.

35. Brisard and Dasquié, *Forbidden Truth*, p. xxix.

36. Much of the narrative about the Carlyle Group is drawn from Dan Briody, "Carlyle's Way — Making a Mint Inside the Iron Triangle of Defense, Government and Industry," *Red Herring*, 8 January 2002.

37. Briody, "Carlyle's Way."

38. Robert Baer, *Sleeping with the Devil: How Washington Sold Out Our Soul for Saudi Crude* (New York: Crown, 2003), p. 70.

39. Quoted in "Evolution of the Terrorist Threat and the U.S. Response, 1983–2001" (Top Secret, declassified). Appendix in the *9/11 Report*.

40. See *Joint Inquiry into Intelligence Community Activities Before and After the Terrorist Attacks of September 11, 2001*. Report of the U.S. Senate Select Committee on Intelligence and the U.S. House Permanent Select Committee on Intelligence, December 2002. H. Rept. 107–792. Henceforth this will be referenced as the *Joint 9/11 Report*. On pages 152–56 of the report, the analysis details the all points bulletin to federal agencies to find and arrest Khalid al-Mihdhar and Nawaf al-Hazmi, the ringleaders who later attacked the Pentagon.

41. The NSA was running the intercept. It was established in August 1998 in the course of a lead coming from the East Africa investigations. See "Deadly Mistakes," *Die Zeit*, 1 October 2002, p. 18.

42. See "Additional Views, Senator Richard Shelby," pp. 40–41. *Joint 9/11 Report*. Interview: Richard Shelby.

43. *Joint 9/11 Report*, pp. 172–73.

44. *Joint 9/11 Report,* p. 152.

45. Confidential interview 12 (FBI special agent, New York office).

46. See PBS *Frontline,* "The Man Who Knew," produced by Jim Gilmore.

47. Quoted in Additional Views, (Richard Shelby), *Joint 9/11 Report,* p. 82.

48. The e-mail is dated 29 August, 2001, and is cited in PBS *Frontline,* "The Man Who Knew."

49. Confidential interview 12. The e-mail was dated 29 August 2001.

50. PBS Interview: Chris Isham.

51. The article appeared in the *New York Times,* 19 August 2001, p. 18.

52. Miller et al., *The Cell,* p. 305.

53. PBS Interview: Frances Townsend.

54. John O'Neill to Lou Gunn, 22 August 2001.

55. Quoted in *Joint 9/11 Report,* p. 205.

56. Woodward and Eggen, "Aug. Memo Focused on Attacks in U.S.," *Washington Post,* 18 May 2002.

57. The President's Daily Briefing is described in the *Joint 9/11 Report.*

58. Jim Stewart, "Ashcroft Flying High," CBSNEWS.com, 26 July 2001.

59. During that summer of 2001, Gary Hart, who had coauthored the report on terrorism preparedness, continued to appeal, both publicly and privately, for urgency. On September 6, he addressed the International Air Transportation Association meeting in Montreal. The paper the next morning said that "Hart Predicts Terrorist Attacks on America." Later the day of the speech, he saw Condoleezza Rice. "Please get going more urgently on homeland security," he told her. Hart is interviewed in *Buzzflash,* 19 February 2003.

60. PBS Interview: Valerie James.

61. Interview: Wesley Wong.

62. Linda Robinson, "What's In the Report?" *U.S. News and World Report,* 11 August 2003, p. 20.

63. Confidential interview 4.

64. *New York Times,* 4 September 2003.

65. See BBC News, 6 November 2001.

66. *New York Times,* 27 September 2001.

67. William Safire, *New York Times,* 29 September 2001.

68. Watson's quote in the *New York Times* is as follows: "[The Saudis] were not subject to serious interviews or interrogations" (4 September 2003).

69. Confidential interview 32.

Chapter 7   Rendezvous: September–November 2001

1. Confidential interview 9 (a senior member of the Clinton National Security Council and colleague of Clarke's). See also Benjamin and Simon, *The Age of Sacred Terror,* pp. 342–46.

2. Ibid, p. 350.

3. *Times of India,* 12 October 2001. The FBI's deputy assistant director of counterterrorism, John S. Pistole, later told the U.S. Senate Governmental Affairs Committee that the U.S. had "traced the origin of the funding of 9/11 back to financial accounts in Pakistan, where high-ranking and well-known Al-Qaeda operatives played a major role in moving the money forward, eventually into the hands of the hijackers located in the U.S."

4. *Washington Post,* 18 May 2002, p. 5.

5. Quoted in Jane Mayer, "The Search for Osama," *New Yorker,* 29 June 2003.

6. Quoted in the *Joint 9/11 Report,* p. 309.

7. General Hugh Shelton is quoted in the *Joint 9/11 Report,* p. 307.

8. *Washington Post,* 30 November 2001.

9. Robert Young Pelton, "The Legend of Heavy D and the Boys," in Nate Hardcastle, ed., *American Soldier: Stories of the Special Forces from Iraq to Afghanistan* (New York: Adrenaline, 2002).

10. Confidential interview 27 (a Green Beret sergeant).

11. Interview: Johnny Spann.

12. Quoted in Moore, *The Hunt for bin Laden,* p. 63.

13. Kukis, *"My Heart Became Attached,"* pp. 112–13.

14. Ibid., p. 115.

15. CNN, "House of War."

16. Interview: Shawki Mohammed.

17. Interview: Abd al-Haribi.

18. Klein, "If Anything Happens to Me . . .", *Parade,* 18 August 2002.

Chapter 8   *The United States of America v. John Walker Lindh*

1. Interview: George C. Harris.

2. *Los Angeles Times,* September 11, 1992.

3. The Iran/Contra scandal is well covered in Bob Woodward's book *Shadow.* The other five individuals who were pardoned were Elliott Abrams, former assistant secretary of state for inter-American affairs, former national security adviser Robert McFarlane, CIA agent Clair George, and Bush lieutenants Alan Fiers and Dewey Clarridge.

4. The Consortium News, 16 August 2000, www.consortiumnews.com.

5. President George W. Bush, in comments to the press the day before his father's insights, had referred to the fact that the government had heard from "Lindh's attorney."

6. CBSNEWS.com, 1 February 2002.

7. Between 1958 and 1962, when Rehnquist was a private attorney in Arizona, he served as the director of Republican "ballot security" operations in poor neighborhoods in Phoenix. Rehnquist was part of Operation Eagle Eye, a flying squad of GOP lawyers that swept through polling places in minority-dominated districts to challenge the right of African-Americans and Latinos to vote. At the time, Democratic poll watchers had to physically push Rehnquist out of the polling place to stop him from interfering with voting rights. In 1964, Rehnquist demonstrated his segregationist sentiments when he fought the passage of a Phoenix ordinance permitting blacks to enter stores and restaurants.

8. "Letter to an American Taliban," CBSNEWS.com, 19 December 2001.

9. Confidential interview 28 (a Green Beret sergeant).

10. Kukis, *"My Heart Became Attached,"* pp. 156–157.

11. Ibid., pp. 157–161.

12. Confidential interview 28 (a Green Beret sergeant).

13. "Measuring Betrayal," interview with Jane Mayer, *New Yorker* Online, 10 March 2003.

14. "The Lindh E-Mails," the *Bulletin* (with *Newsweek*), 19 June 2002. Also Jane Mayer, "Lost in the Jihad," *New Yorker,* 10 March 2003.

15. Tape-recording is discretionary in FBI interrogations. Second agent presence is standard Bureau practice. Interview: FBI special agent (ret.) Gene Ward.

16. FBI agents use one of two procedures to sustain the integrity of their interrogations. They can either have the accused read and sign the statement, initialing any interlineations or crossed-out words, or they can file an FD 302 form, while preserving their original notes for review by the defense and the court.

17. Interview: Ward.

18. Ibid.

19. "The Lindh E-Mails," *Bulletin*, 19 June 2002.

20. Mayer, "Lost in the Jihad," *New Yorker*, 10 March 2003.

21. Memorandum to Assistant Attorney General Michael Chertoff, 19 December 2001. "Lindh Prosecution," Criminal Division, Department of Justice.

22. Interview: Tony West.

23. "American Taliban's Day in Court," CBSNEWS.com., 25 January 2002.

24. Affidavit in Support of a Criminal Complaint and an Arrest Warrant, Anne E. Asbury, *United States of America v. John Philip Walker Lindh,* United States District Court for the Eastern District of Virginia, 15 January 2002.

25. "American Taliban Due in Court," CBSNEWS.com, February 12, 2002.

26. *Virginian-Pilot,* 2 December 2002.

27. The official biography of Paul Joseph McNulty can be found at www. usdoj.gov. He was appointed U.S. attorney for the Eastern District of Virginia in September 2001.

28. In 1997, Bellows received the Attorney General's John Marshall Award for Outstanding Legal Achievement. In 1999, he received the Attorney General's Award for Excellence in Furthering the Interests of National Security. In September 2002, Virginia governor Mark Warner appointed Bellows to the Fairfax County Circuit Court.

29. Frank Shults of the U.S. attorney's office, Eastern District of Virginia, was helpful to the author.

30. Confidential interview 37 (an assistant United States attorney in the Eastern District of Virginia).

31. Senators Orrin Hatch (R–Utah) and Arlen Specter (R–Pa.) were not so easily fooled and subjected Attorney General Janet Reno and FBI director Louis Freeh to tough questioning under oath. See Online *NewsHour,* 26 September 2000.

32. Quoted in ABCNEWS.com, 17 August 2001. See also *Washington Post,* 14 August 2001.

33. Freeh testified three times on the Lee case. See CNN.com, 26 September 2000.

34. In testimony before the House Judiciary Subcommittee on Crime, quoted in Wikipedia, the Free Encyclopedia, undated.

35. In addition to his report on the Wen Ho Lee case, it was felt that Bellows unnecessarily revealed incompetence in FBI internal security in the Hanssen case, an impression not supported by the trial record.

36. Interview: David N. Kelley. In 2003 Kelley became the deputy United States attorney for the Southern District of New York.

37. *Washington Post,* 13 October 2001.

38. The complaint stated: "Walker was moved to a lawn where others whose interrogations had been completed were also moved" when he "heard shots and screaming from the basement." The indictment simply stated that "after being wounded, Lindh retreated with the other detainees to a basement area."

39. Lindh impressed everyone on the defense team interviewed for this history with his sincerity and high intelligence.

40. Rohan Gunaratna is the author of one of the better books on bin Laden and Al-Qaeda, *Inside Al-Qaeda: Global Network of Terror* (New York: Columbia University Press, 2002).

41. Dr. Sonn's biography can be found at www.islam-democracy.org.

42. Sonn is quoted here in Jane Mayer's article in the *New Yorker,* "Lost in the Jihad."

43. Transcript of interview with John Walker Lindh, CNN, 1 December 2001.

44. Interview: David Fecheimer.

45. "Did American Taliban Voice Regrets?" CBSNEWS.com, 15 March 2002. Interviews: Harris and West.

46. Transcript of Pre-Trial Hearing, 1 April 2002. *United States of America v. John Walker Lindh.*

47. See "Lindh Prosecution Wins One," CBSNEWS.com, 1 April 2002. See also legal analyst Andrew Cohen's lucid commentary in CBSNEWS.com.

48. "Evidence Ruling in Lindh Case," CBSNEWS.com, 5 April 2002.

49. *New York Times,* 12 April 2002.

50. *Seattle Post-Intelligencer,* 1 June 2002.

51. Confidential interview 24 (a Marine captain seconded to Lindh's transportation detail).

52. Radack was interviewed by Jane Mayer. See "Lost in the Jihad," *New Yorker,* 10 March 2003.

53. *Newsweek,* 24 June 2002.

54. Interviews: West, Harris.

55. "Lindh Seeks Mazar-e Sharif Witness," CBSNEWS.com, 19 April 2002.

56. Interview: Harris. Permitting himself a brief smile in interview, Harris commented, "We particularly liked that one. We felt it was very progressive."

57. Carlotta Gall and Neil A. Lewis, "Tales of Despair from Guantanamo," *New York Times,* June 17, 2003.

58. *New York Times,* 26 September 2003. The Air Force had tried to keep the charges against Airman al-Halabi secret but was overruled by the United States Air Force Court of Criminal Appeals, which ordered them opened.

59. A first-rate review of Miranda case law in terms of the Lindh case can be found in Edwin Dobb, "Should John Walker Lindh Go Free?" *Harper's,* May 2002, pp. 8–19.

60. *St. Petersburg Times,* 11 July 2002. Tampa attorney Ralph E. Fernandez had represented Cruz and the others.

61. Confidential interview 16 (a retired Defense Intelligence Agency analyst knowledgeable on the subject).

62. The author interviewed several surviving family members about the formation of the 9/11 Commission. Interviews: Robert McIlvaine, Anne Mulderry, Trish Galagher, Holly O'Neill.

63. The furor about Kissinger's appointment began in June. His resignation was in December. *The Guardian,* 14 December 2002.

64. See p. 333, note 40. *Joint 9/11 Report,* December 2002, pp. 316–24.

65. Mike Allen, "Questions Swirl around Bush over 9-11 Attacks," *Washington Post,* 16 May 2002.

66. Elisabeth Bumiller, "White House Strategy: From Attack to Admit," *New York Times,* 6 June 2002.

67. Michael Isiskoff and Mark Hosenball, "The Secrets of September 11," *Newsweek,* 30 April 2003. "Scores of contacts" is the characterization of Senator Bob Graham, the then-chair of the Senate Intelligence Committeee. Another individual associated with the Saudi Intelligence agents was Fahad Al-Thumiary, who worked in the Saudi Consulate in Los Angeles. When press approached Al-Thumiary about his role in the 9/11 plot, the U.S. government deported him in May 2003. He was not questioned by the FBI owing to his diplomatic status. "Expelled Saudi Diplomat Not a Terror Suspect, says U.S.," Agence France Presse, 13 May 2003.

68. Cohen's analysis can be found on CBSNEWS.com, 11 July 2002.

69. Mark Kukis interview with McNulty, *"My Heart Became Attached,"* pp. 172–75.

70. Interview: West.

71. "Plea Bargain," Online *NewsHour,* 15 July 2002.

72. Team Lindh tended to dignify this sort of double-talk — and continues to — in the interest of John Walker Lindh. The government continues to police the gag order (the Special Administrative Measures) that extends to witnesses and attorneys, and the federal Bureau of Prisons has full discretion over what sort of a prison life Lindh will lead. The government formally regards Lindh as a potential threat to the state.

73. *New York Times,* 23 September 2003.

74. Interview: Johnny Spann.

75. Interviews: Mohammed Niazi, Saleem Khalili. Johnny Spann's written summary of the four witnesses he spoke with in his trip to Afghanistan in December 2002 (updated: Jan. 2003).

76. Inteview: Khalili.

77. One account of Tyson's efforts can be found in Kukis, pp. 125–27.

78. Interview: Johnny Spann.

79. Interview: "Jack" (Keith Idema). Jack, a former Green Beret, was on contract to fight with the Special Forces in Afghanistan.

80. Criminal Docket for Case #1:02-cr-00037-306, 10/04/02.

81. Interview: Abd al-Haribi.

82. Kukis, pp. 191–92. The author also questioned Kukis about his findings. Interview: Mark Kukis.

INDEX